Hugh Butcher, Patricia Collis, Andrew Glen
and Patrick Sills

Community groups in action
Case studies and analysis

Routledge & Kegan Paul
London, Boston and Henley

First published in 1980
by Routledge & Kegan Paul Ltd
39 Store Street, London WC1E 7DD
9 Park Street, Boston, Mass. 02108, USA and
Broadway House, Newtown Road,
Henley-on-Thames, Oxon RG9 1EN
Set in 10/11pt Times Roman
by Input Typesetting Ltd
London
and printed in Great Britain by
Lowe & Brydone Ltd
Thetford, Norfolk

British Library Cataloguing Data

Community groups in action.
   1. Citizens' associations – Great Britain –
   Case studies
   I. Butcher, Hugh
   322.4'3   JS3008   80–40442

ISBN 0 7100 0492 3
ISBN 0 7100 0493 1 Pbk

Contents

Illustrations

Preface

Reviewing the legacy of the May 1968 'évènements' in Paris, Peter Jenkins wrote that

> it is the style rather than the content of the politics of 1968 which have the more survived as people . . . have turned from the 'politics of ultimate ends' to a politics of more specific ends. Ten years later, citizens' action of one form or another is the characteristic mode of political activity in a good many of the western democracies.[1]

Yet serious and sustained analyses of the new forms of citizens' action remain few and far between. Most surprisingly, there has been little detailed study of those local community-based self-help and campaign groups that have become so much part of the everyday scene.

When this project was initiated, the authors were struck by the absence of research studies on which we could build. Although some interesting case study material has since begun to appear, the field remains largely unexplored; we hope that this study will stimulate others to give more attention to this neglected area of contemporary social reality.

When we began meeting as a 'working party', our main common interest was in finding appropriate methods of evaluating the effectiveness of community work interventions with local groups. We soon found it necessary to broaden this area of interest to include a concern with the structure, dynamics, resources and goals of the community groups themselves. A concern with some of the sociological and organisational features of neighbourhood groups, initially seen as a ground clearing prerequisite to a proper examination of community worker effectiveness, became a compelling – indeed the central – interest in its own right.

With the help of a modified version of the Gulbenkian Community Work Group's 'Framework for Analysis'[2] a series of detailed case studies were compiled. These studies, of locally based self-help and campaign groups, were then subjected to comparative analysis under the following headings: goals and goal achievement; organisation process and structure; strategies, tactics and resources; and the role of the community worker. We would be the first to admit that our findings are tentative, drawn as they are from a narrow empirical and geographical base. Nevertheless our conclusions do derive, directly and inductively, from in-depth data collection, reflection and analysis carried out over an extended period of time. We hope that both our approach and conclusions will prove stimulating to all those involved, professionally or otherwise, in community groups, as well as those observers of the contemporary scene who are attempting to make sense of what is happening in neighbourhoods and estates up and down the country.

Part One of the book provides introductory and background information: it traces the development of the York-based working party, records our reservations about available literature on community groups, and introduces the reader to the research methodology adopted in this study. The checklist used to guide data collection is presented in full, and the community groups studied and the settings in which they operated, are introduced.

Part Two comprises five detailed case studies of 'community groups in action'. They have been written up according to a common format and, to help the reader, a brief chronology of key events is appended to each one.

The chapters that make up Part Three consist of comparative analyses of the case study material around a number of key themes. The generalisations and conclusions presented have, for the most part, been developed inductively from our own empirical data. However, insights and perspectives have been drawn from the literature of sociology, organisational analysis and other disciplines; and where this has happened sources have, of course, been acknowledged.

The final part of the book draws together, in list form, the main findings and propositions of the study, and suggests some avenues for future research development.

We hope that the book will prove of use and interest to four main groups of reader. The first comprises those research workers and academics engaged either in the currently embryonic field of the sociology of community groups or in more established, but related, disciplines like community studies, organisation theory and political science.

The second is the growing number of social workers, community workers, adult educationalists, planners and other welfare state professionals who 'work in the community'. The two Gulbenkian reports on community work have stressed that this 'typically consists of work with groups of local people who have come into existence because they want to change something, or do something that concerns them',[3] and that, for practice to be effective, 'an understanding of group relationships and dynamics, inter-group tensions and social pressures is essential'.[4]

The third audience is educational: those community work trainers based in both colleges and the field who are concerned to provide appropriate study programmes – programmes which the Pinker report recommends should include 'examination of the way groups form in relation to their goals and objectives, membership and size and the effects of these on group behaviour, group roles and interaction'.[5]

Fourth, we hope that the book might be found useful by activist members of community groups in providing a frame of reference for the planning and review of their activities.

Hugh Butcher
Patricia Collis
Andrew Glen
Patrick Sills

Acknowledgments

The authors would like to thank all members of the groups and local authorities studied for their readiness in 'taking part'; our colleagues in the CDP teams and the Department of Social Administration and Social Work, University of York, in particular the two community workers studied, Professor Kathleen Jones and Eric Butterworth for providing support and resources for the project, and Dilys Page who initially helped to pull the group together and draft some early manuscript; Mike Lovitt for his careful scrutiny of, and helpful comments on, the final draft script; and Audrey Freeborn for typing the final script, as well as the many others who have typed drafts of different chapters.

Abbreviations

1 The groups

SCAG   Senior Citizens Action Group
WCAC West Cumberland Action Committee
GAG   Glodwick Action Group
FCA   Failsworth Community Association

2 The community development programme

NCDP   National Community Development Project
CDP   Community Development Project (in a local area)

3 Abbreviations in SCAG case study

CI   Community Industry
CMS   Cumberland Motor Services
FE   Further Education
MP   Member of Parliament
OAPA Old Age Pensioners' Association
PC   Parish Council
RDC   Rural District Council

4 Abbreviations in the WCAC case study

CIAC   Community Information and Action Centre
DES   Department of Education and Science
PTA   Parent-Teacher Association
WPST Working Party on Schools Transport

5 Abbreviations in the Glodwick Action Group case study

CAB   Citizens' Advice Bureau
CPO   Compulsory Purchase Order
FHA   Family Housing Association
NATA   New Abbeyhills Tenants' Association

6 Abbreviations in the Failsworth Community Association case study

FAS   Failsworth Amenity Society
HSC   Home Safety Committee
OPWC   Old People's Welfare Committee
TAVR   Territorial Army Volunteer Reserve
UDC   Urban District Council

7 Abbreviations in the Joint Working Party on Vagrants case study

DHSS   Department of Health and Social Security

Part one
Introduction

Chapter 1
The background to the study

Parents organising to run a playgroup or start an adventure playground; residents protesting against an urban motorway plan; tenants forming an association to resist a rent increase or press for an improvement in estate facilities; mothers of handicapped children campaigning for an improvement in local social services – regular reports of these, and countless other examples of community groups in action, are to be found in local newspapers serving towns and villages up and down the country. The media, indeed, create an impression that the past decade or so has witnessed an explosion in grass-roots organising; the picture is painted of ever increasing numbers of voluntary action groups taking up, in new and challenging ways, an ever wider range of issues.

Although evidence concerning the incidence and prevalence of such groups is fragmentary, the few studies that do exist tend to reinforce the picture created by the media. Newton, for example, in his study of politics in Birmingham – which, on a number of criteria was deemed to be 'a fairly typical example of British cities in general' – identified 4,264 formally organised voluntary associations.[1] A nationwide survey of local amenity and civic societies by Barker similarly documented a dramatic increase in the formation of such societies since the beginning of the 1960s.[2]

In the absence of more comprehensive surveys of community groups and organisations we are forced to rely on the limited evidence available from local or specialist studies of the kind carried out by Newton and Barker. As Newton has remarked, researchers 'rarely ever pose such basic questions as "how many groups are there in the city" or "what proportion of them are active at any given time", never mind set out to answer such elementary queries'.[3] But ignorance about the answers has not inhibited academics and others from offering commentary about qualitative changes in the aspirations, style and strategy of voluntary action groups during recent years. The growth of the

3

modern self-help movement,[4] the increase in state interest in the sponsorship of participation and voluntary activity,[5] and the development of more combative forms of community action[6] have all been seen as evidence of significant changes in the extent and nature of grass-roots community involvement.

Although the primary organisational vehicle for this increasing grass-roots action is the local community group, this has been the subject of remarkably little disciplined data collection or analytical reflection. While theorists of formal organisations have contributed to a burgeoning literature devoted to the analysis of large-scale bureaucracies – including those social welfare organisations that employ professionals to work with community groups[7] – there has been little empirical study of more informally organised and locally based, mutual aid and campaigning groups. It is in this field that the present volume attempts to make a contribution through a detailed and comparative examination of the activities and achievements of five such groups. The aim is twofold: to provide useful additions to the growing, but still relatively small, number of case studies of community groups' initiatives and development; and, through a comparative analysis of this case study material, to generate some hypotheses about the goals, organisation, strategies, worker support and effectiveness of such groups. This research approach – the development of testable propositions from a comparative examination of carefully documented case study material – was not the only one open to us. Like much work in the social sciences, its adoption was not based wholly on scientific criteria, but resulted from a mixture of methodological preference and contingent opportunity. It is essential, therefore, that the ensuing case studies and commentary be read with some understanding of how the research developed, and of the methodology used.

CDP research group on community groups

The origins of this study can be traced back to a research working party that began meeting at York University from early 1974. The working party comprised university academics with teaching and research interests in community work, along with members of the research teams attached to the Oldham and Cumbria Community Development Projects (CDPs).[8] The University of York's Department of Social Administration and Social Work was responsible for the research teams attached to three CDPs[9] and had established a 'central unit' to encourage inter-project comparative work, facilitate dissemination of findings, and provide a forum for discussion of common problems.

The working party was specifically concerned with research into the initiatives of community groups. Its members broadly conceived such groups as collectivities of people who voluntarily joined together for the main purpose of promoting change, either in the form of new service provision or through the exertion of influence on the policies of external bodies. The groups were further conceived as 'community based' in so far as 'their membership activities and headquarters (if any) were located'[10] within the boundaries of the particular local authority from which consumers of the service were drawn or in relation to which influence efforts were directed. Where the target body[11] was not a local authority, the equivalent local area was deemed to be that covered by the organisation's most immediate and accessible level of administration.

The original focus of the working group was a concern to find an appropriate methodology for evaluating the effectiveness of project support for community groups. It soon became clear, however, that in order to effect a proper evaluation of worker intervention with particular groups, it was necessary to take account of many other features of group life. The membership of the community organisations, the goals and strategies which they adopted, the influence of the environment on aspects of group structure and process: all these would interact in a complex way with worker-related variables (such as the role adopted and the resources deployed) and confound any simplistic approach to evaluation. The focus of interest, therefore, broadened out, and a search was undertaken for studies that had examined the dynamics of community organisations in all their evident complexity. This search proved disappointing; while it served the limited purpose of clarifying some of the key variables to be taken into account, it failed to reveal a systematic body of field-tested propositions on which our own work could be based. Some of the limitations of this literature can be illustrated with reference to three research traditions: research into community work practice, sociological and political science research into community dynamics, and the socio-psychological studies of small-group behaviour.

Empirical and theoretical evaluations of community work practice suggested themselves as sources that might offer insights into the sociology of community groups. Goetschius, for example, categorises groups as primary or secondary, friendship or interest, simple or complex, formal or informal, and his study of tenants' associations, social clubs and community associations in

London provides an analysis 'of factors affecting the development of the groups'.[12] Brager and Specht similarly type community groups as socialisation, primary, organisation-development and institution relational – a categorisation that is fruitfully utilised in a study of British community work by Taylor et al.[13] We certainly gained valuable insights from studies like these, but in the end they failed to provide an appropriate theoretical foundation upon which to build. One difficulty stemmed from their adoption of a 'worker' perspective. Not only did a great many groups have little or no contact with a paid community worker; we did not want to make any prior assumptions about the relative importance of a worker's role. This was a clearly evident danger if we relied too heavily on typologies developed by practitioners for practitioners.

Other difficulties were presented when we turned to the work of academic sociologists and political scientists. Pickvance has noted that sociologists have traditionally taken an interest in voluntary associations.[14] Their studies have focussed, for example, on the relationship between voluntary associations (their membership, leadership, concerns) and aspects of social stratification. They have studied the ways in which voluntary organisations may or may not contribute to social integration. For political scientists, a concern with processes that preserve and enhance pluralist democracy has led to an interest in the way voluntary associations mobilise people for democratic involvement and participation or mediate between state and 'mass'. The academic is, therefore, rarely interested in voluntary action groups in their own right – as organisational forms worthy of independent study – and is inclined to focus upon them only in so far as their examination can illuminate a wider problem. The community studies of the sociologists and the power studies of the political scientists provide useful, but incomplete and partial, insights to the student of voluntary group action. As Baldock says of community studies, 'the difficulty with using this evidence is that the groups have usually been of subordinate interest to the researcher and one has to look at a number of studies before patterns and their significance begin to emerge'.[15]

If we believe that community groups are organisations worthy of study in their own right, then a further field of research suggests itself: the socio-psychological study of group behaviour. Alas, this field also failed to provide the framework of theory and findings that we were seeking. We reached the same conclusion as Derricourt who, after reviewing the usefulness of small group research, came to the conclusion that there was no 'clear, coherent set of theories . . . the main model implicit in most group work is the therapeutic model used in social work'.[16] Although one or two writers – most notably McCaughan[17] – have begun the task of teasing out from the vast socio-psychological literature findings of particular value to those with a primary interest in community groups, in the end we found this literature too fragmentary, interventionist and therapeutically biassed to serve as a systematic basis for our own work.

The comparative case study method

If existing approaches could not provide us with an adequate framework, what was to be the most appropriate way forward? Various writers, including some of those already mentioned, have advocated the compilation of carefully documented case studies as the most productive strategy through which greater understanding of group life may be attained.[18] Although as recently as 1974 Milson could lament the shortage of case study material, particularly of British origin,[19] later years have, in fact, seen an increase in published studies.[20] It was in the belief that the case study method provided the most promising way forward that the York working party embarked on a programme of recording and documenting the experience of community groups. Case studies can, however, take us only so far. They can provide valid and interesting sociographic material, and they may prompt compelling insights and generate useful hypotheses for further testing. In the current under-developed state of knowledge about community groups these contributions are not to be lightly dismissed.

The formation of our inter-project working group provided an opportunity to move one step beyond the compilation of discrete case studies and to adopt a common framework that would enable data to be collected on a comparable basis. This approach was in keeping with a recommendation in the second Gulbenkian report that the development of a common 'framework for analysis' would encourage consistency in reporting of community work initiatives and enable a bank of comparable data about community projects to be established.[21] The Gulbenkian framework, however, contains a practitioner bias – many of the suggested headings for analysis assume that some sort of intervention has occurred; and the working party began to explore ways in which it might be modified and adapted.

The Gulbenkian report was not explicit about the way in which research workers could most profitably use the data generated through use of the framework:

> The framework for analysis . . . should be capable of
> being used by anybody, within or outside the situation
> and with practical or theoretical interests. Similarly an
> analysis may be carried out for any one of several
> purposes and the same project may be usefully analysed
> by different people.[22]

For the working party a compelling research 'purpose' entailed
the employment of comparable case study material to help to
develop empirical generalisations upon which middle-range
theoretical propositions could be advanced. The study group
decided to complement case description with commentary and
analysis, and to review collected data under the following
headings:

1 Group goals and goal achievement
2 Organisation
3 Strategy, tactics and resources
4 Worker role

It should be noted that the twin processes of data collection and
theory generation were seen to be part of a total process. As
Glaser and Strauss pointed out in their discussion of grounded
theory:

> Generating a theory from data means that most
> hypotheses and concepts not only come from the data,
> but are systematically worked out in relation to the data
> during the course of the research. Generating a theory
> involves a process of research.[23]

It is important to be clear that such an approach to theoretical
work does not entail ignoring the insights and tentative generalisations provided by other research workers. Indeed it will be
seen from the later thematic commentary and analysis that the
sources of many of our ideas emanate from outside our own
data. The crucial point about adopting an inductive approach to
analysis is that generalisations are harmonised with data, that a
good 'fit' is achieved between theory and data.

The inductive, grounded theory, approach to developing
hypotheses seemed to be particularly appropriate to work in this
field. We had the opportunity of adopting both case study and
comparative methods: to utilise, in other words, the 'intensive-
comparative' approach advocated by Mouzelis. He points out
that it has become commonplace to talk of the case study/survey
dilemma. The case study method is said to provide insights and
fruitful hypotheses, but to offer no basis for testing such

hypotheses. On the other hand, a survey study does offer the possibility of generalised and methodologically more valid findings, but often of a superficial and rather trivial character. There is a way out:

> By strategically choosing a few cases (say two to five), it is possible to combine intensity of study with comparative variations of significant variables. . . . By the 'intensive-comparative' approach of a few similar cases, generalisations can be built up, valid in well circumscribed and narrow organisational contexts.[24]

Mouzelis's context is bureaucratic organisations. But the same arguments apply – perhaps even more strongly, given the relative paucity of studies – to the study of informal organisations of the community group variety.

To recapitulate then, our aim has been twofold: to augment the still small number of case studies of community groups in action; and to suggest some hypotheses about the aims, structure and dynamics of these kinds of organisation. Methodologically, a modified version of the Gulbenkian 'framework for analysis' was used to help to ensure a common format for case study reportage. Finally, a broadly 'intensive-comparative' approach to analysis was adopted. Clearly the depth and power of comparative analysis rests upon selecting the most appropriate range of topics to be addressed in the case studies. We discuss below our specific modifications to the Gulbenkian framework and present the checklist we eventually used in the construction of our case studies. Before embarking on such detail, however, one other matter of an introductory nature needs to be touched on: the reader will require some background information about the groups and their settings.

The community groups and their settings

Two of the case studies that follow are concerned with the activities of community groups in the small town of Cleator Moor. This town, on the coastal industrial belt of West Cumbria, had its origins in the nineteenth-century iron-ore mining boom.[25] Only intermittently during this century has Cleator Moor – in common with the rest of West Cumbria – enjoyed any measure of economic prosperity. Since the turn of the century, the absence of a viable economic base has resulted in high levels of unemployment, low wages, old and unimproved housing stock and the withdrawal of community services. This solidly working-

class town has, as a consequence, experienced a steadily declining population as young adult members forsake the area in search
of better living standards elsewhere (leaving a community of
7,500 people with a higher-than-average proportion in the
younger and older dependent population groups).

The first of our case studies focusses upon the Senior Citizens
Action Group (SCAG), a mutual aid and action group run by,
and for, pensioners in Cleator Moor. The second account traces
the operations of the West Cumberland Action Committee
(WCAC), an organisation that developed out of the work of a
number of groups formed in the towns and villages of West
Cumbria to protest about increases in bus fares, particularly as
these increases affected the cost of children's journeys to school.
While SCAG channelled most of its energy into organising and
running self-help schemes – its campaigning activity remained a
relatively small part of its overall work – WCAC was wholly
concerned with protest and influence exertion to achieve local
policy change.

Cleator Moor was part of Ennerdale Rural District Council
before the reorganisation of local government in April 1974.
Both the Council and the Cleator Moor representatives were
traditionally dominated by the Labour Party. After the reorganisation, Ennerdale was amalgamated with two similar councils to
form Copeland District Council. The Conservatives gained
minority control of the Council through an alliance with representatives of Ratepayers' Associations. At county level, the
Cumberland County Council which existed before reorganisation
was merged with Westmorland and parts of Yorkshire and north
Lancashire to form the new Cumbria County Council. Both this
and its predecessor were controlled by an alliance of Conservatives and independents.

Our next two case studies are concerned with the activity of
community organisations in Oldham, a metropolitan district
within the Greater Manchester conurbation. Oldham grew rapidly during the nineteenth century, its economic prosperity
rooted in the expansion of cotton and related industries. Population reached a peak of 194,000 in 1901, after which it declined
in parallel with the fortunes of the cotton industry. Although
there has been some influx of engineering and service industries
over recent years, this has not been sufficient to halt the economic decline of the area, with associated patterns of social
deterioration. A Department of Environment report describes
matters in the following way:

In the matter of its physical environment, Oldham suffers

from large scale obsolescence of its housing stock, public
amenities and industrial premises, reflecting the massive
building boom of the last century and the town's
subsequent economic decline. It displays a worn out
physical fabric and inadequate provision to meet today's
needs and standards . . . in summary, Oldham is a
deprived community by modern standards of a good
environment. . . . It vividly illustrates all the problems of
urban obsolescence which affect so many towns in the old
industrial areas of this country.[26]

Both the Oldham Metropolitan District Council, and the
County Borough Council which preceded local government
reorganisation, were Labour Party strongholds. The metropolitan district area extended beyond that of its predecessor, and
incorporated the old Failsworth Urban District Council, which
had also been controlled by the Labour Party. The Glodwick
area, in the east of the metropolitan district – from which our
third case study group, the Glodwick Action Group (GAG),
takes its name – was in the early 1970s an area of acute housing
and social stress. Consisting of some 2,000 late-nineteenth-cen-
tury terraced houses, largely in owner occupation, the area had
faced two major recent changes: an influx of large numbers of
people of New Commonwealth origins, and extensive urban
renewal and re-development. The area, said to fill a 'sump'
function for the private housing market in Oldham,[27] was facing
five declared or prospective Compulsory Purchase Orders (covering 800 properties) with the remainder of the area designated
for rehabilitation in a series of Housing Action Areas. The study
of GAG focusses on how local people organised to challenge a
CPO designated in October 1972 on about 250 houses.

The second Oldham case study concentrates on the activities
of the Failsworth Community Association (FCA). Failsworth lies
between the former county borough of Oldham and the city of
Manchester, and in the reorganisation of 1974 might, in the
opinion of some of its residents, have been better incorporated
into this latter area than into the new Oldham metropolitan
district. Like Oldham, Failsworth's past was mainly linked to the
cotton industry and its fortunes, but as these declined between
the wars new industry connected with aircraft and rubber came
into the area. However, even up to the 1950s, agriculture formed
quite an important part of Failsworth's economy; although latterly more and more of the area has been given up to housing.

Associated with this has been a rise in population, which
contrasts with a gradual decline in the population of Oldham.

The area also has appreciably more owner-occupied housing than Oldham, and the housing generally, as judged by its amenities, is in better condition. While more of the population of Failsworth than in the former Oldham borough are in white-collar occupations, and to some extent the area has become a commuter zone for Manchester, it is still a mixed community economically, with many of its residents engaged in manual work. Within the area there are particular pockets of deprivation, which have led to the inclusion of a small part of Failsworth in Oldham's inner areas programme.

The Failsworth Community Association grew up both with particular concerns about local physical planning issues and health and social welfare needs, and with a general brief to protect the interests of the whole population of the former Failsworth Urban District Council area. The Association came into existence, in fact, shortly after the 1974 reorganisation of local government, as a direct result of local fears that the views of Failsworth people might receive less attention within the enlarged local government system.

The northern British town[28] in which the fifth of our case study groups was located has a population of approximately 105,000, a further 50,000 people living in adjoining suburban areas beyond its governmental boundary. The class breakdown of the population is comparable to that of the country as a whole. The industrial base is mixed in terms of public and private ownership, heavy and light engineering, and large and small enterprises. Confectionery and transport are particularly prominent in the manufacturing sector. Another sizeable employer is the tourism industry, catering for the many visitors attracted to the town's architectural heritage. The town is a commercial and cultural centre functioning as a mini-metropolis to its wider area. Although the scale of environmental deprivation is limited in proportion to the town's overall size, the housing stock has a level of amenity lower than the national average, and the town includes neighbourhoods which have been or are due to be designated as general improvement areas or, in one case, a housing action area. The tenure mix is similar to the national distribution. There is considerable interspersion of public and private housing, and, outside the town centre, housing has a high density within the urban area.

Historically, the town's politics has a Liberal tradition, but in the last fifteen years the electoral balance between the Labour and Conservative parties has been close. This has resulted in frequent fluctuations in the control of the local council. During the period of the case study, the Labour Party regained control in April 1972 for the final two years before local government reorganisation. The town's status changed on 1 April 1974 from a county borough to one of eight district councils within a largely rural county council. The Conservatives gained minority leadership of the new District Council and retained their long-standing control of the county council, whose boundaries were not significantly changed in the reorganisation.

The initiative described in the case study arose from local concern about the numbers of single homeless men in the town. In 1972 a Joint Working Party on Vagrants was formed and this body went on to establish an overnight shelter near the town centre. After much public and political controversy, responsibility for this provision was taken over by the incoming District Council in 1974.

Research methods and problems

Peter Marris has suggested that research into community action 'is contemporary political history, interpreted for its relevance to future action'. The methodology of such research, he says, 'is straightforward, if not very reassuring: to be everywhere, know everything that happened and how it happened, to record all this – and then, behind the mass of detail and the accidents of personality, to discern the general pattern of issues which determined these events'. Marris's conception of this kind of research is worth quoting at length since it closely reflects the difficulties experienced by the working party at all stages:

> In many ways it is more demanding than the interpretation of a scientific experiment, because so little can be taken for granted – neither the way the aims were defined, nor the methods, nor the perceptions of relationships which informed the actions, nor the meaning of the outcomes. And it cannot afford to be any less careful in recording its data. Yet the findings will not have the conclusiveness of a scientific experiment, because there is no single frame of reference by which they must be evaluated. Every indicator used to measure change itself implies assumptions about relevance, whose political and ideological implications have to be articulated.[29]

It seems appropriate at this stage to present and discuss the research instrument used to guide the collection, and order the analysis, of our data – what we have called the 'case study checklist'. We will then outline the main sources of information used and the different relationships which research workers had with the groups. Finally we will return to consider some of the dilemmas which arose in carrying out the research role.

The case study checklist

As noted above, a checklist was adopted and refined in response to the need for a common analytical framework for recording working party members' data. Drawing upon earlier work by the authors, and more particularly upon the Gulbenkian 'framework for analysis'[30], the checklist became an important aid in the collection and organisation of case study material. The checklist that is reproduced here is the outcome of a number of revisions undertaken during our attempts to use it, though we are aware that further refinements and additions could still be made. In introducing the checklist, therefore, we emphasise that it represents a practical research tool, something that has evolved through application in compiling the case studies, derived through practice rather than developed from theory.

Local community groups   *Case study checklist*

Name of group
Name of research worker
Relation of research worker to the group
Sources of data and methods of research
Documentary evidence
  – quality of records kept by the group; whether or not meetings are adequately recorded, if at all; other documentation; newspaper reports.
Chronological summary of events.

Introduction

– an overview of the group's activities; a general description and summary of what the group does and what its main concerns are.

The context

– describe the situation as it existed before the group was

formed: was any other body or group of people, or individuals, taking up any of the issues subsequently taken up by the group; how much awareness was there of the problems or issues subsequently taken up by the group?

The constituency

– describe the constituency of the group, or those whose interests the group wants to represent.

1   *Formation of the group*

1.1   Were there any particular events which precipitated the formation or emergence of the group?

1.2   Where did the initiative come from during the emergence of the group? Who were the main activists at this stage? Did they remain active? Were any of these people outsiders or newcomers to the area, or professionals (community workers, CDP workers, etc.)?

1.3   Did the group have a sponsor (i.e. someone or some body who provided material or other help to the group)?

1.4   How was support obtained in the early stages? Were there any open or public meetings, for example, to launch the group?

1.5   What were the most important factors in the formation of the group?

2   *Objectives and general aims*

2.1   Why was the group formed? Distinguish the specific objectives from more general, long-term aims, if possible. Note that the group's immediate objectives may subsequently have changed. What is required here is an account of the group's perception of its objectives in the early stages of its development.

2.2   Objectives and aims of any professional community or CDP workers involved in the group at this stage. Why did the worker support or initiate the group or encourage its formation?

2.3   Have the objectives or the general aims changed since the group was formed? Specify changes, giving reasons. Include changes of emphasis.

3　　*Organisation and development of the group*

3.1　Membership; numbers; fluctuations in support by active members. Distinguish core active members from less closely involved supporters and describe any formal structures which distinguish active participants from other supporters (e.g., it might often be officers who are the activists, and the focus of a group's identity or image).

3.2　Previous or other organisational experience among core activists.

3.3　Structure of the group in terms of its organisation into subcommittees, etc. Any further comments on leadership if not already dealt with under 3.1 above.

3.4　Frequency of meetings; meeting-place; degree of informality or formality; are minutes of meetings recorded?; general style of operation.

3.5　Manner of making decisions; degree of dissent. Problems, if any.

3.6　Resources for organisational and other administrative aspects of the group's activities. For example, are there any costs in running the group, and if so, how are these borne? Do the members pay subscriptions?

3.7　Conflicts, tensions and problems within the group or core group.

3.8　Learning from experience; the running of the group – does it get easier as more members become experienced in organising its affairs?

4　　*The role of the community worker*

4.1　Why did the worker become involved in this particular group?

4.2　How does the work of the group fit in with the general aims of the Project (CDP cases only) or sponsor (if any)?

4.3　The worker's role as a newcomer may have affected the development of the group – did it help or hinder?

4.4　How much does the worker direct what goes on? Does he ever initiate activities?

4.5　Has the worker ever made efforts to keep the group going when but for those efforts it might have lapsed?

4.6　How does the worker operate in situations of internal conflict?

4.7　How much time does the worker give to the group and its activities? Does he feel it is enough? Has the degree of the

worker's involvement changed over the period of time covered by the case study?

4.8   Has the worker had any influence on the strategy of the
group?

4.9   Assessment of dependency of group on the worker. Has
this changed?

4.10   What have been the worker's main contributions to the
group?

5   *Strategy*

5.1   Action taken to gain support for the group.
5.2   Action taken to achieve objectives.
5.3   Any major disagreements among members or supporters
on matters of strategy or tactics.
5.4   Use of publicity material, leaflets, posters, etc.

6   *Achievements, impact and failures*

6.1   Achievement of short-term objectives; the main factors
contributing to those successes.
6.2   Progress to longer-term aims.
6.3   Failures and problems. Have any objectives been abandoned? Why? Has the continued existence of the group at
any time been at risk? Why was this and how was the
difficulty avoided or resolved?
6.4   Impact of the group within its constituency.
6.5   Impact of group outside the constituency; press, radio, TV
coverage. Support and influence from local leaders, MP,
etc.
6.6   Reaction of any relevant existing structures to the group
– e.g., Labour Party, trade unions, local authority officers,
councillors. Was support or influence sought from these
bodies or individuals?

7   *The future of the group*

7.1   What factors will determine whether or not the group
survives?
7.2   Does its existence depend on any outsider(s), community
worker or any other person whose interests are distinguish-
able from those of the local community?
7.3   If CDP is involved, will the group outlive CDP?

8   *Concluding comments*

- points arising from the case study which seem significant to the research worker and which are not covered, or sufficiently emphasised, elsewhere.

One of the major dilemmas encountered in devising this checklist was how to combine the provision of a chronological account of a group's development (the approach most frequently adopted in other case studies) with the more factorial mapping of activities, progress, problems and achievements which would be conducive to systematic comparative analysis. We chose to emphasise the latter approach, but were concerned that the content of each section, while necessarily compiled at a particular point in time, should as far as possible be considered developmentally and in terms of the groups' own time perspectives. The inclusion of a summary of events was also intended to provide a chronological backdrop and reference point for the case studies in order to help to overcome the snapshot flavour liable to creep into such accounts.

The factorial basis of the checklist does, of course, have implications for its users. The balance and integration of description and commentary is left to individual research workers. There is also a risk of repetitiveness; of events and factors which were closely connected becoming fragmented because of reporting procedures. In addition, the headings need to be used selectively in so far as they are differentially relevant to particular groups and research purposes. It would be unreasonable to expect the checklist to be equally appropriate to the enormous variety of local groups to which it might be applied; and we will review our own experience of its application in the concluding chapter. It is our general hope, nevertheless, that publication of the checklist might suggest and encourage more systematic approaches to the recording and evaluation of case study data.

Sources of information and group-research worker relationships

While the five case studies all follow the framework of the checklist in their presentation, there were some variations in the relationships between the groups and research workers and in the sources from which information was derived. At one extreme, the case studies of the Senior Citizens Action Group and the Joint Working Party on Vagrants were undertaken by people closely involved in the groups, committed participant observers, particularly in the latter case. At the other extreme, the Failsworth Community Association was made the subject of a case study largely because the working party members wanted to test the checklist as an interviewing guide for use with groups about which the research worker had little, if any, prior knowledge. The Failsworth material was mainly secondary data obtained from an interview with the Association's secretary; the only first-hand evidence was gained through the research worker's attendance of one executive committee meeting.

Levels of data are part and parcel of the question of the 'distance' of the research worker from the group. Most groups are likely to have some written material and notes of meetings (although these will not necessarily be accessible to the research worker), but the quality of the first-hand evidence will be a function of the closeness of the worker to the group. The two case studies in this book written from first-hand observation (the Joint Working Party on Vagrants and the Senior Citizens Action Group) differ in the nature of the workers' participation. In the case of SCAG the research worker was performing the role of community worker to the group, and saw observation and evaluation as integral to his involvement. The role of the author of the Joint Working Party study was the reverse – he was able to write about the group because he was fully participant in it – that is, he was participant before taking the role of observer and researcher.

The accounts of the Glodwick group and the West Cumberland Action Committee illustrate cases where the research role was uppermost (although as members of their respective CDP teams both authors were committed to the groups in a general sense). In the case of the Glodwick group the research worker's involvement was long-standing and was much closer than that with the West Cumberland Action Committee. More first-hand data was available to the writer of the Glodwick case study by virtue of the fact that over a considerable period she attended most of the group's meetings, albeit primarily as an observer rather than as a participant in the group.

The Glodwick and West Cumberland Action Committee cases both illustrate the use of secondary data by authors with some degree of involvement in the groups. In the case of Glodwick, the research worker's own observations were supplemented by material obtained by interviewing the community worker, several members of the group, and an officer of the local authority. But while in this case the research worker maintained a continuous involvement with the group over a considerable period, the West Cumberland Action Committee was examined intensively over a short period. This is the situation which is most usual in the kind of exercises carried out by students, where intensive investigations are feasible only over a short period of time. In the Cumbria case, evidence was drawn from written material and also from a few interviews with key people.

Assuming that the ideal is the 'being everywhere and knowing everything' role, we should perhaps conclude that the Joint Working Party, SCAG and Glodwick groups have been given the fullest examinations. On the other hand, the short-term but intensive approach used with the WCAC has a great deal to commend it in terms of the degree of detachment the research workers could bring to their material. This can be illustrated in numerous ways but best, perhaps, in terms of access to opposing perspectives. A 'visiting' research worker, particularly if this person is not known to those involved with the group, is more likely to obtain evidence from all sides than is the person who has been closely involved with the group over a long period of time. It has to be acknowledged as a defect of the intensive, short-term investigation, however, that interview situations yield material in a second-hand form which cannot reproduce events as they actually took place. Not only do interviews produce only that person's view of events, but they produce reflections after events.

The more the better is probably the only conclusion consistent with the 'everything everywhere' ideal. The fact remains that it is the discerning of 'the general pattern of issues which determined' the events which is the research proper, rather than the collection of material, and this brings us to problems in the research role.

Some research dilemmas

Some of the problems of the research worker's role have been touched on in the preceding section, in particular the discrepancy between events and events remembered, and the conflict between close involvement and objectivity, which may stand in inverse ratio to one another. The former may be countered by reference to contemporary written records, where these exist, but the latter can probably be guarded against only by the research workers' attempts to be aware of possible prejudices.

A further problem in some cases may be the possible effect of the research on the group's operation. In theory this could be a favourable or unfavourable influence, but the negative effect is the one more likely to cause concern. The group in our case studies most likely to have been adversely affected by research, because of its frequent volatility and insecurity, was probably the Glodwick Action Group. The research worker was struck by the unease shown by members of this group when she first attended meetings, compared with the easy acceptance of her as an observer at the Failsworth Community Association committee meeting she attended. Whether she presented less of a threat when present only at a single meeting, or to a group confident of their ability to run a formal committee meeting, or whether her role as a research worker was more easily understood and accepted by the Failsworth group, is not clear. Whatever the explanation, there was no sign of the discomfort caused by her presence at an early GAG meeting, which prompted one member to say, 'Why don't you ever say anything? Why do you always just sit there?'

If we are interpreting contemporary political history 'for its relevance to future action', then the subjectivity of interpretations is one of the major stumbling blocks the research worker is aware of from the outset:

> From the perspective of differing ideologies and interests, the same history reveals different patterns, which are all insights into its meaning, though their implications may be contradictory. Hence the researcher has to decide for whose interest he speaks, and whom he is seeking to influence, while still recognising that the force of his argument depends on the intellectual integrity of his analysis, not his commitment.[31]

Nobody, Marris thinks, can be 'at once a detached, reflective observer, as interested in failure as success, and an energetic schemer'. Can anybody, though, interpret events in community groups with any more authority and integrity than anybody else? Who is the best person to do it? There is surely no obvious answer to questions like this; each contribution has to be judged for what it is. We judge each case in relation to our perception of the author's role in the events described and interpreted.[32]

Part two
The case studies

Chapter 2
The Senior Citizens Action Group

Introduction: an overview of the group's activities

The Senior Citizens Action Group of Cleator Moor was formed in October 1973, when a group of pensioners discussed with a Community Development Project worker what could be done about a problem troubling many elderly people in the town: difficulty in getting small repairs done around the house and garden. Committed to promotion of social change and social welfare objectives at a local level, the group embarked on a range of self-help schemes and pressure group activity on behalf of persons of pensionable age in the town.

In pursuing such aims the group's work both complemented and overlapped the activities of the other three pensioners' organisations in the town. The first of these, the Cleator and Cleator Moor Welfare Committee, had made the welfare of the handicapped, housebound and the very elderly its main concern. It organised outings and trips and raised funds to provide holidays for the housebound. A small committee met regularly to conduct business and members of the group operated their own good neighbour scheme, making friendly visits and generally keeping an eye on the welfare of the frail and housebound. The other group, the local Old Age Pensioners' Association, operated from a prefabricated hall – known locally as the Pensioners' Hut – built a few years ago after protracted fund-raising by the association. The OAPA ran bingo and other entertainments from the hut, the accumulated proceeds of which provided a handout to the town's pensioners at Christmas time.

Besides these two organisations mention should also be made of the Companions Club, another well-established body catering for pensioners in the town. Unlike the Welfare Committee and the OAPA it was not a separate organisation as such, but was the name given to the regular Thursday evening sessions run from the local Further Education Centre. Funded and supported as an FE class, it was run by a committee of pensioner members in conjunction with the centre tutor. A normal evening's activities included a talk by an invited speaker, followed by a discussion and social.

The self-help orientation which characterised these established organisations was mirrored in the work of SCAG, but in the case of this latter group was complemented by attempts to operate as a local pressure group, bringing to the attention of decision makers and others the concerns of retired and elderly people in Cleator Moor.

It may be helpful, before describing SCAG's activities along the lines suggested by the checklist, to mention briefly the issues taken up by the group.

Small jobs service for home and garden
Many pensioners locally found it difficult to get tradesmen to do small jobs around the house and garden; for example, attending to a dripping cistern, planing down a sticking and draughty door, and replacing a pane of broken window glass. One of SCAG's early successes was to get a number of organisations interested in helping with these problems. Local secondary school children undertook some household and gardening tasks as part of their community service, and SCAG managed to negotiate with the local Community Industry[1] scheme for that organisation to employ some of their teams of young workers on repair and decorating jobs for local pensioners.

Pedestrian safety
Elderly people found it both hazardous and time-consuming to get shopping done and to collect pensions in Cleator Moor on certain days (particularly market day, when roads around the central square became swollen with traffic). SCAG took the matter up with the local road safety committee, the parish and district council and the police. When it became apparent that traffic levels failed to meet the Department of the Environment's requirements to warrant a pedestrian crossing, negotiation with the police was stepped up, resulting in a promise of increased police presence on the square.

Chiropody services
Rationalisation of services all too often results in the withdrawal of local provision. The continuation of the National Health Service chiropody provision in Cleator Moor was threatened in this way. SCAG lobbied the community physician and eventually the

local community health council, with the result that the service was reinstated.

Restrictions on use of concessionary bus passes

Councillors were lobbied and a delegation met the management of the local bus company over the issue of what were felt to be unnecessary time restrictions on the use of pensioners' bus passes. The group did not, however, prove able to get any change in the regulations governing use of the passes.

Weekly socials

A weekly 'tea and crack' afternoon was instituted in the local OAPA hut and became a regular feature of activities. Originally intended primarily for the disabled and housebound, a minibus was loaned every Wednesday afternoon from the local community resource centre,[2] and two members of the group undertook the fetching and carrying of the less mobile to the hut. As numbers multiplied, the help of the social services department was obtained: they provided a personnel carrier and driver to bring a further dozen or so of the more handicapped. Although originally organised around the needs of those who would otherwise have had little chance to get out of the house, other pensioners were also encouraged to drop in. Numbers fluctuated between 65 and 95 a week, with more when parties and entertainments were organised.

Welfare rights course

The regular Wednesday afternoon socials provided a springboard from which other activities could be organised. A variety of coach trips, pie and pea suppers and parties were arranged, along with a short welfare rights course. The latter consisted of sessions (with visiting speakers) on housing benefits, income and social security rights, and social services provision for pensioners.

Emergency help cards

A simple means of summoning help in times of emergency – a large red HELP card to be placed in a front room window when emergency help was needed – was distributed throughout the town and used to good effect on a number of occasions.

Food and household goods club

This venture began to operate every Wednesday afternoon from April 1975. A small group of SCAG members purchased each week vegetables and fruit, tinned goods, dairy produce and household goods like soap and washing-up liquid at cost price from market gardeners and wholesalers. They were then sold at cost (some items were marked up with a small addition to cover breakage and spillage) from a stall set up at the weekly social. Membership of the shopping club stood at over 60, and it assisted in a small, but direct, way to help fixed incomes to stretch further.

Background to group activities

It was clear from the inception of SCAG – from the time that the first group of people met to discuss the problems associated with getting small jobs done around the house and garden – that most of the issues taken up were seen as important by substantial sections of the retired population of Cleator Moor. Some of the issues (for example, immobility and lack of social contact among the housebound) had been identified and partially tackled by existing community groups. Other issues, like the absence of local chiropody services and the cost of transport to larger adjacent towns had been forcefully brought to the attention of CDP workers right from their initial contacts in the area.[3] The response to the activities and initiatives of SCAG provided a further indication of the salience of the issues tackled; for example, discussion and debate at the Wednesday afternoon socials reinforced the impression that chiropody services and concessionary bus passes were important local issues. Similarly, pensioners accepted with enthusiasm the emergency HELP cards and took full advantage of the co-operative shopping club, the socials and outings – all testimony to the fact that the issues selected by the group for attention were significant ones.

Formation of the group

The particular event which led to the formation of the group was a visit paid by a member of the CDP action-research team to the local Further Education Centre's Companions Club. Following a brief talk about the CDP and social survey work planned, the community worker invited people to exchange views on the problems and issues confronting people of pensionable age. Substantial agreement was reached that getting small repairs and other odd jobs done around the house and garden caused anxiety and discomfort far out of proportion to the actual work to be done. Other issues were mooted, but it was this one in particular that brought an immediate positive response when it was suggested that those interested might meet again to take the issue further. Names and addresses of those enthusiastic about such a follow-up meeting were collected. The worker then circulated a reminder of the agreed date and venue, and a week later the group that was eventually to call itself the Senior Citizens Action Group came together for the first time.

Three out of the nine people who attended this original meeting remained core members[4] of SCAG. Other core members joined either by personal invitation, through participation in group activities (turning up, for example, to the group's welfare rights sessions or socials), or through the notices of meetings posted in the window of the local Information and Action Centre.[5] The group (both core and fringe) was almost wholly composed of local people, many born and bred in West Cumbria and mostly long established residents of Cleator Moor and Cleator. The worker stood out as the only real 'off comer'.

Objectives

From the group members' point of view, the original impetus to form a new group was simple enough. As already noted, it was a wish to see if anything could be done about the problem of getting small jobs done around the house and garden. It was clear that a degree of self-interest motivated people to work on the issue; indeed, most early participants supplied examples of difficulties they were currently experiencing.

Before considering the ways in which the objectives were modified and extended, it may be appropriate to outline the objectives of the worker and CDP in supporting the formation and growth of this new community group. It is clear that a mixture of reasons was involved.

It is not difficult to account for the CDP's involvement with community groups; we need look no further than the original briefs and statements prepared at the inauguration of the national CDP experiment. At the time of SCAG's inception, the Cumbria Project utilised the familiar top-down/bottom-up formulation to describe its community work activities. Bottom-up work involved CDP workers in performing roles as an enabler and catalyst – helping groups of local residents to define and articulate needs and issues as they saw them and work for some resolution in a way acceptable to them. Work with SCAG was seen as an instance of this approach, complementing the top-down method (of, for example, social surveys, health screening, and welfare rights campaigns among pensioners), in which CDP personnel set about identifying needs, setting up experimental projects and stimulating the development of participatory and power-sharing mechanisms in a more directive fashion.

The organisation of pensioner action and pressure around felt needs and issues along the lines of the bottom-up approach was justified for the worker in terms of particular political and value assumptions. This is not the place to debate the range of values that inform and motivate activity in the community work field. Suffice it to say that, put baldly, the worker believed that an important set of reasons that help to account for the disadvantages and problems experienced by particular population groups (like pensioners) are to be found in the lack of power of such groups, power to prevent resource allocation in favour of other, less deprived and more influential segments of the population. His attitude echoed that of Miliband who, when conjecturing about whether poverty – a disadvantage or problem, it will be noted, confronting many elderly people – would be tackled or not, concluded that:

> It depends first and foremost on the respective strengths of conflicting forces operating in society, some making for the persistence of poverty, and others working against its persistence; and the trouble for the poor is that the forces operating against them are very much stronger than those working in their favour.[6]

Miliband went on to say that it is not, then, a question of the recognition of poverty, or the selection of the right policies, or even the creation of the right administrative framework; rather it is a 'question of the distribution of power in society'.

Such a perspective inevitably raises more questions than it answers. We can ask, with respect to pensioners and their organisations, for example, how can retired people best organise to pursue their collective interests? What alliances can they form with other social groupings to increase their strength and influence? One of the important aspects of the worker's involvement with SCAG was to explore with people in the CDP area the answers to some of these questions. A concern to develop an understanding of people's predispositions to engage in collective action along with an exploration of the potentialities for, and constraints upon, community action by pensioners constituted important underlying questions for the worker in his involvement with elderly people in Cleator Moor.[7]

If the general rationale for working with pensioners was clear, why work with this particular group? There were, after all, established pensioner organisations in Cleator Moor; why not support them, why work towards the establishment of yet another group? In the first place it should be noted that other workers already had an existing, if limited, contact with both the OAPA and the Cleator and Cleator Moor Welfare Committee. As it happened, CDP came to invest more manpower resources in SCAG than in these other organisations, but at the time of SCAG's first meetings there was no notion of making a choice to work with one group more than another. In the light of the enthusiasm at the first meeting 'to get on and do something' about the odd jobs issue, it seemed less than helpful to direct energy into the question of whether other organisations were not more appropriately placed to pursue the issue. Here were people willing to get to grips with a problem themselves – a problem, moreover, outside the normal purview and concerns of existing groups. It was preferred, then, to work with an organisation that did not have established and accepted approaches and traditional areas of concern. Finally, it should be noted that membership of existing groups seemed to be divided along religious lines; it was thought that an organisation which might wish to move beyond self-help approaches might be more effective if unencumbered by such limitations.

Changes in objectives

Returning to group members' objectives, the original concern with odd jobs became largely displaced. Considerable energy was expended early on in setting up the small jobs scheme: obtaining necessary sponsorship and finance, negotiating with Community Industry to make a work force available, and organising referral mechanisms and publicity. As initial difficulties were overcome, the objective shifted from initiation to maintenance. Later, Community Industry extended the small jobs scheme to Whitehaven and other parts of West Cumbria, and at the same time relieved SCAG of almost all of the organisational and promotional work that it had found itself responsible for in the early stages. As road safety, chiropody services, socials for the housebound, the household goods club and other issues gained prominence, so other initial objectives, in their turn, became displaced.

It is interesting to note that new goals sometimes grew from attempts to implement earlier aims and objectives. The identification of need among the housebound was brought home forcefully to the group when members set about distributing the emergency HELP cards throughout Cleator Moor. The regular

monthly meeting heard graphic accounts of pensioners who had
received no visitors for days or even weeks, or who had not been
out of their house for many months. The effect of such isolation
on other aspects of life was debated; the group heard about the
person who, when visited, maintained that he could not be bothered to cook for himself and, apparently, had not eaten anything
at all for several days. The organisation of activities to help to
meet some of these needs was seen as an immediate and practical
step that the group should take. From that time on the Wednesday afternoon socials, the outings, the pie and pea suppers and
parties were given a high priority by the group.

Another example of one thing leading to another was the spin-
off effect that the concern with local chiropody services had on
reinforcing and buttressing an interest in the deficiencies of the
local concessionary bus pass scheme. The link was clear; if little
could be done immediately to restore a local chiropody service,
then transport to other towns that did offer a service was a
primary concern.

In general, situations did not arise that forced conscious
choices between issues to be taken up. This is not to say, of
course, that energy, time and ideas did not conspire to keep
some issues low down on agendas while others were brought to
the forefront of attention. The kind of factors that seem to have
influenced the implicit ordering of priorities were concerned with
resources and local norms.

Resources
As pensioners, many group members had the time to engage in
labour-intensive operations (like the social and household goods
club). This encouraged a self-help or self-organising approach to
meeting needs and tackling problems. The availability of small
pump-priming grants from CDP was another significant resource.
It appeared to the worker, on more than one occasion, that the
availability of grants of up to £250 influenced consideration of
solutions and actions that could utilise such money. This was
exemplified in extreme form on one occasion when a member of
SCAG (who was also a member of the pump-priming committee)
announced at a meeting that there was a substantial amount
remaining in the pump-priming budget to be allocated before
the end of the financial year and 'could we think up any useful
schemes on which to spend the money?'

Local norms
There were culturally accepted ways of responding to pensioners'
needs in Cleator Moor; for example, outings, fund-raising activ-

ities to ensure a handsome Christmas handout, and pie and pea suppers. In many ways group members seemed most comfortable when they were engaging in activities of this kind.

Overall, then, the group had a succession of goals, one or two occupying the centre of attention and activity at any one time. While group activity itself can help to stimulate a demand for action on new fronts, some issues and problems seem destined, as it were, to remain in the wings until energy, time and ideas bring these forward for attention. Yet other issues vanish from the agenda, either because group action has run its course to a successful conclusion, or because it is recognised that, for the time being at least, nothing else can be done.

Aspects of internal group organisation and development

Membership

Core membership numbered about ten to twelve people. Most of these people attended the regular monthly meetings of SCAG, along with another four to ten fringe members. A monthly meeting, in other words, generally consisted of about 12 to 20 people. As already noted, core members were nearly all pensioners (all but one were over pensionable age) and about half of them were members – often key members – of other community groups. SCAG included active members from the other three pensioners' organisations in the town, the OAPA, the Further Education Centre's Companions Club and the Cleator and Cleator Moor Welfare Committee. This was in addition to the ex-chairman of a tenants' association, an ex-parish councillor, and an ex-trade union branch secretary.

Fringe members consisted of two local councillors, who were intermittent attenders, as well as others who attended meetings when specific issues interested them. For example, two people were particularly concerned when concessionary bus passes were on the agenda, as they had to make regular visits to relatives who were long-stay patients in Whitehaven Hospital. Both participated in a delegation to meet the manager of the bus company, but were subsequently irregular attenders at meetings.

At the beginning, members were nearly all women, but later the proportion of men grew to about a third. Members were almost entirely working class in family background and prior occupation, and for the most part they lived on the council estates and in the older, smaller, terraced properties in the parish.

Leadership
Leadership, both formal and informal, was more or less co-extensive with membership of the core group. Officers, who provided a formal leadership, were elected for one year and consisted of a chairman, deputy chairman, secretary, assistant secretary, treasurer and assistant treasurer. Other members of the core group acted as significant opinion makers. In general, members carved out particular areas of interest and activity, their influence often being decisive in their own selected areas; for example, a sub-group of three men did most of the work in connection with the shopping club, three or four women under-took most of the organisational work in connection with the socials, and two other men with work experience of lorry and van driving were deferred to on transport matters.

A constitution drawn up nearly two years after the group's formation formalised a number of organisational matters, including the circumstances under which decisions had to be put to a vote. Formal voting on formally drawn up motions, however, rarely took place, the bulk of decisions being arrived at after extensive, and often exhausting, airing of views.

The CDP worker
The worker, as already acknowledged, was heavily involved in bringing the group together in the first place, and for the first 9 or 10 months convened and chaired the meetings. Officers were then elected, and from that time the worker held no official position in the group.

The worker tried to play servicing and group maintenance roles by, for example, helping members to clarify options and think through the consequences of particular suggested courses of action. In the early days, when convening and chairing meetings, all temptations to influence the overall direction taken by the group, or the basic means it was to use to achieve its goals, were resisted, and any ideas offered were advocated in a tentative and circumspect manner. Most worker energy was put into attempts to draw out the implications of ideas offered by members, and to discourage early foreclosure of debate. Later the worker moved from this stance to some extent, throwing in ideas of a more contentious and committed nature. This was due in large part to a feeling that the group was then in a position to treat his views as just another contribution to be weighed and accepted or rejected without being invested with any automatic halo of expertise. Overall, then, the worker tried to remain fairly non-directive in approach, while identifying with the group's aims.

It can be confusing to talk about worker dependency in a general way. The group was autonomous in terms of deciding the directions it wished to take, but as far as implementation of decisions was concerned the group used the worker's support to a greater or less extent according to the initiative in hand. For example, the worker gave considerable assistance to SCAG's secretary in following up the chiropody service issue, but was only minimally involved in the organisation of the socials for the housebound, the emergency HELP cards, and the food club.

It is difficult to discuss the amount of worker time involved in supporting the group, as this varied greatly from week to week. Formal meetings took up about two hours one evening per month. There was also regular attendance for an hour or so at some point during the Wednesday afternoon socials; and various members of the group used to drop into the CDP offices; for example, to discuss points, bring in minutes for typing, and book the minibus. Overall, the worker probably spent something in the order of 1½ to 2½ hours per week on SCAG matters.

Utilisation of resources
The group applied for, and made use of, various small CDP pump-priming grants: £250 was made available for the socials (including trips and parties) and £250 for the household goods club. Another £25 was forthcoming to help to start off the odd jobs scheme and £48 for production of the HELP cards. Another small grant of £110 was obtained for production of simple, easy-to-read leaflets to be used in conjunction with the welfare rights sessions. The CDP-sponsored community resource centre helped with the typing of minutes and preparing posters, and made their minibus available every Wednesday and for special outings (some of the money from the various pump-priming grants found its way back to resource centre coffers for the use of their facilities). Finally, for convenience only, the group elected to hold their monthly meetings on CDP premises. Other non-CDP resources included the use of the OAPA hut for socials (a rental was paid), the use of the social services department's tail-lift personnel carrier, and a £25 grant from the local district council to assist in setting up the small jobs scheme. Fund-raising activities like bring-and-buy sales and raffles were organised to help to keep bank accounts in credit. Finally, stress must be given to the amount of voluntary time and effort members put into SCAG affairs.

Meetings
As already noted, SCAG met at least once a month to conduct its business, and practically everyone who attended the meetings put in an appearance at the weekly social. Much of the business at the monthly meetings consisted of talking out and ratifying or rejecting suggestions and decisions made at the more frequent Wednesday afternoon sessions. One-off meetings were held by sub-groups as and when necessary to thrash out the details of a particular initiative (for example, a sub-group met twice when the welfare rights sessions were in the planning stage).

Decision making
As implied already, many ideas were discussed informally between group members outside the regular monthly meetings. Sometimes this led to very swift decision making at formal meetings, but at other times to extended discussion (often over small but contentious points). While, generally speaking, everyone had an opportunity to put their point of view at meetings, sub-groups of people – as already noted – had more or less influence according to the topic under consideration.

   A number of lines of tension existed within the group. One was between those who favoured caution and remaining true to original aims and objectives and those more adventurous members who were enthusiastic to follow up new schemes and were open to modification of existing plans. A second dividing line was between those who generally preferred to see energy invested in self-help activity and those more enthusiastic about pressure-group activities. There were also frequent disagreements between those members who were on personal and friendly terms with influential local councillors – and were keen to enlist their support, advocacy or patronage in pursuit of given aims – and those who were, or became, disillusioned with their local representatives.

Tactics and strategy

Action taken to gain or increase support for the group
Besides some attempts to engage the active interest of two of the town's local councillors, the group took action to increase support on a number of fronts. For example, when the small jobs scheme was getting under way invitations were extended to people in other pensioner organisations in Cleator and Cleator Moor to act as referral points for the scheme. These people were invited to meetings, and became regular attenders at the

Wednesday socials. Similarly, because of possible duplication of activities with the Welfare Committee and through the use of OAPA premises, contact was maintained with those organisations, and this also led to some recruitment of members to SCAG. Efforts were also made to present the group's point of view through press and local radio coverage.

Action taken to achieve objectives

SCAG's multiple goals required a variety of tactics. Among other things the group invited 'target' personnel to its meetings: for example, the secretary of the local community health council, the district road safety officer and the chief superintendent of police. It organised deputations to push a point of view (to the parish council and to the management of Cumberland Motor Services). The group also lobbied through letter writing to, and personal contact with, district and county councillors, and it encouraged media publicity on the road safety issue.

A brief account of the initiation of one project – the small jobs scheme – will illustrate how a variety of activities and tactics were combined over one particular issue:

1 Following a talk given to the Companions Club a meeting was called by the worker. The group decided to pursue the issue, first by contacting other groups to establish the demand for an odd jobs service.

2 A talk was given by a member of the Community Industry (CI) team, when the group was informed that CI could possibly provide a labour force, given that SCAG could organise sponsorship,[8] finance and referral. Discussion took place about the prospective participants, and the position concerning work on council-owned properties. Two people agreed to act as referral points, and three others to invite further people to act as referral points for different localities. A local councillor promised to explore the possibility of the rural district council (RDC) sponsoring and financing the scheme.

3 Contact was made with the RDC, CDP and parish council (PC) concerning finance, with the PC about sponsorship (difficulties in obtaining sponsorship delayed the scheme for a long time, due to misunderstandings and a changeover in clerk to the council). The manager of CI attended a PC meeting to explain the responsibilities of sponsorship, particularly concerning fidelity insurance. Still unclear, the PC clerk requested written clarification and referred the question of insurance responsibilities to county council solicitors for expert advice.

4   A further meeting took place with representatives from other organisations, and a network of referral points was established. These were incorporated into a poster advertising the scheme which was distributed to the Post Offices, the library, the OAP Centre, chip shops, pubs and the Information and Action Centre.
5   Administrative aspects of the scheme were settled; a referral form and standard letter were designed. A policy concerning the priority to be given to different jobs was formulated.
6   The scheme got underway; the time from original discussion of the need at the FE Centre to completion of the first round of jobs was 7 months.

An assessment of achievements and failures

In general, the group was successful in achieving its self-organising and self-help objectives (for example, the socials, the shopping club and the HELP cards scheme), but remained less successful in influencing the policy and practice of external agencies (though partial success was achieved over the chiropody, road safety and small jobs issues). This latter point is particularly noteworthy in view of the limited – many would say marginal – policy objectives the group had set itself. Not only were the returns from pressure activity extremely modest; they were achieved only after substantial expenditure of time and effort. It is only too easy to speculate about the reasons for the relative success of different initiatives. However, a number of plausible hypotheses relevant to a consideration of the group's pressure activities suggest themselves. The strong tradition of self-help among local people – particularly influential when attempts to meet the needs of pensioners are being considered – contrasted with the prevailing absence of militant grass-roots community action in Cleator Moor over the previous two decades. Such generalisations do, of course, require explanations in themselves; the role of councillors as spokesmen and advocates for particular community interests (a jealously guarded role which they found threatened by the CDP's attempts to encourage self-organisation among local people) may have been an important element. Councillors tended to be long-standing residents, 'close to the people' in the sense of having been neighbours and workmates. Some members of SCAG had personal ties with their local representatives, and this inhibited the adoption of a militant stance towards the council and councillors. It seems possible that the slowness in achieving results over some issues may have been partly due to reluctance to use direct action methods; for example, ways of deliberately disrupting traffic for demonstration purposes were considered when the group seemed to be getting nowhere with the pedestrian safety issue, but were rejected in favour of argument, persuasion and lobbying as the main tactics.

Overall, SCAG developed into an organisation whose members were prepared to give a considerable amount in time and effort to issues that concerned them. It was not identified (in terms of membership) with any particular geographical or religious segment of the community, and had the potential to act as a bridge between other groups working for elderly people's interests in the parish.

Impact of the group within the constituency
Short of conducting a survey of pensioners in Cleator Moor it would be difficult to say precisely what impact SCAG's activities had upon their constituency. There is, however, some evidence from a separate enquiry that people praised the trips, the raffles, the household goods club and the bring-and-buy, and that SCAG's action on concessionary fares was supported by people who compared what happened in Cleator Moor with the concessions that senior citizens in other parts were entitled to. In general it was found that pensioners were aware of SCAG's existence, and that action was being taken on issues which concerned them. It is interesting to note that in some ways SCAG officials came to behave in a similar way to local councillors: some SCAG members particularly mentioned that they had been invited to approach committee members with any problem which worried them.[9]

Impact of the group outside the constituency
Press, radio and television: As well as two or three local press reports on group activities, the worker was involved in a short news interview, and a ten-minute feature was made by Radio Carlisle on the household goods club.

Sponsorship and influential support: Members of the group, as noted, felt it worthwhile to encourage the interest, and hopefully the support, of two local councillors (both parish councillors, one a county councillor and the other a district councillor). Both were considered to have made constructive contributions to group discussions and both supported group initiatives at parish council meetings (small jobs, road safety); the district councillor also lent support over the chiropody issue (through his position on the community health council) and other matters.

Reactions of other existing structures

The group's activities were relatively uncontroversial. Only the shopping club generated a flurry of excitement; a newspaper report entitled 'Pensioners Go Bulk Buying' caused some concern among local traders, and there were dark mutterings about the possibility of abuse and of its 'getting out of hand'.

The impression was gained that in the eyes of established organisations and decision makers old people and their groups were a worthy and highly respectable cause that all could support as a 'good thing' without too much further thought. This, to the worker, seemed to be the attitude of most local politicians in the project area, at parish, district and county council levels. The low profile of the group evoked little overt reaction from other significant interests and organisations in the town.

Future of the group

At the time of the worker's withdrawal from the group, a number of factors seemed to point to its survival in some shape or form: members' commitment, the development of group identity, and the development and organisation of initiatives without worker involvement. The question mark hung over the phrase 'in some shape or form'.

While the experience of this and other pensioner groups in Cleator Moor reflected a considerable reservoir of skill and knowledge that could be mobilised to organise activities, there was much less evidence of growth in the skill and confidence needed to deal effectively with organisations and agencies external to members. In so far as the majority of pensioners' interests could be affected only marginally by self-help activity, a central goal had to remain the evaluation of methods that would help members of the group to learn to confront external targets effectively.

In so far as internally executed initiatives remained central to the group, the continued existence of CDP-instituted organisations (the resource centre) and funds (pump-priming grants) would remain important influences on achievement of goals. The question 'would the group outlive CDP?' partially became an aspect of a larger question: how much of the CDP apparatus constructed to support local groups would remain after the central CDP team had been dismantled?

Concluding comments

Certain themes are discernible if we stand back and review both the selection of issues taken up by the Senior Citizens Action Group, along with the level at which these issues were tackled. Put crudely, we can say that the group had a fairly consistent predisposition to take up issues that allowed themselves to be tackled at a local level; and that, whenever possible, members opted to take self-help and self-organising initiatives rather than attempt to influence outside bodies and decision makers. This, of course, is a gross over-simplification. The group did embark on pressure-group tactics in attempts to influence decision making, but members were most comfortable when pursuing a broadly self-help strategy. The underlying strategic sequence seemed to run as follows: first try to confront the issue or meet the need through local grass-roots resources and efforts; if this approach was ineffective (or inappropriate) then, second, to explore strategies of local influence; finally, if local pressure-group strategies were in their turn ineffective or inappropriate, to explore strategies that could be pursued at a national level.

Attempts to confront the chiropody issue furnish a good example of this sequence. Soon after the problem of withdrawal of local services had been identified, members began to explore action possibilities on two fronts: first, how to entice a (personally known) chiropodist, at the time practising in Whitehaven, to provide a sessional service in Cleator Moor for the National Health Service; and, second, how to set about fund-raising and other initiatives in order that the group could sponsor a local person for professional training. When neither of these self-help avenues seemed to present much hope of success the group began to lobby local decision makers, first the community physician and then members and the secretary of the local community health council with requests for a limited reinstatement of local services. Later, with the threat to local provision continuing, the group decided to lobby national decision makers. Contact was made with county councillors, the MP and Age Concern England, requesting support for the group's effort to raise the linked issues of pay and training for chiropodists with the Minister of Health and Social Security.

It could be suggested that selection of issues and strategy heavily slanted towards the local is not surprising and hardly needs explaining. After all, the group had its roots in a very limited geographical area and never had any pretensions to be more than locally based. Such a response will not do. On a variety of issues members quite clearly came to see the major causes of problems as rooted outside their local area, linked to decision making and resource allocation at a county, regional or national level. It was clearly seen, for example, that Department of Environment regulations concerning siting of pedestrian crossings had blocked achievement of a satisfactory solution to the local problem of pedestrian safety. The household goods club was seen to be valuable, but only because state retirement pension levels were too low. The comparative tardiness of concessions to pensioners in West Cumbria (for public transport, etc.) was put down to county council policy and the lack of adequate central government guidance to local authorities on such matters. In other words, members of SCAG did see the root of many problems in wider social and decision making structures; so why did the group maintain a preference for tackling problems at a parochial level, as far as possible within the compass of their own resources?

If the case study material allows us to dispense with explanations that suggest a failure to see the wider ramifications of issues, it also enables us to query simplistic theories that focus on the supposed lack of organisational experience among members. As we have seen SCAG did include people with organisational experience in other community organisations and groups, and included a one-time active trade unionist and parish councillor. A criticism, if any, to be levelled at the make-up of the group is that it provided yet another vehicle for the already organised and active in the town and failed to provide an opportunity for the organisationally inexperienced to come forward. Moreover, we must also remember that at the self-help level the group surmounted some not insignificant organisational problems. If lack of organisational ability is to be used as a partial explanation then its exact meaning and application must be specified.

Perhaps a more cogent set of explanations for the group's strategic performances is to be found in what we might call the balance of opportunities for action confronting SCAG. The case study material offers some clues to the way in which particular facets of the group's social environment conspired to channel its efforts in particular directions.

At one level we have seen how the existence of small pump-priming grants to help community projects to get under way encouraged SCAG to look for solutions that could make use of such bounty. The community resource centre provided other facilities that exerted a similar influence. The group, it will be remembered, turned to the resource centre for a minibus to bring the handicapped to the 'tea and crack' socials. It was only when numbers expanded and further transport was required that the possibility of the social services department providing a vehicle and driver was explored. Had the resource centre been able to offer the use of a second minibus it is fairly certain that the group would have looked to additional voluntary effort to meet their transport needs rather than seek provision from a statutory authority.

It can, of course, be argued that pump-priming grants, minibuses and all the other group-supportive services available in the area were neutral in the sense of not predisposing any particular use. A minibus can take a group of activists to lobby their MP just as well as convey handicapped people to an afternoon social. A pump-priming grant can be used to mount a campaign for better pensions or housing just as well as inaugurate a household goods venture. Or can it? The full significance of expanded opportunities to undertake self-help activities is perhaps only fully grasped when the complementary restrictions on opportunities to influence external targets is considered. Again, the case study gives illustrative material. SCAG found that local councillors jealously guarded their role as advocate, spokesman and patron. Local representatives liked to represent in a particular way and they felt uncomfortable (and had not come to terms) with groups of people who approached them in a non-deferential fashion. At its most extreme one local county councillor publicly complained that the 'proliferation of action groups could be the downfall of society', while a district councillor claimed that 'they kick the legs from under authority'. Many would not go this far but would agree that independent action groups can come perilously close to trespassing on their role. Those local groups that attempt to maintain their integrity and independence and are not prepared to have their aims and objectives taken over by their local representatives seem to come in for most criticism.[10]

The close-knit nature of community networks – in which councillors have often been personally known over long periods – also serves to inhibit action which is innovatory (in the sense of challenging norms governing people's relationships with their representatives). Divisions over strategy within SCAG sometimes reached stalemate because while on the one hand members would have liked to challenge the actions or opinions of particular councillors, on the other hand they felt inhibited from doing so because of personal ties and traditional normative expectations.

If local councillors play their role in such a way as to narrow the opportunities for successful intervention by independent pressure groups, then representatives of local official agencies and other bodies are no less adept at protecting their own organisation from the impact of local grass-roots feelings and demands. All we can do here is illustrate this point with one or two examples from a whole range of simple but effective tactics. Blurring, or not divulging, the divisions of responsibility in particular areas of policy and policy implementation can be one effective way of limiting the extent to which a group can make its voice heard and get its demands met. SCAG's action on the pedestrian safety issue was a case in point. Where should pressure be applied to get a satisfactory discussion (let alone solution) of the problem of local pedestrian safety? The road safety committee of the district council? The police? The highways department? The county road safety officer? The district council road safety committee referred local problems to relevant parish councils for their recommendations. The police controlled the deployment of traffic wardens. The highways department carried out traffic censuses if a pedestrian crossing was under consideration. The county road safety officer and police could recommend that Department of Environment standards concerning crossings should be set aside if there was a particular problem or hazard. It is only too easy for a group to find itself communicating with a variety of organisations and officials, none of which will explicitly define their area of responsibility in relation to the others. It is not that they deliberately attempt to evade responsibility, so much as that they are reluctant to volunteer information and suggestions that would effectively serve the group. Delays in replying to letters and other irritations can also help to dissipate a head of steam as group members find themselves bounced hither and thither between the cushions of the departmental and agency pin-table. Even when, as in the case of the small jobs scheme, there was an apparent willingness by all concerned to help meet a need, it took seven months to get a viable project off the ground.

These are only examples of the organisational frustration that local groups must overcome if they are to influence the actions of target agencies. It is hardly surprising that on many occasions members turn inwards and ask themselves 'How can we meet this need from our resources? If we have a go ourselves we will at least see some results'. Community resources and small grants re-enter the scene to encourage the take-up of this option.

Chronological summary of events: October 1973 – October 1975

19 October 1973   Following the worker's meeting with

Companions Club, invitations circulated to interested pensioners to discuss further the problem of getting small jobs done, and the question of pedestrian safety.

23 October 1973   Nine pensioners and the worker meet to discuss these problems. Decisions taken to invite Community Industry to discuss small jobs at Companions Club, to write to the road safety committee about the possibility of getting a pedestrian crossing for the market square, and to form the Senior Citizens Action Group.

22 November 1973   Parish council agrees to back the request for a pedestrian crossing. Decision to have a further meeting with Community Industry to work out the details of a small jobs scheme.

4 December 1973   Working meetings to take further the establishment of an odd jobs scheme, sponsorship for Community Industry, fund raising and publicity.

14 March 1974   Decision to open a bank account and to make contact with other local pensioners' groups.

27 March 1974   Referral points for the odd jobs scheme decided. Ennerdale Road Safety Committee replies to SCAG that they are unable to authorise a pedestrian crossing; decided that other alternatives should be examined. Decision to take up the difficulties of gardening for pensioners, and to contact the council in regard to this.

30 May 1974   Odd jobs scheme goes ahead. Decision to write to the police about traffic round the square on market days and Saturday mornings.

18 June 1974   Discussion about extending the hours of the lollipop man in the square. Area Health Authority contacted about the poor chiropody service in the area.

16 July 1974	First round of odd jobs completed successfully. Decision to write to Copeland Council and request discussions about SCAG's proposals on a grass-cutting scheme for pensioners. Reply from community physician about chiropody services. Decision to write to him suggesting that transport be arranged for all Cleator Moor patients to go to a special afternoon clinic in Whitehaven.
13 August 1974	Community physician replies suggesting that Cleator Moor people should receive their treatment in Cleator Moor rather than travelling. SCAG decides to approach the community health council. Decision to write again to Copeland requesting a meeting. Police say that restricted parking might be introduced in the square in the interests of pedestrian safety. SCAG fears that this will speed up the traffic and make the situation worse. Decision to write to the press.
19 August 1974	Letter to Whitehaven News concerning a pedestrian crossing.
10 September 1974	Report that chiropody services are to be discussed at the community health council. Report that Copeland Council and SCAG are to meet to discuss grass-cutting. Decision to hold welfare rights course for pensioners, with information booklets printed for all pensioners. Pump-priming grant to be applied for.
	Pedestrian safety; following the rejection of SCAG's suggestions, decision to approach the education authority about extending the hours of the lollipop man.
	HELP cards enthusiastically received but supply exhausted. Decision to apply for pump-priming grant to print more.
	Distribution of HELP cards reveals a number of housebound pensioners.

	Decision to investigate the possibility of an afternoon social.
17 September 1974	Pump-priming committee agrees to a £134 donation towards the welfare rights course, and £48 for printing HELP cards.
19 September 1974	Decision to go ahead with a social afternoon, and to apply for a pump-priming grant for transport and refreshments.
20 September 1974	Press report of Copeland's environmental health and housing committee: cost to council of doing pensioners' gardens would be prohibitive.
9 October 1974	First 'tea and crack' organised in Pensioners' Hut.
18 October 1974	Community physician announces to SCAG that chiropody services are to be resumed in Cleator Moor, and that a domiciliary service is to begin.
November 1974	Welfare rights course.
18 November 1974	Pump priming grant of £250 approved for 'tea and crack'.
2 December 1974	Discussion of preparations for Christmas party. Follow-up of problems of pensioners from CDP's social survey announced.
Christmas 1974	Christmas party.
6 January 1975	Decision to remind Copeland of their planned meeting with SCAG about gardening. Decision to write again to the Director of Education about extending the hours of the lollipop man.
	Decision to discuss community service by young people with teacher from Ehenside School.
	Decision, on basis of survey follow-up, to support the move to have all electric wiring in pensioners' houses inspected,

and to discuss the problem of loneliness among the elderly with Ehenside School.

Agreed in principle that the idea of a household goods co-operative is a good one, that the idea be taken further, and a pump-priming grant be applied for.

3 February 1975   Decision to co-operate with Ehenside School on community service. SCAG to refer those in need of help or company. Decision to contact education authority again about pedestrian safety, and Copeland Council about the meeting over gardens.

25 February 1975   Pump-priming committee defers decision on grant for household goods club, and receives reports on the HELP cards and the 'tea and crack'.

3 March 1975   Decision to enquire about Copeland's policy on help with TV licences for pensioners.

20 March 1975   Decision to write to Copeland Council and Cumberland Motor Services about removing the time restrictions on concessionary bus passes.

26 March 1975   Pie and pea supper and entertainment.

7 April 1975   Decision to remind Copeland Council of SCAG's enquiry about TV licences. Decision to invite secretary of the community health council to SCAG meeting to discuss ways of getting a chiropody service in Cleator Moor.

21 April 1975   Secretary of community health council comes to discuss chiropody services with SCAG. Explains shortage of chiropodists in the area. Further planning of community service scheme with Ehenside School.

28 April 1975   Pump-priming committee approves grant of £250 to set up household goods club.

1 May 1975   Press article at instigation of SCAG

drawing attention to poster in Cleator Moor urging people to use pedestrian crossings, and the urgent need for one in Cleator Moor. Press article about the household goods club organised by SCAG, which alarms local Cash and Carry concerns.

5 May 1975   Cumberland Motor Services invites SCAG to send a delegation to sit in at CMS meeting.

Decision to invite the police to a SCAG meeting to discuss traffic management for pedestrian safety. Report that the Cash and Carry wholesaler used by SCAG for the household goods club is refusing to serve SCAG. Decision to meet the manager and explain the position to him.

8 May 1975   SCAG receives letter from Copeland Council that no money is available this year or next for help with TV licences.

Delegation to meet Cumberland Motor Services agreed.

Secretary of the community health council expresses his willingness to meet SCAG again on chiropody issues.

Decision to write again to police about pedestrian safety in market square.

SCAG still awaiting decision of Cash and Carry wholesaler. Decision to contact manufacturers to see if direct buying is possible.

11 June 1975   Trip for 80 members.

16 June 1975   SCAG delegates meet Cumberland Motor services manager about time restrictions on bus passes. Each side explains its position.

2 July 1975   Regular group meeting hears progress report on community service scheme from organising teacher. Scheme making

satisfactory progress and will resume after the summer vacation.

10 July 1975   Letter to all local councillors outlining difficulties over time restrictions on concessionary bus passes. Councillors asked to press the matter. Letter sent to the Director of Finance.

1 August 1975   Reply from Cash and Carry wholesaler that he cannot supply goods for reselling.

4 August 1975   Chief superintendent of police and road safety sergeant attend monthly meeting and give assurance that extra policing of the square on Fridays and Saturdays would be arranged.

21 August 1975   Outing for 'tea and crack' members.

19 September 1975   Group holds a special meeting to draft a constitution.

6 October 1975   Monthly meeting. Extended discussion of aspects of group strategy, relationship between the group and 'tea and crack', etc. Agreement to pursue chiropody issue at wider level.

10 October 1975   Letter sent to Chairman of Cumbria County Council Policy and Resources Committee asking him to support the group's efforts in bringing the dire state of chiropody services to the attention of the Minister of Health.

Chapter 3
West Cumberland Action Committee

Introduction

> 'It is a government responsibility, whoever is in power, to make journeys to school free for all school children throughout the country' (A Cumberland county councillor, June 1973).

The mood of many people in West Cumberland turned to such thoughts in the summer of 1973. The editorial of a local newspaper described the mood as a product of the 'age of protest', citing the activities of the West Cumberland Action Committee as an example. Articles and features appeared in the Cumberland press describing children and their parents marching to school, come rain or shine, carrying banners and placards in protest against the way free bus passes were allocated. Meetings rallying support were closely followed in the press; pronouncements in support of free travel to school by councillors and local dignitaries were regularly reported. Petitions were organised and presented to the local MP, who addressed an open air rally in Whitehaven. Three hundred people heard the speeches and plans of campaign put forward by the local protest groups, the WCAC, and councillors at all levels of local government. The campaign generated an enthusiastic momentum revealed in statements like 'the protest will spread throughout Cumberland and even the country nationally', 'the push should be from Cumberland and we should march and march and let England know that all school children must have free passes', and, in talking of the children's involvement, 'youth has lain dormant long enough and now is their chance to show what they can really do if given the chance'.

Petitions, protest and demonstrations in localised parts of West Cumberland indicated an emotive response to a number of issues. The banners that read 'Small Children, Small Fares',

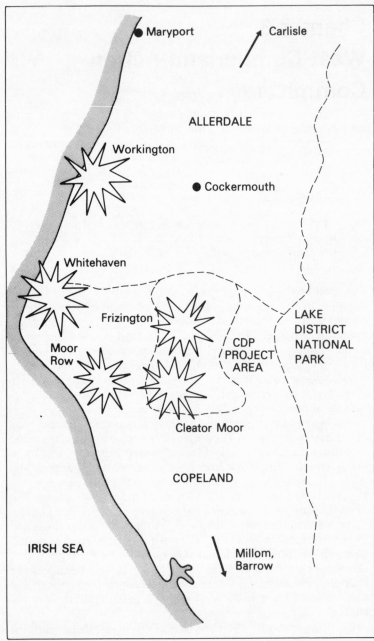

Figure 1   Where the bus fare protests erupted in West Cumber-land, July 1973

'Free Passes for our Lads and Lassies', 'Give us This Day our Free Pass' illustrated the fervour. The West Cumberland Action Committee was born amidst this furore to help to co-ordinate the protest and lobby the bus company, the local authority, the national government, or whatever body might be able to make free travel passes to school a reality.

What is not explicable, however, is why this particular fare increase led to such vehement public reaction when previous increases had passed with little comment. From 1966 to 1973, the Cumberland Motor Services had altered its fare structure once a year.

Context and background

The 1944 Education Act made it a duty for parents to send their children to school. To reduce the transport costs of those children living some distance from school, passes were introduced to provide free travel for under 8-year-olds who lived over two miles away, and for 8- to 14-year-olds who had more than three miles to travel. This policy has often been criticised both locally and nationally on the following grounds:

1 The mileage limit is enforced inflexibly according to map measurement as the crow flies, no matter whether the actual distance travelled by public transport exceeds this limit.
2 The limit is measured from school to home irrespective of the position of the bus stop. Consequently whilst the child next door might qualify for a pass, your child might not.
3 The use of distance as a qualification for a free pass in no way eases the financial burden of bus fares to school for those households with limited incomes.

In some areas education authorities have used their discretionary powers to reduce the effects of these anomalies; for instance, by subsidising bus companies to the extent that school children up to a specified age (in a few cases school-leaving age) merely pay a low flat-rate fare. Cumberland Education Department granted pupils passes only on the basis of the 1944 Act.

At the time the protest erupted in West Cumberland, the Conservative government had already begun to look at school transport. The Department of Education and Science had set up a Working Party on Schools Transport (WPST), part of whose brief was to review the costs of getting to school and to recommend ways in which these could be reduced. In Spring 1972 the Secretary of State for Education and Science and the Secretary of State for Wales requested the working party to 'review the present arrangements for, including the existing law affecting, the provision of school transport and to report on any changes which might be needed'.

Along with other parts of Britain, West Cumberland in the summer of 1973 was undergoing re-organisation of local government. It was a muddled situation with new and old councillors assuming new responsibilities; some maintained their position on the old councils, others also held positions on the steering committees of the new authorities, and others had just been elected to represent their constituents for the first time in the new local government structure. The different responsibilities of the new county, district and parish councils were also being worked out. Counties and districts needed to define their responsibilities, among other matters, in the public transport field. What contribution should districts make towards the subsidy support of uneconomic routes? Should district councils be able to continue to run their own municipal bus services? What should Cumbria's relationship be with the National Bus Company subsidiaries? What would be the implications of the Transport Policies and Programme report for public transport services?[1] Amidst all these rearrangements, plans, and the setting up of appropriate committees, the National Bus Company subsidiary in the West Cumberland area, Cumberland Motor Services, raised its fares and generated an angry public reaction.

The Community Development Project became associated with the bus fares protest shortly after the marches started. The Project had been established in the two parishes of Cleator Moor and Arlecdon/Frizington (part of the Ennerdale Rural District Council) since May 1972. A profile of the area had been completed[2] and, on the basis of this, action and research strategies were being formulated. By the summer of 1973, when the bus fares protest escalated, CDP was beginning to take up local issues and carry out research. All of the action team had been appointed, as well as two members of the research staff. A Community Information and Action Centre was opened offering support, advice and advocacy to individuals; it was also ready to respond to community groups' needs. Initially, it operated from the same building in which the rest of the CDP staff were based.

Towards the end of June, a group of mothers living on a new estate at the edge of Cleator Moor contacted CDP requesting support and advice in planning a meeting through which to consolidate the hitherto independent actions of parents and children on the bus fares issue. All of them had taken part in the marches to schools.

Formation of the group

The event which precipitated local protest and eventually led to the formation of the West Cumberland Action Committee was an increase in children's (and adults') bus fares. The Cumberland Motor Services bus company had successfully applied to the Northern Traffic Commissioners with the effect that the lowest child's fare was increased from 3p to 4p.

It was the Cleator Moor mothers who suggested the idea of calling a meeting to co-ordinate the campaign through a centralised committee. The Chairman of the Ennerdale Rural District Council, who had on occasions led both the Frizington and Cleator Moor marches, agreed to chair the meeting; with the help of CDP letters were sent to all known protesting groups of parents and to parish, district and county councillors. The venue was to be Whitehaven, and a large public notice advertising the meeting was placed in the *Whitehaven News*. It was hoped that not only would a committee be formed, but also that plans would be made to organise a mass rally and the serving of petitions on the National Bus Company and the Cumberland County Education Committee. About 100 supporters attended this first meeting, including councillors from Frizington, Cleator Moor, Moor Row, Workington and Whitehaven and representatives of the bus fares protest groups in each of these places. Numerous councillors pledged their support and agreed to raise the issue of free travel passes at the next Cumberland Education Committee meeting. Twenty-eight supporters (none of whom were councillors) became members of the group, which was named the West Cumberland Action Committee. Three hundred people attended the subsequent open-air rally at which the local MP for Whitehaven made an address in support of the campaign. The following day, the committee attended the Cumberland County Council meeting in Whitehaven and handed a petition with 3,000 signatures to the chairman.

During June and July, the Cleator Moor group undertook most of the work involved in organising the inaugural meeting and the rally, lobbying councillors and inviting them to meetings. The numbers attending WCAC meetings, however, declined over the following months (the Whitehaven and Workington members particularly fell away), as the activities of the Committee became more concerned with lobbying at county and national levels. After the first public meeting when the WCAC was formed only one new member joined the committee.

Group objectives

From the events that led to the formation of the WCAC, it is clear that the overall objective of the committee was to bring about a change in the basis on which travel passes were allocated. It was a campaigning issue group in that it could see no solutions locally to the problems created by the national legislation, nor did it set itself the goal of trying to make alternative transport provisions by using members', or obtaining other, resources. The WCAC sought either a change in the legislation nationally or a reallocation of the county's financial resources to subsidise the cost to households of home to school bus fares. The committee also sought to mobilise public support and organise meetings to air the issues.

The main concern of the committee was not unnaturally for the children in West Cumberland. In a circular, the committee stated that it was hoped to bring about 'the provision of free passes to all school children travelling to and from school regardless of cost'. This statement encompassed the slightly different concerns of the protest groups. For example, the Moor Row bus fares protest group emerged more as a direct reaction to the constant increases in fares, while the Frizington group specifically objected to the mileage limit travel pass system. Some of the groups had publicly identified a number of other objectives prior to merging with the WCAC. The Frizington group had earlier raised localised problems; for example, some estates in the village were not well served by school buses, and buses to the secondary schools in Cleator Moor did not connect well with the finishing of school at the end of the day.

CDP objectives

As mentioned above, the bus fares protests occurred at a time when the Project was beginning to carry out action-research initiatives. In the Initial Study, Project workers were described as generalists, ready to respond to the queries and demands put to them by local people. The Project wished to portray itself as a community resource centre:

> While people often know what needs to be done or

changed, the difficulties experienced in trying to bring this about are great. Yet unless the residents of small communities put forward their ideas and do what they can to put them into practice, there is the danger of losing any chance of creating the type of communities that are wanted by those who live and work in them. A primary function of CDP will be to act as a resource to people who wish to try and do something in the community . . . CDP staff will be available to talk over ideas and explore the possibilities of turning them into action. Alternatively, someone will attend meetings of organisations to discuss particular issues and see whether some course of action can be worked out. The resource centre will undertake to find out relevant information on behalf of an individual or group . . . and can offer to community groups a variety of secretarial assistance.[3]

The Cleator Moor Bus Fares Protest Group, and subsequently the WCAC, were seen as the sort of groups that the resource centre should service in terms of supporting and encouraging action in response to local needs and local problems. However, Project workers recognised that they did not have the technical expertise to suggest to the group what policy options there were, or which channels should be used to influence the relevant bodies. At the time, the Project had no experience in the transport field and responded to the request for advice in terms of organisational support. The West Cumberland Action Committee was one of the first groups with which CDP associated itself. A worker at the Information and Action Centre subsequently became the community worker to the group.

Changes in the group's objectives

Whilst the specific nature of its objectives were modified over time, the conception upon which WCAC evolved withstood substantial change. Over the initial months the definitive 'free travel to school' was used as a banner for the campaign. In practice, however, the WCAC's criticism of the system of pupils' passes became broader. They took into consideration the raising of the school-leaving age, and, in a letter to the Director of Education in April 1974, pressed that all school children should travel to school free or at a low fixed charge, not just the 5- to 14-year-olds. The committee also argued that, while the present system existed, the anomalies mentioned earlier should be ironed out.

Initially most of the committee's work was aimed at obtaining public sympathy and support: planning the marches, organising the mass rally, and collecting signatures for the petition. Later, the objectives of the committee were modified by the responses received from the local authority and DES; for example, when the Cumbria County Education Department's estimates for 1974–5 revealed no change in the subsidy allocated to travel costs, and when Education Ministers announced cutbacks in education expenditure.

More and more it became clear that the WCAC was up against not just an *ad hoc* fare increase, but the national policy on free passes. It was sympathetic councillors who quickly reinterpreted the issue into the need to influence policy. The Chairman of the Ennerdale Rural District Council, for instance, stated that 'the long-term policy for Cumbria should be free bus passes for all school children . . . in the short term local authorities should consider subsidies for school bus services'.

The initial marches and demonstrations of protest can, therefore, be seen as an attempt to gain the sympathy and support of local and county councillors. Through this sympathy and support it was hoped that a change in county policy on subsidising fares would occur. At the same time, or in response to the county's rejection of such subsidies, WCAC became concerned to effect change in national policy; for example, in the provisions of the Education Act of 1944.

The secondary objectives of the local protest groups were not taken up by the West Cumberland Action Committee. The committee was established as a campaigning group, with the issue of the travel pass allocation system in the forefront. Over time, as the committee found that its proposals were being rejected, it attempted to redefine its objectives and adopt a more general role as a public transport watchdog group.

Changes in CDP's objectives

In terms of its commitment to working with community groups, CDP's objectives remained unchanged. Partly through its association with WCAC the Project had begun to pursue other issues related to public transport; for example, the constraints on work opportunities created by inadequate public transport services.[4] Some six months after the WCAC was formed there was unease in the Project over the committee's limited use of alternative strategies. By then the committee's strategies were totally directed at county and national levels. Although the WCAC was still holding monthly meetings, no attempts were being made to harness the support of local people, to stimulate local protest action or to engage in examining ways of reducing the hardships on large families caused by the costs of sending their children to school. The committee was no longer a local action group serving a local function; it was felt by some Project members to be in danger of isolating itself from the local constituency in focussing its efforts on effecting changes in the structures and policies of local and national government. The Project did not, however, dissociate itself from the committee.

Aspects of internal group organisation and development

Membership

Over the first year, the WCAC's membership decreased from the original 28 to about 10, with some fluctuations in attendance at meetings. Originally the Cleator Moor group was the most active in planning activities, making representations to councillors and stimulating the amalgamation of the groups. The Whitehaven group always retained a measure of independence and, like the Cleator Moor mothers, occasionally held separate meetings. Eventually the Workington group too became isolated from the committee.

Nearly all the members of WCAC were young mothers in their late twenties.[5] The majority were housewives with no daytime work commitments (this was particularly true of the Cleator Moor group). About half of the members had previous experience in community self-help or voluntary organisations; for example, Women's Institutes, helping out with pensioners' clubs, and pre-school playgroups. Some of the Cleator Moor women drifted away as they became involved with a playground venture established in September 1973 on the new estate where they lived. Most of the Committee members were working class, though some of the Moor Row women were professionals' wives.

That the committee members were mainly women probably characterised some of the local reactions to it. The CDP worker felt that the bus company officials and councillors tended to patronise them: 'after all they're only a bunch of women, not to be taken seriously'. On the other hand, because they were women, they may have found it easier to get face-to-face meetings with officials and councillors. Meeting the ladies in the afternoon could have been seen as a pleasant interlude in the day.

Tensions and difficulties occurred in the home for some women who had had little experience in community affairs. The CDP worker thought it necessary to give personal support to those women who found that their involvement in the WCAC led to difficulties in their marital relationships. Some husbands (in Cleator Moor and Frizington particularly) resented their wives' involvement with the committee and their association with male CDP workers during the committee's early days. Hence, despite the long-term support of the CDP worker (who was female), the cultural view that the woman's place is in the home may have pressurised some of the women to terminate their involvement with the committee.

It is also worth noting that neither schoolchildren nor councillors became members of the committee. The youth who had 'lain dormant long enough' were never involved. Towards the end of the summer of 1974, the worker was in touch with a group of pupils from a local grammar school who had begun protesting independently about school bus fares, but they did not respond to her invitation to meet WCAC. Likewise, councillors who had pledged their support and even attended one or two of the early meetings, never actively associated themselves with the membership.

Leadership

The amalgamation of groups from five areas seemed to the CDP worker to present difficulties in terms of establishing formal leaders. However, because of the amount of work carried out by the Cleator Moor women and the fact that one of them acted as spokeswoman for the WCAC, this group came to be the leaders.

In stimulating ideas and action following the original local hyperactivity the CDP worker also played an important role. In addition, discussion and formulation of strategies at the meetings were influenced by the stronger-willed representatives of the independent groups. Those with more experience in community organisation also had relatively more influence. Some members from Frizington apparently felt at a particular disadvantage due to what they felt to be their lower education. Only in March 1974 was there in fact a formal election of officers, more in response to the need to open a bank account than to structure the committee's roles. The elected officers included representatives from Moor Row, Frizington and Cleator Moor. The worker was elected secretary.

Role of the CDP worker

In no way did CDP workers take an active part in the formation of WCAC. A number of CDP workers had joined in the local Cleator Moor marches; this probably influenced the Cleator Moor women to come to the Project's offices seeking advice on how to arrange the co-ordinating meeting. Three workers were in touch with members of the Cleator Moor Protest Group in different capacities. Subsequently one worker provided support for the West Cumberland Action Committee. She was based full-time in the Information and Action Centre.

The worker saw her immediate function as the servicing of the committee with technical information on tactical matters. How could the committee translate its local protest into policy influence? Who had the power to enable home-to-school bus fares to be subsidised? What was the National Bus Company's policy in Cumbria on child fare subsidies? What was the county council's? Which committee of the new county authority should be approached regarding the desired change in policy? Who were sympathetic councillors, who were the influential ones? How did you make an objection to the Northern Traffic Commissioners?

Such were the technical questions that the committee had to resolve and such was the political mapping of the new and old local authorities that had to be carried out. Apart from those problems arising from local government re-organisation, both the worker and the committee soon discovered that the procedure for influencing policy on school transport was confused and unclear. It was difficult to find out how the policy channels of the bus company, the local authorities, the Traffic Commissioners and the government slotted together.

In addition to helping to trace the political decision making channels, the worker assisted in drafting letters and suggesting a variety of tactics that could be used. She also acted as convenor of meetings and secretary to the committee. This, she felt, was a means of avoiding conflict between the village-based groups. A particular problem for the worker was that she saw it as important not to lose the momentum of the campaign; and yet at the same time she had to give members of the committee the time and opportunity to get to know their way round local government procedures. Between the meetings, and particularly during the first six months, the worker made personal contact weekly with members of the Cleator Moor and Frizington groups. The Cleator Moor women used to drop into the Community Information and Action Centre. The Frizington women often used to visit her at the CIAC mobile van session in the village. Home visits were also made to the Cleator Moor and

Frizington women and occasionally to members from Moor Row. Contact with the Moor Row, Workington and Whitehaven members was mainly by telephone, usually to the spokeswoman of each group. By this level of contact, the worker acted as the central co-ordinator. She acknowledged that WCAC offered her *carte blanche* to act on her own initiative, particularly in making contact with county councillors and officials at the Department of Education and Science. On one or two occasions the worker was the sole representative of the committee when presenting the case to a potential sympathiser. The content of these meetings was always fed back to the committee. However, rather than construing these methods of working as inducing a dependency where the group leant heavily upon the worker, she saw herself as an equal member of the group and identified completely with its aims and objectives. Along with other members of the committee she felt that she had responsibilities in implementing the decisions and tactics agreed on and in using her initiative should a situation arise that demanded it.

As secretary, the worker was largely responsible for drawing up the agenda and putting forward suggestions and ideas for action. In the early days, when action and tactics were directed at the local level, the worker had been less instrumental in suggesting possible strategies, and conflict within the group seldom led to the worker's intervention. Her more directive role developed later, when the committee moved into the more general policy field.

Overall, the worker felt that the long-term goals of WCAC determined her role. The need to maintain momentum led her to take on a co-ordinating and actively directive role. In her own view, had she not performed this role, it was doubtful whether the committee would have survived the strategic move from the local to the county and national levels.

Use of CDP resources
Throughout its life WCAC made heavy and continuous use of the Project's typing, photocopying and poster-making facilities. The CDP offices and the Information and Action Centre were both used as meeting places, and the Project's vehicles were used to ferry people to and from meetings. The CDP market stall was used in Whitehaven when signatures were being collected for the petition. The research team was also asked to help the committee in putting together a questionnaire on the financial hardship of families resulting from the increase in bus fares. Two small grants (each of £40) were received from CDP's pump-priming committee in March 1976.

Use of other resources and facilities

Prior to the formation of WCAC most of the local protest groups held meetings in public buildings, schools or private homes. The meeting at which the committee was formed was held at the Catholic Men's Society Club in Whitehaven. A fund-raising fashion show was held in the Civic Hall in Cleator Moor in March 1974; previously, fund-raising had been carried out autonomously by the groups and planned outside WCAC meetings. The only donation (£5) towards its funds was received from the Ennerdale Rural District Council.

Meetings

The committee held a regular meeting every month, with additional meetings when necessary. Most of the initial meetings were devoted to planning the lobbying and publicity campaigns and to talking through transport problems; for example, the isolation of rural areas caused by cutbacks in services. A considerable amount of contact occurred between meetings when members were planning the mass rally, preparing the financial burden questionnaire and organising fund-raising events. Special meetings were called to discuss particular tactics, for example when WCAC decided to present a copy of the petition to the Parliamentary Under-Secretary of State for Education on his visit to the area in September 1973. The Workington and Cleator Moor groups also held their own meetings from time to time, as already noted. In general, the meetings were conducted informally, and members were encouraged to put their points of view. Though an agenda was constructed, new issues and proposals were often raised in the course of meetings.

Decision making

From the records there is little indication of how decisions were arrived at. The worker tended to record the broad substance of the discussion and the final decision made without clarifying the options considered, how much time was devoted to discussing them and who, if anyone, tended to be influential in making them. Even so, it was clear that the committee had some problems in accommodating the views of the previously independent groups. Tensions arose when planning and discussing future strategies; the leader of the Workington mothers, for example, was particularly vocal in advocating more aggressive tactics.

The making and implementing of decisions also reflected some disagreement on priorities within the committee. Although it was readily agreed that a dossier of information on cases of financial hardship should be presented to the DES Working

Party, this was never completed, the Frizington group having particular difficulties in collecting the material.

Tactics and strategy

The WCAC wanted to effect and change policy, a change which would ultimately mean the reallocation of the County Education Committee's resources and/or a change in the provisions of the 1944 Education Act. The committee continually attempted to identify the channels through which its influence could be exerted. In attempting to achieve its objectives, as with many other protest groups, WCAC operated in a number of ways to gain support:

1 At the outset it located and brought together those groups of mothers protesting at the increase in bus fares; in particular, it organised a mass rally.
2 Councillor interest was established through the preliminary activities. Five local district and parish councillors publicly acknowledged their full support. Influential councillors were also invited to attend some of the committee's meetings or were lobbied on the face-to-face level.
3 Local radio broadcasts, leaflets and press coverage publicised the committee's aims. WCAC meetings were not publicised in advance in the press, though accounts occasionally appeared afterwards. Notices of meetings were sent out to those who joined the committee at the Whitehaven meeting.
4 The committee dealt with an individual case that arose from the anomalies that could occur through the 3-mile limit of the 1944 Education Act. The case was referred to the WCAC by the Community Information and Action Centre. The mother of the child concerned subsequently joined the committee.
5 Letters were sent out to schools in West Cumberland seeking support, but the reaction was poor (though these letters were addressed to school governors, many of them were dealt with by the headteachers; indeed the worker questioned whether the item had been allowed on to the agenda for the governors' meetings as the Education Department provided the secretariat and was responsible for preparing the agendas for such meetings).

6 Contact was made with Parent Teacher Associations (PTAs) and voluntary organisations whose representatives were invited to attend WCAC meetings; for example, the Socialist Action Group.

Action taken to achieve objectives

Over the twelve-month period considered in this case study, the action taken by the committee went through two broad phases, the former directed at the local level, and the latter directed at official policy making structures in the county council and central government.

First phase: This was the period of the marches. Parents refused to allow their children to pay bus fares to school (buses were boarded and no fares offered), and children marched with banners to schools in protest.[6] The season of protest culminated in the creation of WCAC at the meeting in Whitehaven and the organised mass rally. Petitions were co-ordinated through WCAC and presented to the chairman of the county council, and to the Under Secretary of State for Education when he visited the area.

The first and second phases merged in that they both aimed to influence policies but, from August 1973, no attempts were made to generate the kinds of localised protest that had characterised activities in June and July.

Second phase (county and national level): Following the formation of the committee its strategy was conducted along the following lines:

1 Lobbying for support through local societies, voluntary bodies and schools (including Boards of Governors).
2 Lobbying parish and district councils to press the Cumberland and Cumbria Education Committees to use their discretionary powers to reduce school children's bus fares and to lodge objections with Traffic Commissioners against the increases.
3 Meetings with officials and councillors, presentation of the WCAC case to the county's Education Finance and General Purposes Sub-Committee.
4 Collection and preparation of cases to demonstrate hardship.
5 Submission of evidence and comments to the DES Working Party on Schools Tranport. This was carried out in part through contact with the local MP.
6 Inviting sympathetic and non-sympathetic

organisations and councillors to WCAC meetings to
discuss the issues.

Achievements and failures

Prior to the formation of WCAC, the local campaign attracted
a great deal of public sympathy, as was indicated by the strong
support for the marches and attendance at the public meetings.
The committee successfully advocated on behalf of a child
adversely affected by the anomalies of the 3-mile limit. A substantial amount of support was also realised through the strong
backing given to the committee by councillors. They were able
to persuade the Cumberland County Education Committee to
carry out a review of their subsidies to school bus fares. This was
conducted by the Director of Education, and a project group
was set up to look at the implications of free travel to school.
Members of WCAC were invited to attend the project group's
one and only meeting to present their views. They were asked
to supply evidence of need, which the committee was also preparing for the DES Working Party. The survey work was never
completed. In December 1973 the Director of Education
reported to the Cumberland Education Committee that the possibility of subsidising school travel was feasible but the costs
involved were high: £80,000.[7] Nevertheless it was recommended
that 'the Cumbria Education Committee should give sympathetic
consideration to the general problems involved in the provision
of transport for school children within the limits of the funds
available in the financial estimates'. In addition WCAC asked
that due consideration be given to the DES Working Party
report.[8] As a result of the February 1974 general election and
the subsequent cutbacks in national expenditure, Cumbria
County Council felt it was unable to reallocate any of its
resources to allow for additional subsidies to be made to reduce
school transport costs. Having created a special project group to
examine WCAC's case, and achieved a favourable response, the
Council was prevented by national circumstances from further
consideration of the issue.

Whilst it has not been possible to trace through with committee
members the impact of the financial changes in policy making
circles, it would not be surprising to find that this was a frustration. The frustration of gaining so much political sympathy
locally and then failing to bring about any change in policy can
only make government appear remote and covert, and groups
like WCAC feel weak and powerless.

When the Cumberland Motor Services applied for another increase of fares in January 1974, WCAC was again successful in asking local councils as well as the county council to lodge objections. It was due to the actions of the West Cumberland Action Committee that the new Copeland and Allerdale district councils regularly placed 'fixed' objections before the Commissioners when fare increases were announced. Prior to the formation of WCAC local authorities had often made 'interim' objections but never fully prepared or argued their case; indeed, in many instances this was withdrawn before the Commissioners' hearing. The Committee also had some degree of success in making public Cumbria County Council's discussions on the finance of public transport expenditure. For example, the Public Passenger Sub-Committee was to have discussed the accounts of CMS and another Cumbrian bus company behind closed doors. Following a letter that was read to the full council and sent to the Policy and Resources and the Highways and Transportation Committees, this discussion was carried out with the public and press admitted.

Impact

Press reports confirm that the committee initially gained substantial public support. But there is no evidence to indicate the local reaction to the activities of the committee. Indeed, this would be difficult to assess. The committee's constituency was fluid because of the changeover in the school population. In addition its constituency could equally well be conceived either as all parents and children in West Cumbria, or simply as those who were resident where the initial protests sparked off.

There were two radio broadcasts during the local campaigns, but the most extensive form of coverage was in the press which responded to the public sympathy to the bus fares protest. Subsequently, WCAC gained little coverage, though an article appeared in a community newspaper in Frizington towards the end of 1974.

The committee consistently made attempts to gain influential support. Members sustained links with the local MP, through whom they channelled their national action. At the county level the committee had the support of a local councillor who sat on the Education Committee and the Sub-Committee's project group; the group was also supported by the chairman of the local district council. These contacts were particularly helpful in providing information on policy changes, and in recommending the aims of WCAC to respective councils or committees.

The CDP worker reported some disenchantment with councillors among some of the committee. Their pledges of support came when public interest was high, but their active association was nil. The WCAC could have been seen as a popular body to which councillors attached themselves for political capital shortly after the new local government elections. The committee subsequently located potentially influential councillors and invited them to their meetings; for example, the Chairman of the Economic Development Committee of Cumbria attended a meeting to inform the committee of the likely policies of the County Council.

Through the worker, the committee also made contact with the Transport Road Research Laboratory agency, which had ready access to the evidence submitted to the Working Party on School Transport.

Reactions of other existing structures
Initially the committee's strategies were visibly conflictual. It was at this stage that verbal support from local councillors was most forthcoming. This period of activity formed the basis on which the reputation of WCAC was established. The involvement of Project workers in some of the marches linked CDP with this activity.

There was some reaction amongst local establishment figures that this sort of action was unduly abrasive; and the Project became to some extent identified with such strategies.

Subsequently WCAC lobbied schools and voluntary organisations, receiving an ambivalent response from the former and tacit support (particularly from the Cumberland Parish Councils Association) from the latter. The committee's image became less controversial through its appeals to such more recognised organisational structures. In general the response from statutory bodies was one of sympathetic understanding.

Future of the group

In this case study we have attempted to draw out how the committee took up the issue of a bus fares increase and led a public protest directed at both local and central government. The nature of the issue – the travel to school costs and the anomalies of the mileage limits – was the backbone of the objection to the June 1973 and January 1974 fare increases. The Committee chose to draw attention to the anomalies of the Education Act and to seek a change in the legislation. For this reason the committee became involved in attempting to influence the then fluid policy making process.

Despite the fact that Education Committee resources were not allocated to school transport subsidies, and despite the government's continued deferment of the DES Working Party report,[9] WCAC continued to meet. Two grants were obtained from CDP's pump-priming committees to send letters to MPs at the House of Commons to ask them to raise the issues again. The committee accepted the long-term approach to policy change, thus confirming the commitment of its members to their original objectives. The committee, however, made little headway, and attempted to concern itself with more general public transport issues. But even with its liaison with other local voluntary organisations concerned with public transport, the committee's activities became largely limited to periodic meetings. While attempting to redefine its focus, the committee had great difficulty in establishing itself as a 'public transport watchdog', and led no further local campaigns despite continued fare increases.

The central role of the worker proved crucial to the convening of WCAC's meetings. When the worker left the Information and Action Centre the Project's involvement with the group diminished considerably. It became questionable whether the campaign for free travel passes to school was still the prerogative of the WCAC in West Cumbria. The group's prospects for survival as a county and national pressure group were bleak.

Concluding comments

The experience of WCAC points to a difficulty which is common to many community groups: that the local problems which stimulate their formation have national causes that are not affected by the limited influence which groups can bring to bear. The West Cumberland Action Committee seems to have fallen between two stools; first it became isolated from its local constituency (its main source of public support), and second, it proved unable to establish links with other organisations throughout the country to pursue an effective national campaign. This may have been caused by its decision to direct most of its energies into influence-exertion at the intermediate level, that is, the county council, which eventually proved unwilling to use its discretionary powers to alleviate the problems. By then, the committee had moved too far from the bases from which it originated to continue pursuing individual grievances to the mileage limits or mounting public campaigns against further increases. But it had not moved far enough to be able to contemplate co-ordinating a national campaign.

Chronological summary of events: June 1973 – May 1974

June 1973   Cumberland Motor Services raises bus fares.

Mothers and children in Moor Row, Cleator Moor and then other parts of West Cumberland begin protest marches.

Cleator Moor Bus Fares Protest Group seeks advice from CDP on organising a co-ordinating meeting. Protest groups begin lobbying councillors and officials.

2 July 1973   Open meeting in Whitehaven of all protest groups (Cumberland Motor Services does not attend). WCAC formed and arrangements made for a mass rally and organisation of petition.

3 July 1973   Workington bus fares group holds separate meeting.

5 July 1973   First WCAC meeting (28 attend); plans for mass rally discussed.

Cumberland Education Committee moves that the Director of Education 'be asked to examine the financial implications of a reduction in mileage for children attending school'.

15 July 1973   Open-air mass rally in Whitehaven chaired by the Mayor of Whitehaven (300 attend). MP addresses meeting. Support pledged by local councillors.

16 July 1973   Cumberland County Council ratifies its Education Committee's recommendation (5 July) and extends the brief of the Director of Education's project group 'to look at the whole question of school transport . . . and

that constituent local authorities be invited to submit their views'.

WCAC presents chairman of the council with the 3,000-signature petition.

18 July 1973   WCAC sends letters to all schools and local councils in West Cumberland seeking support.

26 July 1973   WCAC meeting; discussion of Department of Education and Science (DES) Working Party on School Transport. Decision to collect evidence of financial hardship caused by anomalies of the mileage limit.

2 August 1973   WCAC deals with the case of a child adversely affected by the 3-mile limit.

mid-August 1973   CDP helps to produce questionnaire to collect evidence of financial hardship.

late August 1973   Letter received from Cumberland Education Department: the child unfairly discriminated against will receive a pass.

12 September 1973   Some members of the committee meet the local MP to discuss future plans.

WCAC Meeting; agreed that a letter should be handed to Lord Sandford (Parliamentary Under-Secretary of State for Education) with a copy of the petition when he visits the area. Questionnaires being completed. Decision to broadcast on local radio.

17 September 1973   WCAC meets Lord Sandford and hands petition to him.

20 September 1973   WCAC member addresses a local PTA regarding the school bus fares campaign.

1 October 1973   Cumberland Education Finance and General Purposes Sub-Committee appoints members to the director's

	project group 'to examine the financial implications of a reduction in mileage for children attending school'.
12 October 1973	Cumberland Education Finance and General Purposes Sub-Committee notes the existence of the DES Working Party. Agrees to defer consideration of the Director of Education's note on the financial consequences of reducing mileage limits pending the publication of the DES Working Party's report.
	WCAC meeting; discussion of the Education Finance and General Purposes project group. Decision to contact all PTAs.
12–18 October 1973	CDP worker contacts other Education Departments in Britain and the Road Research Laboratory for information regarding local authority subsidies to school bus fares.
23 October 1973	Letter sent by WCAC to the local MP to ask him to press the DES Working Party for the early publication of a full report.
24 October 1973	Contact made with local and national Parish Councils Associations.
early November 1973	Letter sent to Chairman of Cumberland Education Finance and General Purposes Sub-Committee requesting a meeting with WCAC.
	Replies received from schools and local authorities in West Cumberland offering support, or not, to WCAC's campaign.
13 November 1973	Question tabled in House of Commons by the MP regarding publication of the Working Party report.
15 November 1973	WCAC meeting; worker reports contact with other Education Departments. Radio Carlisle present.

27 November 1973   Local radio broadcast.

12 December 1973   WCAC meets Education Finance and General Purposes project group and presents its case.

Small WCAC meeting discusses meeting with Education Committee project group.

19 December 1973   News item on Radio Carlisle about WCAC.

20 December 1973   Cumberland Education Finance and General Purposes Sub-Committee resolves that the Director of Education's project group's report be noted but that until the DES Working Party on School Transport report is published, no action be taken. Agreed that the full Education Committee should recommend 'the incoming Cumbria Education Committee to give sympathetic consideration to the general problems involved in the provision of transport for school children within the limits of the funds available in financial estimates'.

17 January 1974   CMS applies for a further bus fares increase.

Final meeting of Cumberland Education Committee. Ratifies the recommendation put by Finance and General Purposes Sub-Committee to Cumbria Education Committee.

1 February 1974   WCAC meeting; Chairman of Cumbria Economic Development Committee attends.

5 February 1974   Following request from WCAC, Director of Education informs the committee that the Education Committee will now discuss the DES Working Party Report on School Transport.

11 February 1974	Letter received from Ennerdale Rural District Council and Cleator Moor Parish Council saying that they have lodged objections to the fare increases.
14 February 1974	Traffic Commissioners reject the objections.
19 February 1974	WCAC meeting; representatives from Cumberland Parish Councils Association attend.
28 February 1974	General Election; Labour government elected. Labour MPs retain their seats in Whitehaven and Workington.
6 March 1974	WCAC meeting; review of progress to date. Agreement to contact Labour Party on school transport policy.
28 March 1974	WCAC meeting; election of officers. Bank account opened. Fund-raising events planned.
1 April 1974	New local authorities formally take up their responsibilities.
4 April 1974	Worker meets local MP to discuss Labour government's policy on school transport.
29 April 1974	WCAC meeting; fund-raising event finalised.

Chapter 4
Glodwick Action Group

Introduction: an overview of the group's activities

This case study looks at the Glodwick Action Group's activities in relation to the issues arising from the Compulsory Purchase Order made on 248 houses in the Glodwick area of Oldham in October 1972, and covers the period from the formation of the group until April 1975. The group was also concerned with other issues in the area, and this introduction will outline the overall range of its activities from the time of its inception until June 1976.

The group came into being as a result of an initiative by the CDP community worker for the Greenacres and Glodwick areas. His initial enquiries in the area during April and May 1973 indicated that the Compulsory Purchase Order made several months before was an issue of great concern to many people in Glodwick, with a Public Inquiry scheduled for the end of September 1973. The community worker called a meeting in May 1973 of various residents concerned with the problems resulting from the CPO, and from this the Glodwick Action Group was formed.

From an early stage two committees operated; one was specifically concerned with the CPO, and with members drawn entirely from people in the CPO area, while the other was more concerned with the general environmental problems of Glodwick; for example, street cleaning, refuse collection and litter. A number of residents put a large part of the blame for these problems on the Asian population of Glodwick, who were the latest immigrants into the area in the post-war wave which had started with Poles and Ukrainians in the 1940s, changed to West Indians in the late 1950s, and then to Asians in the 1960s.

The group called a public meeting in July 1973 to discuss problems arising from the CPO, and invited councillors for the area and local authority officials. The officers declined to attend and it emerged that the borough solicitor had also advised the councillors not to go; although, as a result of a meeting with two members of the group, he withdrew this advice and in the event seven councillors attended. Over the months relationships with local authority officers slowly improved, despite setbacks from a number of incidents, and various officers were invited to, and attended, group meetings. Other contacts with local authority departments occurred through a complaints and information scheme for residents which was instituted by the group.

In the meantime the group, with CDP help, carried out a survey in the CPO area to discover residents' views and wishes about the CPO. The survey aimed at 100 per cent coverage of the houses in the CPO area, apart from the multi-occupied lodging houses, and succeeded in obtaining replies from 57 per cent of the 197 inhabited houses. As a result of this an evidence paper was written for the Public Inquiry,[1] in which the group, though not challenging the making of the Compulsory Purchase Order itself, questioned whether the local authority could provide for the displaced residents suitable alternative accommodation on reasonable terms, as they were obliged to do by the 1973 Land Compensation Act. The survey had shown that nearly 80 per cent of the residents to be displaced by the CPO expressing any preference had said that they wanted to be rehoused in or near Glodwick, and the group therefore asked that the council should consider a phased redevelopment in the Glodwick area. Further recommendations were that the local authority should examine whether Glodwick residents could be given priority on a small new council estate being built on the edge of the area; that local authority mortgages should be made available to displaced residents; that there should be an improvement programme for any houses in the CPO suitable for rehabilitation rather than clearance; and that there should be full consultation with the Glodwick Action Group over any proposed developments in the area. On this latter point, the survey had asked some questions about the type of redevelopment residents would like to see in the area if the CPO was confirmed and the area cleared. The group was congratulated on its evidence by the Public Inquiry Inspector.

Subsequent meetings were instituted between the group and the housing committee, and the suggestion of phased redevelopment, later accepted by the full council, was pursued there as well as with a committee of officers and at Area Councillors' Committee meetings.[2] The group also raised other related issues, such as the inconvenience of shops in the area closing down once the CPO had been confirmed and compensation become available, its preference for the bricking-up rather than boarding of vacated property, and the possibility of re-letting suitable houses acquired by the council in the area to families who might otherwise be homeless.

In November 1973 an overall Co-ordinating Committee was established, as the group by then had two sub-committees, the CPO and Environment Committees (and a third, the Social, Welfare and Leisure Activities Committee, was formed in January 1974). Attempts were made as a result of the interest of one member to set up a playgroup and there was briefly the beginnings of a Playgroup Committee, but eventually this idea had to be abandoned because of a lack of suitable premises in the area. A weekly Girls' Group (providing social activities for girls aged 8 – 13) was started by someone who approached Glodwick Action Group (GAG) with this idea and organised it on her own under the group's general aegis. This continued to run successfully.

Over a period of months from December 1973 the Environment Committee gradually dwindled in numbers, partly due to the inevitable frustrations of trying to improve an area which was declining, and partly because of the hostility shown by some members to Asian residents, two of whom were members of the committee. Eventually in April 1974 the chairman resigned when the committee was down to three active members, and, although the events were only indirectly connected, this was closely followed by the resignation of the chairman of the Social Committee, as a result of which both committees collapsed and the CPO Committee became the nucleus group once again. This illustrates the general instability of the group which, during the period covered by the case study, was one of its more striking features.

In 1974 the group began to develop the idea of having a separate base for GAG activities and a worker to act as secretary to the group and to develop the complaints and information service. Eventually a four-room terraced house was rented and equipped as an office and information centre. Funds came partly from the group and to a greater extent from CDP. The office opened in July 1974 with a member of the group as part-time worker; she was succeeded by the organiser of the Girls' Group who became the (by then full-time) GAG worker in December 1974. In the meantime discussions took place with the local Citizens' Advice Bureau (CAB) organiser, and after training for the paid worker and interested volunteers the GAG information office became an experimental branch bureau of the Oldham CAB for a six-month period from January to July 1975 (and subsequently continued as a permanent branch bureau). Some members of the group were strongly opposed to the development of a CAB service from the GAG office, and this caused considerable tensions in the group.

The group developed good contacts with staff in a number of local authority departments, including planning, environmental health, and engineering; and many local authority contacts became established by the GAG information officer on individual enquiries. There remained some distrust of local councillors and this partly explains doubts the group had about the value of the Area Committee Councillors' meetings.

Additional concerns which the group pursued included:

1   Liaising with the local authority over the phasing of the redevelopment; one aspect of this was a two-part programme of surveying residents in the phase one step ahead of demolition to see who would like to move into the phase about to be designed and built, and obtaining opinions which the planning department then used as guidelines for their designs.
2   Trying to see that services in the area were maintained and that as few problems as possible arose for residents while the redevelopment of the CPO area took place.
3   The GAG information service.
4   Taking an interest in the conditions of various privately rented, dilapidated and often multi-occupied houses in the area.[3]
5   Involvement in a scheme in collaboration with the local authority and the Oldham and Tameside Family Housing Association whereby habitable houses acquired by the council in the area were let to families or people in particular housing need.

In addition the community worker tried to stimulate interest in the improvement of houses in areas surrounding the Glodwick CPO, the large majority of which had a planned 30-year life, with members of the committee in those areas encouraging the interest of other residents. A survey was carried out by CDP, in conjunction with GAG, of ten blocks of houses, about housing conditions and residents' attitudes. On the basis of the subsequent report[4] CDP, with the approval of the Glodwick Action Group, argued for the declaration of Housing Action Areas on all the improvable housing in Glodwick.

During the period covered by the case study the group became less of a campaigning and more of a management servicing organisation, operating in the interests of the residents of the

CPO area and neighbouring parts of Glodwick. However, following up the issues raised in the Housing Action Area report meant a return to a campaigning strategy by the group, which came together in 1976 with the East Glodwick Group and the local Pakistan Society (all three retaining their independence and individual interests) to form the United Glodwick Residents' Group to press for action on Glodwick's housing problems.

The context[5]

Glodwick is a distinct neighbourhood of triangular shape situated to the east of, and close to, Oldham town centre, being separated from it by the southern internal by-pass and the main railway line. Its other boundaries are equally clearly defined by Alexandra Park and Glodwick Road.

When the Oldham Community Development Project was established in 1972 the area contained over 5,000 people (1971 census), was the major multi-racial neighbourhood in Oldham, and had been in the process of rapid population change for ten years. The 1971 census suggested a Pakistani-born population of 16 per cent, West Indian 5 per cent, and Eastern European 5 per cent. Findings of later surveys by CDP[6] and the local authority[7] suggested that these figures should be doubled to give a more accurate impression of the proportions of Asian and West Indian residents in the mid-1970s. The coloured immigrant population tended to be younger and to live in larger households than other residents. Housing was almost entirely terraced and built prior to the turn of the century. The quality of building varied but there was in general a lack of household amenities (only 43 per cent of occupied dwellings in Glodwick had a hot water supply, fixed bath or shower, and an inside lavatory). The local authority had adopted two basic policies towards the area: compulsory purchase, demolition and redevelopment; and improvement. When the community worker began work in May 1973 roughly 700 houses were in current or proposed clearance areas, and the remaining 1,100 were in proposed improvement areas; this meant that all but about 40 of the 1,800 houses in the area were scheduled for clearance or improvement. In tenure terms, approximately 75 per cent of all properties were owner-occupied (1971 census). A proportionately larger number of the tenanted properties were in the CPO areas, and these included some particularly poor quality privately tenanted dwellings, some of which were multi-occupied lodging houses.

The community worker's account of the area written for the

CDP's First Report[8] referred to the population being ethnically mixed, with religious and other schisms within different ethnic groups often being as divisive as those between them; the same was also said to apply to the white residents. Nevertheless, the residents of longer standing tended to blame the Asian immigrants for the decline of property values in the area, for taking over local shops and thus reducing their shopping facilities, for problems of rubbish, and for the CPO itself. Other problems were also evident in the area; issues relating to the CPO concerned the place and type of rehousing, compensation, closure of shops, accumulation of rubbish, disrepair of property, and the type of redevelopment planned for the area. There were economic problems for residents in improvement areas of finding the outlay if they wished to take advantage of improvement grants, particularly as residents' incomes were generally low.[9] There was a lack of play space and facilities, and playgroups; and there was the proposal that there should be a gypsy site (later established) on the edge of the area.

Accounts of the area by some residents seemed to subscribe to a past golden age of Glodwick: one said that fifteen years ago

'You really were somebody if you came and lived in Glodwick because the area was noted for the professions – solicitors, accountants, doctors, the type of people you'd expect to smoke a cigar. When we first came here you had to have a reference to come and live in this district. It was one of the nicest districts in town bar none. Now you want a reference to get out of it.'

While one may doubt whether the area was quite like this at the time, this was a view commonly held by white residents. In some cases the feeling that the local authority had neglected the area and let it run down by default was elevated into a conspiracy theory, it being suggested that the council had deliberately directed Asians into Glodwick: 'The way that I see it the council put these people in the district. We know for a fact that the council said that they wanted them all this side of the railway.' Similar sentiments were expressed more coolly by another group member:

'Over the past ten years it's been obvious that the area was being neglected and nobody seemed to care what was happening about it, and obviously when this begins to happen property comes empty, it's taken over – as you can see, it's made into so-called flats, lodging houses and things like that – people drifting in and drifting out – you can see the population moving practically from week to week'.

It was hardly surprising, in these circumstances, that Glodwick people sometimes expressed bitterness and suspicion about local councillors and council officers. At best they saw the local authority as having a non-policy of neglect towards the area. The result was a feeling of demoralisation and frustration in the face of the council's apparent indifference.

Formation of the group

Trying to decide what led to the formation of the group, the community worker argued that it would be wrong to take the CPO alone as the precipitating event. If it had been, the group would already have been in existence by the time he began to take soundings in the area in April 1973. But while the CPO was undoubtedly the local talking point, it had not provoked any organised action. Without the CDP initiative there is little likelihood that a group would have been formed; a view supported by three of the members interviewed: 'Without CDP nothing would have happened. The community had disappeared.'

One reason for this may have been that, as far as the community worker could make out, there had been little history of organised action in the area. There had once been a brief flurry of indignation about the plan for a gypsy site in Glodwick, but it had amounted to no more than a public meeting and a few protest letters. Indeed, a residents' association of the GAG type was apparently a novelty in Oldham as a whole. There was a concept of what a tenants' association was, but the only kinds of residents' association which had existed before were either ratepayers' action groups or amenity societies like the Failsworth Amenity Society (which is discussed in the next chapter). A further factor which seemed relevant was the long-standing sense of identification of many local people with the Labour movement, which made them reluctant to challenge or attack the (then Labour-controlled) council. But a more significant reason for residents' collective passivity was the fact that they perceived the CPO threat in terms of their own house, not in terms of the area as a whole. The initial motivation to come to the meetings about the CPO was not concern about the area generally, but arose from individuals wondering what was going to happen to their house. The idea of forming a group around the CPO issue, therefore, seems not to have been mooted at all before the community worker started to talk to people in the area.

The first move the community worker made towards initiating some kind of group round the CPO issue was to bring together in May 1973 a small number of people who he knew were concerned or who had had some previous organising experience. Seven of the thirteen invited to the meeting attended. At this first discussion the decision was taken to organise a public meeting the following month, to be preceded by intensive leafleting of the CPO area. The fact that only 40 people came to the first public meeting is consistent with the community worker's view that the CPO was not by itself something which would have motivated people to act collectively, and even at this meeting he felt that few of those who attended were really convinced that an organised group could do anything. But a measure of breakthrough occurred when a Jamaican resident (who afterwards became a CPO Committee member) recounted his experience of CPO groups in Nottingham and Moss Side. This had a perceptible effect on the people attending. The meeting finally elected a committee of nine people to plan an organised programme of action.

One factor which was apparent from the earliest soundings in the area was tension between the white and Asian residents. But at the first public meeting (at which CDP arranged for an Urdu-speaking translator to be present) there was a general atmosphere of tolerance which was never subsequently repeated. The community worker's view was that CPO was of such immediate importance that even racial tensions faded as an issue. By contrast, later meetings brought in Glodwick residents from outside the CPO area who were more concerned about the general problems of the area, and some of them made it quite plain that they were blaming the Asians for these problems. Support for the group in these early days was sought both by the public meeting in July and by the production, with CDP help, of a handbook on CPO and of two newsletters (the second of which was also available in Urdu translation). The handbook was distributed by group members to all households in the CPO area and the newsletters to all 1,800 houses in Glodwick. All these activities enabled group members and the worker to talk to residents about the group's aims, and what they hoped to achieve.

Objectives and general aims

The immediate task in the early days was to get to grips with the CPO process, to understand the technicalities of it and to prepare

a case in time for the Public Inquiry in September 1973. Despite
the fact that the CPO had been declared over six months before,
people were still very uncertain as to precisely what happened,
what their rights were, and generally how the process operated;
some were unaware that they had any power to appeal against
the local authority's declaration of the CPO at the Public Inquiry
– they thought the CPO was already confirmed. The reports
written by the community worker on his work with the group
clearly show that the concerns of the group in its first three
months – prior to the Public Inquiry – were mainly immediate
worries about just what the CPO would mean to the individuals
affected. The twelve main questions which emerged from the
first meeting in May 1973 reflected people's fears (dereliction,
loss of facilities, shops, etc.), their resentments (at the way the
CPO had been imposed on them, and at the inadequate information they had been given), and their hopes (their wish to be
rehoused locally, their interest in seeing the council's plans for
redevelopment). The questions were in fact mainly requests for
information: when would the clearance begin? Would empty
properties be bricked up? What rights did people have when
rehousing offers were made? Would local rehousing be offered?
Were there any new community facilities in the plans for the
area? And what kind of compensation would they get?[10]

It was clear from the outset that beyond the need to understand the CPO process there was no common view among the
residents of the CPO area. Some wanted to stay in the area,
some wanted to go; some wanted to hang on to their houses,
and others were happy to see the area redeveloped. So a common awareness existed among residents only to the extent that
they were all in a crisis situation; there was no consensus about
how (or, indeed, if) the problem should be tackled. The worker,
very aware of these divergent views, suggested that the group
should look for collective objectives which might gain general
support. This led to his suggestion that a survey should be conducted in the area; he pointed out that if the group wanted to
be seen by the local authority as representative of people in
Glodwick they had to take the views of other residents:

> 'From there on they saw themselves as the champions of
> the interests of the people of Glodwick. Once the survey
> was in they had a clearly defined set of requirements
> from people in the area – local rehousing, but a wish for
> the houses to come down, and cheap housing, and so on,

and they had a case to present. And once the case was
presented at the Public Inquiry that became their
objective.'

In summary, goal succession occurred early in the life of the
group, when the initial aim of acquiring at least the basic information about CPO had been achieved (although this process
continued in respect of individual queries, later usually dealt
with by the information centre). This objective became replaced
first by the carrying out of the survey, and then by the presentation of evidence to the Public Inquiry. Goal succession, as the
worker pointed out, occurred again after the inquiry, as the
requests made in the group's evidence subsequently became its
objectives.

In some instances the group's general objectives were further
developed; for example, they carried out a survey in phase two
of the CPO area about what people would like to see in the
phase one development (under the phased redevelopment proposals it was hoped that all of the people in phase two who
wished it would be rehoused in the phase one redevelopment),
and subsequently two consultation meetings took place between
the group and the planning department about the design of the
redevelopment. In addition, some issues related to the CPO
were incorporated into the committee's objectives over time; for
example, seeking the agreement of Oldham and Tameside Family Housing Association to the management of council-owned
houses in the CPO area for temporary re-letting; and obtaining
written guarantees from the local authority that those residents
who wished to stay in the Glodwick area, but had to be moved
out during redevelopment, should be able to return at a later
date.

Because this account is concerned only with CPO issues, the
aims and objectives of the other two (Environment and Social)
committees of the group are not dealt with here, but there were
a number of objectives which were pursued by the group as a
whole. One such goal was the establishment of a councillor's
clinic in the area. Other objectives which the group adopted
after its initial stages were the promotion of a Glodwick Exhibition, the setting up of the GAG office, and the employment
of an information and advice worker. The latter were not original
objectives of the group; but having been achieved they were in
turn supplanted by the goals of maintaining and developing the
services.

CDP's aims and objectives

The Oldham CDP First Report said that

> The work of community development lies in providing the means for people to identify clearly the problems they experience and to assist in working out solutions to these problems. The process is initiated by the establishment of local groups around real issues, or in helping existing groups to be more effective. Assistance will be given to such groups by means of advice, support and finance.[11]

The initial aims of the Project were largely concerned with working with community groups.

In addition, the community worker thought, there was an element of getting something going 'to justify our existence'. In his view it would be dishonest to say that this had not been a factor in the formation of all the CDP groups; the Project at that stage was trying to demonstrate what it was about and what the processes of community development were, 'so we had a vested interest in that group producing something fairly significant as a base from which the Project could work'. But, in any case, once the Project staff knew what was happening in Waterloo Street it seemed essential to attempt some action; they wanted to respond to what was clearly an urgent need. Over time the worker thought there was little change in CDP's aims in working with the group; the intention was always that the Project should enable people 'to obtain their ends, providing those ends are legitimate in the sense that they don't damage the interests of others in the area'.

Organisation and development of the group

At the beginning the two GAG committees (CPO and Environment) were not formally linked; indeed, originally it was thought that the Environment Committee would be a separate group and for a while it operated as the Glodwick Environment Group. But a number of the committees' interests overlapped, and after the Public Inquiry joint meetings were held at the suggestion of the community worker. This was an attempt to graft on to the Environment Committee the more liberal racial attitudes of the CPO Committee and their better knowledge of committee procedure. Before the joint meetings racial arguments in the Environment Committee proved completely disruptive to its work, and had the temporary amalgamation not occurred it is very likely that it would have collapsed at that time.

In the lull after the Public Inquiry the worker suggested that the joint committee should now prepare a constitution (this had previously been left to one side because of the urgency of the Public Inquiry issue). As the joint meetings between the two committees were only a short-term measure, some kind of overall committee was needed, so the structure adopted consisted of a co-ordinating committee, with the CPO and environment groups as two sub-committees. There was provision for other sub-committees to be added if appropriate (a social, welfare and leisure sub-committee was added shortly afterwards when a resident joined the group specifically to promote such activities). The structure operated for only a few months, and when both the Environment and Social Committees ceased to operate in April and May 1974 (the former as a result of dwindling membership following racial tension, the latter as a result of the chairman's resignation), the CPO committee again became the nucleus committee, absorbing the few survivors from the other two.

Meetings of the CPO Committee were held weekly, as were those of the group as a whole when the sub-committees ceased to meet in May 1974. For the first year or so of the group's existence meetings were held in the CDP office, but after the group acquired its own premises in July 1974 meetings were held there. Meetings originally were fairly unstructured, despite having an agenda; as time went on discussion tended to follow the agenda more, although in a general sense the meetings remained informal.

There was no general membership of the group; attempts were made to institute this in December 1973; but there was an unenthusiastic response from group members and residents, and the attempt was abandoned so that the group could continue to represent all the people of the area. Members of the group did not pay subscriptions; for the most part the group was financed and provided with resources by CDP. Secretarial help and duplicating of newsletters, papers and general correspondence were initially available directly from CDP, and were later taken over by the GAG office, using equipment and stationery provided by CDP. The GAG worker was paid by CDP. When the group first negotiated the lease for the office and information centre, committee members contributed an amount each month to pay the rent, and also raised money by jumble sales to help towards the initial essential repairs and decoration; the group was also granted £1,000 by CDP towards this work. When the

CPO Committee was formed in June 1973 it had eight members, two of whom dropped out immediately afterwards. The remaining six formed a cohesive committee and all remained active members for the next fourteen months, when one resigned largely for health reasons; subsequently the chairman and another member ceased to be active when they were rehoused outside the area. The remaining three original committee members remained involved in the group and one became its second chairman. Four of the six also became involved as volunteer workers in the information centre, and one became the first paid worker until she resigned on health grounds. These six original members of the CPO Committee were its core members; indeed to a large extent they formed the backbone of the group as a whole.

The members of the CPO Committee had had more organisational experience than members of the other committees; one had been a shop steward, another a Workers' Educational Association committee member, and a third a committee member of a sports club; of the remaining three members, one was a nurse and one a shopkeeper. The community worker thought that in the Glodwick area they tended to be seen as residents who were particularly articulate and able to hold down good jobs.

Rather than having one or two obvious leaders, the CPO Committee operated as a leadership group. Members accepted and respected the chairman's role of controlling and directing discussions within the committee, but when it came to meetings with councillors and officials, as the community worker reported, 'they all had a go'. In the group as a whole, and certainly in the CPO committee, decisions were made mostly by consensus. There was provision for votes to be taken, but this happened only rarely. Disputes sometimes arose around the charge that cliques and sub-groups within the group took decisions prior to committee meetings. In the CPO Committee specifically, while personality conflicts occasionally broke out, the community worker considered it 'amazing how little there was in terms of divisions'. But after the group members came together in one committee from May 1974 crises and conflicts were many and varied, largely as a result of the addition of former Environment Committee members. The earlier cohesion was never regained after this merger, partly because the group was now concerned with two sets of issues, and partly because there were particular personalities who saw themselves as leaders and made bids for such roles.

The major internal conflict (apart from the one about race

which has been mentioned in passing as it became an open conflict only in the Environment Committee) concerned the setting up of the Citizens' Advice Bureau service at the information centre. This dispute hinged on some group members seeing CAB as an institution which was middle-class rather than working-class, and because of this it was suspected of attempting to take power from the group and from local residents. At one stage the tension threatened the group's existence. However, the chairman's role was significant as he allowed the aggression to be expressed again and again in meetings until those opposed to the proposal had talked themselves out, and then found they had still not changed other members' minds. The community worker appreciated that some members were afraid that the proposed affiliation of the CAB service would inhibit the independence of activity of the group, and saw the problem as one of developing an appropriate relationship between the information-giving role of the centre and the activist role of the group. In the event the difficulty was resolved by asking enquirers if they would prefer their problems to be taken up without any reference to the group, and by aggregating from the other enquiries (the great majority) evidence of general trends of problems in the area which the group could then take up with appropriate bodies. The community worker's view was that the information service run on this basis strengthened the representative nature of the group rather than inhibited it, and there was no opposition among members to the arrangement being made permanent when the six-month trial period came to an end.

The process of learning from experience certainly occurred in the group. At the beginning the community worker wrote agendas and minutes and frequently had to guide committee meetings so that subjects were discussed one at a time and decisions taken. In time, however, members of the group learned to discuss subjects in a more orderly way (and this generalised to other meetings, for example, Area Councillors' Committees); and all the other secretarial functions and work on individual enquiries came to be handled by the GAG worker.

The role of the community worker

As has already been said, the community worker decided to stimulate the formation of a group round the Waterloo Street CPO issue because it seemed to him to be a matter of great concern to many people in the area. Despite his initiative, however, he held the view throughout that 'it's up to residents to determine what they want to do and what their solution to their problem is'. He was aware of suspicion when he first started approaching and talking to people in the area. There was 'a great deal of hostility and suspicion about me. They couldn't understand why I was interested, why anybody should be bothered'. The resident who became the first chairman of the CPO committee exemplified this wary attitude: 'He bided his time, sussing me out basically. He really gave me a rough ride the first time I went to see him; what the hell did I think I could do? What could a young upstart coming from Nottingham do for them?' Some of the caution with which the worker was viewed may have resulted from his openly stated attitude that immigrants were 'part of the community and had exactly the same rights as everybody else; and we were here just as much to work with them and to meet their needs as we were to meet anybody else's needs'. On the other hand his willingness, as a newcomer to the area, to help residents find out about CPO procedures made a favourable impression. One group member said, 'What really did impress me was that somebody who had come from so far away and didn't know the town could have come into it and given us so much information about who to contact and for what reason. I thought this was marvellous.'

At the beginning the group was heavily dependent on the worker; and for the first eighteen months or so after it had been established it was his major commitment. Initially he was primarily concerned with servicing the group in a secretarial role, giving advice and support, keeping the peace, as well as providing research skills with surveys and technical input on CPO procedure and the Public Inquiry. As time went on the group began to take over some of these functions, particularly after the appointment of its own GAG worker and information officer.

The community worker had an influential role throughout in raising and discussing with the group possible tactical approaches, although they not infrequently chose to reject his advice. In situations where they were unsure about courses of action, or whom to approach, his advice was often sought and taken; it was, for example, the community worker who suggested to the group that they might meet the local authority CDP Inter-departmental Working Party[12] when in 1974 people began moving out of phases two and three of the CPO area in increasing numbers and the area seemed to be becoming even more run down. However, once group members began to establish their own contacts within the local authority they looked less and less to him for this kind of assistance.

In interviews, conducted at a stage when the group had been

in existence for about nine months, three group members commented that the group should be growing more independent of
the worker, one specifically linking this to easing the burden on
him. His commitment to the group in terms of time began to
lessen in the early months of 1975, by which time he was working
actively with four other community groups as well as becoming
concerned with analysing issues common to a number of these
groups.

The worker thought his main achievement after the amalgamation of the CPO and Environment Committees had been
holding the group's disparate elements together. In the various
crises he spent a considerable amount of time 'talking round
problems' individually with the various group members involved,
allowing them to discharge their anger outside committee meetings, presenting to them other points of view, and priming the
chairman in the meantime, so that the effects of conflict were
less cataclysmic.

Apart from being the catalyst for the formation of the group
in the first place, the worker's main contribution to the CPO
Committee was probably the technical information and skills
that he was able to supply. After the group amalgamated into
one committee, however, the peace-keeping role which in many
ways was his most valuable contribution to the Environment
Committee then became more in evidence in relation to the
group as a whole.

Strategy

As already stated, the group never had a general membership
and did not set out to mobilise mass support. Instead, support
was obtained through the use of surveys and occasional public
meetings, which established the legitimacy of the representative
role which the group performed, supplemented later by the taking up of aggregated problems from the information centre.
While members did not wish to have councillors or officials
participating directly in the group, they did want their support
for the group's objectives. In this the Public Inquiry proved
crucial as, according to the Deputy Borough Solicitor at the
time, it established respect for the group among a number of
local authority staff, and almost certainly provided a basis for
the later process of negotiation with various committees and
departments of the local authority. The initial tactic of the group
was simply to ask for information from the local authority about
a number of issues related to the CPO. The brevity of the

answers given, the fact that officers did not attend the July 1973 public meeting, and the way in which councillors used the meeting as a debating exercise rather than a serious discussion with worried residents, necessitated a different line of approach.

It was at this stage that the community worker suggested the carrying out of a survey to establish the wishes of residents in the area; this led to the evidence paper for the Public Inquiry. While the group had obviously hoped that its evidence would be well received, the warmth of the Inspector's praise and his strong endorsement of the group's objectives were unexpected. Its effect, too, on the local authority was striking, with the Borough Solicitor agreeing at the Public Inquiry to give every assistance to the group. Having acquired some status in the eyes of officers, the group was able to build on this and to change its tactics. From this time (October 1973) onwards the CPO group and the officers began to establish a relationship which, while not without considerable setbacks, did at times become co-operative and mutually helpful.

Even when the relationship with officers was positive, the group did not rely solely on the local authority for information; in the summer of 1974, for example, they invited a Manchester architect to three meetings to discuss the background to the design of a scheme like the CPO redevelopment, and the nature of an architect's brief. This enabled the group to cover the relevant points in a questionnaire to residents to be rehoused in the new development, and to be well informed before starting to discuss the proposed plans with the architect's department.

Strategy with local councillors was different, in part because the group was more suspicious of them and also because, unlike with the officers, the group did not have information which the councillors wanted and which could form the basis of some degree of co-operation. The main approach adopted was to raise problems again and again at different meetings.

It seemed to the community worker that the local authority had initially feared that the group might use direct action:

> 'They had no idea how strong it was, and how effective it would be; no idea what the Glodwick Action Group actually represented, how powerful it was, and what kinds of methods it was going to use to achieve its ends. I think there was a vision of a horrific sit-in at the Town Hall and disruption of council meetings. But, the way things developed, there wasn't really any need for direct militant action.'

The group's main effort at publicity to people in Glodwick as a whole was the distribution of the newsletter to all 1,800 houses in the area. The experiment of preparing an Urdu translation was dropped after one attempt as demand was slight, apparently because of illiteracy among the Asian population. Posters were used in local shops to advertise events. Media publicity was used only rarely. There was no radio or television coverage; and use of the press was occasional. The community worker thought that this partly reflected his own scepticism about the press, but even more the fact that the group had not tried to mount a campaign as such. In only one case during the period dealt with here did the group lobby the local MP, and this was over general local issues when he attended one of the councillors' clinics.

Achievements and failures

In the view of both the group and the community worker the main achievement of the CPO group was the phased redevelopment of the area and local rehousing of residents. In addition, the design of the redevelopment came to accord with residents' wishes in that the houses, flats and shops were planned to be of low-rise construction and in brick and tile, and there was to be an exact match of the size of housing to the needs, elicited by group surveys, of the Glodwick residents to be rehoused there. The group was also successful in getting the local authority to give written guarantees (or, in the Deputy Borough Solicitor's phrase, 'an expression of good faith and best endeavour on the part of the local authority') to residents in phase one, who were forced to move out of the area, that they would in due course be given priority in the letting of new dwellings built in the redevelopment.

The community worker thought that the raising of the lodging house issue, and the initiation and implementation of the Family Housing Association scheme (which was designed in part to meet some aspects of this problem) were achievements for which the group could take much credit. In addition there was the success of the information centre, which was dealing with an average of 130–140 enquiries per month in the period covered by this case study. The former Deputy Borough Solicitor also saw the acceptance of the phased redevelopment as a success for the group, as it was the first time to his knowledge that such a scheme had been tried in Oldham.[13] But he thought some officers remained sceptical about its likely success. He thought the group's main achievement was getting priority for the area from the local authority; and although he thought it justified in this case, he felt it also needed to be said that the results of one section of the community pressing its own needs in this way could be a distortion of activities throughout the borough as a whole.

The community worker thought that members of the group perhaps did not recognise the full extent of their achievements because they had adopted a number of different goals at successive stages. They had started off pessimistically, but with each success became more optimistic; and despite the fact that progress had never been smooth or inevitable they had achieved a great deal of what they had wanted in the redevelopment. So latterly, for example, they argued amicably with the architect's department over details such as whether the new houses should have the kitchen at the back or front, without realising how far this was from their experiences in the early days when they were trying, with enormous difficulty, merely to get factual information about the CPO process from the local authority.

In addition, the community worker thought that the impact made by the Glodwick group seemed to be generalising to the authority's dealings with other groups. It appeared now to be recognised that once a CPO area had been represented (that is, declared by the local authority, subject to possible appeal through a Public Inquiry) it was reasonable to get involved with residents in determining what should happen in the area. And, while at the beginning it had been difficult to get the Glodwick councillors to come to the July 1973 public meeting, in the Greenacres area, where a CPO was not even due to be represented for over a year, the Greenacres Residents' Action Group had already had planning and environmental health officers to its meetings and had had good support from their councillors: 'I don't think that would have happened two years ago.'

Major factors in the group's achievement of its objectives appear to have been its impressive presentation of evidence at the Public Inquiry, its success in convincing the local authority that it was a responsible body representative of local people, and, according to the local authority officer interviewed, the quality of a number of the group's members, who were tenacious over matters raised with council officials but yet on most occasions did not antagonise them.

GAG had few failures in pursuing its objectives, such examples as there are being relatively minor; for example, the group adopted a proposal by the planning department that the department should try to attract a small supermarket to set up temporary premises in Glodwick until the new shops to be built were ready; but in the event this came to nothing. Since what success the group had was achieved by its affecting the attitudes and operations of the local authority, an attempt is made here to trace the group's relationship over time with both councillors and officers.

Relationships with councillors

As has already been mentioned, the local councillors were generally distrusted by group members, who saw them at best as being inactive over the area's problems. One member said he thought 'the councillors were very apathetic. I know personally the previous three councillors for the area and I do know that they were a bit lackadaisical in their attitude.' Another said he saw them as 'a group of mediocre people who, year by year, got in because nobody ran against them. We had one councillor in this area who was in office for eight or nine years and I've never seen him in this area apart from around May when we have the elections, no other time.' One member apportioned some of the blame to the way councillors were organised by the party:

'The party system has been developed to such an extent now that the individual is merged, he disappears beneath his party line; the party line is put out by the local caucus which determines how the town is run. It's a shame really: if your personal views conflict with those of the party then the party comes first.'

In his initial discussions with residents in the area the worker observed that some saw the CPO as 'a conspiracy brought about by the councillors'. A specific incident which fostered this view was the comment made by a local councillor to one group member 'when he asked her why anybody should be concerned about the Glodwick area since it was in any case such a mess. This has not been forgotten and is often quoted by members of the committee.' Another comment which has long been remembered by the group was the admission by one councillor at a public meeting that the area had been 'allowed to run down' by the council. One group member thought the councillors seemed 'over-awed by permanent officials', who seemed to exert a strong influence over them. This was borne out by the incident right at the beginning of the group's existence, when the Borough Solicitor told two members of the group that he had advised local councillors not to attend the second public meeting. One member said that on hearing this she was 'amazed; I thought the councillors were free agents.' She had spoken subsequently to one of the councillors who said he had his duty to the council to consider; she rejoined that he also had a duty to the people who had elected him.

Another early issue which caused bad feeling in the group towards councillors was that of the councillors' clinics. After the persistent pressure from GAG for their establishment, it was understood that this would be a joint venture between the group and councillors. GAG undertook to advertise the clinic and act as receptionists, and three clinics were held. With the advent of local government reorganisation it was decided that such clinics should be held throughout the new metropolitan borough and, without reference to GAG, this was implemented in Glodwick. 'To add insult to injury the councillors chose to advertise the clinic with the name the group chose: Councillors' Complaints and Advice Night'. The group's annoyance was further compounded by the fact that, when the CDP sub-committee came in April 1974 to consider the proposal of paid workers for the two proposed information centres, some councillors argued that there was no need for a full-time worker in the Glodwick area in part because so few people had made use of the councillors' clinics. The committee approved the appointment of a part-time worker only for the Glodwick information centre but, somewhat to the group's chagrin, of a full-time worker for the Abbeyhills centre; the Glodwick post was not made full-time until November 1974.

The group debated a variety of issues with councillors at various meetings: Area Councillors' Committees, the special meetings with the housing committee, and two public meetings attended by councillors. In general these meetings, particularly the Area Councillors' Committee, did not increase the group's confidence in their councillors, and after a meeting in October 1974 the minutes of the group recorded that 'it was suggested that the meeting had not achieved very much and that there appeared to have been a great deal of buck passing going on'. The chairman mentioned that a councillor had said after the meeting 'that the councillors had felt that they had let the Glodwick Action Group go too far'. There was general concern that this kind of statement had been made and the question was asked as to why it was that the councillors who were supposed to be representing the wards had not already seen the problems that the Glodwick Action Group was raising. It was felt that it could only indicate their own lack of concern.

The *ad hoc* meetings with the housing committee seemed a little more profitable. After what proved to be the final meeting of a series of three in October 1974 the group's minutes said that:

Although there was some concern that the chairman in particular was ignorant of the questions being raised and that many members of the committee were not as well informed as they might have been, it was felt that the meeting generally had been worthwhile; though there were some differences of opinion about this. It was noted in particular that the committee had given approval to the corporation officials continuing discussion and negotiation direct with the local residents.

But the chairman of the group said he 'was concerned about the statement made by the chairman of the housing committee when he described the phasing as desirable but unrealisable. It was for this reason that he felt that continued effort should be made to work closely with officers of the corporation.'

In December 1974 the group was angered by the failure of the housing management sub-committee to agree to the proposals for some council-owned houses in the CPO area to be managed by the Family Housing Association and used to accommodate homeless families; this resulted from general criticism of housing associations expressed by one councillor at the meeting. The decision was taken despite the fact that the suggestion had the approval of senior local authority officers both individually and as a group. A strongly worded letter from the group was assured that at the next housing committee meeting the decision would be sent back for reconsideration. In the event, however, it was passed, which obviously made group members highly suspicious of the explanation that this was merely 'an oversight'; although in due course at the full council meeting the resolution was referred back and the decision eventually reversed.

By March 1975 the worker felt that there had been some change in councillors' attitudes over the previous few months: 'there had developed a grudging kind of acceptance that you have to make some response, but it's not a commitment to the group'. He thought the Glodwick councillors saw themselves much more as the managers of resources than the representatives of people in the area, as was more common in other wards, and that they felt threatened by some members of the group who were patently as able as themselves. Some councillors did seem to be changing their attitudes but he felt these changes were far from whole-hearted; they resulted from residents' criticisms that they had ignored the area for years and that they were therefore to an extent to blame for its current problems. He felt that there was 'a degree of guilt' in their response to the Glodwick Action Group. At the end of the period covered by this study relationships were beginning to improve, partly as a result of the group's persistence, and perhaps also because local authority officers by this time accepted a number of the group's objectives as reasonable; this in turn probably influenced the councillors' attitudes.

Relationships with local authority officers

In the early days the group viewed local authority officials with considerable suspicion. One member described their relationship as 'a continual skirmish'; it seemed to him that 'personal ambition on the part of local government officers – architects, planners, engineers – depends on CPO development. The furtherance of a career of an engineer or whatever he is depends on developing the town.'

On the other hand, officers were equally suspicious of the group and its intentions, and, once again, it was the Borough Solicitor's advice to both officers and councillors alike not to attend the second public meeting which confirmed group members in their view that the local authority was at best completely unco-operative and at worst was conspiring against the residents of the area. At the Public Inquiry the Inspector raised with the Borough Solicitor the question of whether he had advised the local authority officials not to attend the meeting, and the Borough Solicitor confirmed that this had been the case. But he undertook not to do so again; furthermore, partly in response to the favourable reception given to the group's evidence, he expressed his willingness to attend any future public meeting called by the group and gave an assurance that the group's evidence would be considered at a high level in the local authority. Subsequently he introduced a discussion of the evidence at an officers' management group (which consisted of local authority chief officers) meeting, and afterwards wrote to the secretary of the group saying he thought 'that there was a good chance that the views expressed by the group would receive a good hearing by the corporation'.

After the CPO was confirmed in March 1974 the group called a public meeting, at which the Borough Solicitor, the heads of the housing and environmental health departments, and representatives from the engineering and planning departments answered questions from local residents about the CPO and its implications. The Deputy Borough Solicitor had attended this meeting as an observer and, when interviewed, said it conformed to the pattern he had later observed to be typical of such meetings. It began with 'a blast of hot air' from the residents, but then gradually the relationship between residents and officers became more amicable. As far as he knew this was the first time such a meeting had been held in Oldham, so it was a new experience for officers. He went on to say that his own view was that where *ad hoc* groups like GAG were formed they should be met and listened to by officers; some officers complained about the time this took up, but in his view the time had to be expended. He had come to think that whenever a major housing scheme was proposed the local authority should endeavour to encourage the formation of community groups by, for example, calling a public meeting. This would involve the authority in only a small amount of expenditure, particularly compared with the vast outlay on each major housing scheme.

By March 1975 the community worker thought that the attitude of officers in certain departments, particularly environmental health, solicitors, and planning, and also to some extent housing and engineers, had noticeably changed: 'They're not solving all the problems immediately, but at least you know now if the group has a problem and picks up the phone and gets hold of the right person it usually gets things sorted out fairly quickly.' The Deputy Borough Solicitor also thought that the information centre was valuable, and was an example of what such a community group could do to help residents in an area. He cited as an illustration the information centre's giving details to the local authority of empty houses in the area which needed making secure; he felt it was important for the local authority to have such a channel of local information.

Some of the group's suggestions were implemented by the local authority despite the difficulties they created. For example, the housing manager pointed out that with the FHA scheme his department did not have enough people to be able to cope easily with the new task of inspecting properties to see if it would be worth spending money on rehabilitating them for short-term letting. The department had to inspect owner-occupied properties all over the borough but was also being asked to give priority to Glodwick, work which in the normal course of events would not need to be done at all. Despite this, the officer thought it was reasonable for the FHA and the group to request this use of short-life properties because it tied in well with the proposal for a phased redevelopment in keeping houses in occupation and thus sustaining a feeling of community, as well as reducing dereliction and, hopefully, vandalism.

The community worker thought that while the proposal for a phased redevelopment was in principle agreed soon after the Public Inquiry, a real commitment to the plan by the local authority only developed over time as a result of the group's maintaining its pressure. It was only, he thought, when members of the group met officers at the Inter-departmental Working Party in September 1974 that the real commitment of the authority to the phasing was made. The scheme had

'not worked perfectly since then by any means, but at that point the authority was forced to say "Well, what have we actually done by having a phased redevelopment?" I don't think they'd really thought out the implications and now the group was saying to them, "Look, this is what it means, and unless you're prepared to meet these implications forget the thing altogether, because you're making life worse for us. We'd rather get out as quickly as possible".'

At that stage some officers recognised and were sympathetic towards the problems. One chief officer

'listened to the group's reasons for suggesting bricking-up and then said, "Yes, bricking-up will cost less in the long run because it won't have to be done so many times. Right. I accept your argument; I will go and argue it with my committee for you." And he did, and they've now got bricking-up.'

There was also the example of the group pointing out to the architect who designed the first phases of the redevelopment that he had made no provision for families with more than five members. The community worker thought this showed that contact with the group had changed his view of his role as an architect:

'I think that's highly significant, and it seems to me that's what community development should be about. But that can happen in many ways better through the groups, and the actual face-to-face contact between officers and residents, than it can through the notion of a CDP working on the officers to change their attitudes, because the attitudes don't change till you meet the realities.'

The future of the group

The factors affecting the group's survival in April 1975 were the progress of the phased redevelopment, whether the information centre continued, and whether significant new issues arose in the area. Financially the group depended on CDP, though it was not impossible that some of its activities could have continued on a more restricted budget such as the group might have been able to raise itself. In addition the community worker still performed an advice and support role in relation to the group.

The community worker said in March 1975 that he did not think the CPO group would exist in the same form a few months later, particularly because key people in the group were being rehoused outside the area. But he thought (as indeed happened) that the group would probably continue with a smaller number of people. From his point of view it would, if the group started to flag, be very difficult to decide how far he should try to keep it going, and whether it could survive the process of people having to move out of the area and moving back in. The information centre, he thought, could survive as a basis for a continuing group, but he did not know if that would be the Glodwick Action Group. 'I would think it'll be more a question not of survival of that particular group of people but survival of the notion of group organisation; but how long after CDP is difficult to tell at the moment.'

Chronological summary of events: October 1972 – April 1975

October 1972	Waterloo Street Compulsory Purchase Order declared: 248 houses.
April 1973	Start of fieldwork by CDP.
April/May 1973	Community worker's discussions with local people about problems of the area.
24 May 1973	Initial meeting of interested people about problems relating to CPO and decline of area. Decision to call public meeting on these subjects.
7 June 1973	Public meeting attended by 40 people, at which decision taken to set up Glodwick Action Group. Committee of nine residents formed.
12 June 1973	First meeting of committee which became CPO sub-committee.
19 June 1973	Public meeting on CPO issues, attended by 300 people and 7 local councillors. Councillors agree to suggestion that a

Councillors' Clinic should be held in the area.

August 1973   Booklet on CPO prepared by CDP to answer questions raised by residents and distributed by group to all houses in CPO area. First newsletter prepared by a member of the group and delivered by members to all 1,800 houses in the area. (Up to April 1975 8 newsletters were produced by the group.) Group and community worker conduct survey of households in CPO area for Public Inquiry. Survey asks whether respondents think the problems of the area can best be solved by CPO, whether in the event of the CPO being confirmed people wish to move from the Glodwick area or not; what type of tenure is preferred and what rent/mortgage payments could be afforded; opinions on land use in redevelopment (for housing, shops, industrial development, open space, community facilities); and whether the information given by the local authority on CPO is adequate and understandable.

25 September 1973   Public Inquiry: group gives evidence based on results of the survey, arguing for: a phased development of the area; local rehousing; the provision of adequate mortgage facilities for those who wish to buy houses elsewhere; improvement for those houses suitable; and consultation with GAG on matters relating to the CPO.

Inspector conducting Inquiry congratulates group on its evidence.

10 October 1973   Public Inquiry evidence discussed at officers' management group (committee of chief officers of local authority). Possibility of phased redevelopment and local rehousing considered.

October 1973   Second newsletter produced, with Urdu
                      translation available on request.

                      Complaints and information form
                      procedure set up, with form attached to
                      back of newsletter.

23 October 1973   Community worker suggests idea of
                      Glodwick Exhibition.

8 November 1973   Local councillor attends GAG committee
                      meeting to discuss problems in the area;
                      says Councillors' Clinic to go ahead.

15 November 1973   Public meeting to report progress and
                      adopt constitution for the group; 6
                      councillors attend to answer questions
                      about local issues.

30 November 1973   First of monthly (later bi-monthly)
                      Councillors' Clinics held. After local
                      government reorganisation these were
                      held on a borough-wide basis.

November 1973   Community worker suggests idea of
                      group having its own worker, particularly
                      to develop the work on complaints and
                      information.

18 December 1973   First meeting between CPO committee
                      and the local authority housing
                      committee to follow up GAG's evidence
                      to the Public Inquiry. GAG's suggestion
                      of a phased redevelopment of the CPO
                      accepted. Possibility raised that at least
                      some of the people in the first phase of
                      clearance could be rehoused on nearby
                      council development. Group raises
                      problem of the bad condition of some
                      multi-occupied lodging houses in the area
                      and their high rents, and also suggests
                      that houses in good condition acquired
                      by the council in the CPO area some
                      time before they are due for demolition
                      should be let on a short-term basis to
                      homeless families and others in housing
                      need.

January 1974	Community worker suggests idea of group having its own premises.
February 1974	Survey by CPO committee members in phase one of the redevelopment area to find out demand for rehousing on nearby council development.
12 March 1974	Further meeting of CPO committee with housing committee: subjects discussed are: shops; possibility of a community centre; lodging houses; use of good property for re-letting. Group to be consulted about designs for redevelopment.
14 March 1974	CPO confirmed, with the exclusion of two houses.
25 April 1974	CDP sub-committee agrees to provision of premises for the group and to appointment of a worker to provide secretarial services for group and to develop complaints service; but agrees only to a part-time, not full-time, appointment.
16 May 1974	Public meeting, attended by about 70 people, to discuss redevelopment of CPO area now CPO confirmed. Six local authority officers (heads of solicitors, housing and environmental health departments, and representatives from planning, engineering, and additional officer from environmental health) come to meeting and answer questions from residents.
12 June 1974	Joint meeting of Glodwick Action Group, New Abbeyhills Tenants' Association, and Holts Tenants' Association with local Citizens' Advice Bureau organiser to discuss information and advice services and the possibility of running these in conjunction with the CAB service.
15 July 1974	Official opening of GAG office,

providing meeting place and office for the group and an information and advice centre.

18 July 1974   CDP sub-committee approves the commission of a report on lodging houses in Glodwick area.[14]

22 July 1974   First paid GAG secretary and information officer starts work.

15 August 1974   Joint meeting of GAG, New Abbeyhills Tenants' Association, and Holts Tenants' Association with CAB area advisory officer. Agree that there should be a six-month experiment of GAG and NATA information centres operating as branch CABs, receiving CAB information service and training and under the overall responsibility of the local CAB organiser.

29 August 1974   Group attends second meeting of Area Councillors' Committee. Subjects discussed are CPO issues generally, and the appointment of a youth worker in the area.

18 September 1974   Special meeting of GAG with council officers to discuss problems arising in the CPO area. Officers attending are heads of engineering and planning, and representatives from solicitor's, housing, environmental health, public relations, libraries. Officers agree to recommend to respective committees:

1 That houses in phases two and three of the CPO area (and likely to remain standing for some time) should be bricked up rather than boarded up.
2 That a letter should be sent by the local authority to all households in the CPO area telling them the expected date of purchase of their property.
3 That the housing department should consider giving to people moving from phase one of the CPO area to council

houses outside Glodwick a written
guarantee of rehousing later back in
Glodwick as it is redeveloped.

4 That the council should consider
proposals for the re-letting of well-
maintained property which it acquires
in the area to families in need.

5 That the planning department should
pursue the possibility of persuading a
supermarket to open temporary
premises in the Waterloo Street area,
to help with difficulties caused by
shops closing down as a result of the
CPO.

The first four proposals were all
subsequently implemented.

September 1974   First GAG worker resigns for health
reasons. Survey by group in phase two of
the CPO area about preferences for type
of development, housing, etc. to be built
in phase one.

2 October 1974   Further meeting with housing committee;
subjects discussed are general
environmental state of the area, the
rapidly declining number of shops, and
the question of rehousing people from
the CPO on a nearby council
development.

3 October 1974   Housing director and housing manager of
Oldham and Tameside Family Housing
Association come to committee meeting
to discuss with the group the possibility
of FHA's managing council-owned
houses in the CPO area for temporary
re-letting.

10 October 1974   Second GAG information officer (like
the first, a member of the group)
appointed by the group.

19/20 October 1974   First CAB training weekend for potential
and existing advice workers in GAG and
other tenants' and residents' groups in
the Project area.

24 October 1974   Group attends third meeting of Area Councillors' Committee. Items discussed are: the inclusion in a social services department accommodation list of several properties in bad condition and for which very high rents are charged; the problems of a particular family living in one of these properties; the possibility of the Family Housing Association managing council-owned houses for re-letting in the Glodwick area, and the provision of a community centre. At a subsequent committee meeting GAG members query whether these meetings are having any useful result.

October 1974   After one year of operation of the complaints and information form procedure (complaints initially having been dealt with by members of the group, latterly more often by the GAG worker), the group has dealt with 179 enquiries for local residents, 97 of which involved approaching local authority departments for action or assistance. Main areas of complaint are about street cleaning, refuse disposal services, CPO and improvement, pavements and street lighting, landlord and tenant and other housing problems.

4 November 1974   Meeting with members of planning and architect's departments to discuss plans for redevelopment of first part of CPO area following the group's survey. Some of the group's suggestions were being implemented; for example the houses and flats are to be of brick and tile and thus fairly traditional in appearance, and six shops and a supermarket are to be the first buildings to be put up.

14 November 1974   CDP sub-committee agrees that GAG worker appointment should be full-time and not part-time.

25 November 1974	New GAG information officer starts work.
30 November/ 1 December 1974	Second CAB training weekend.
7/8 December 1974	Third CAB training weekend.
19 December 1974	Group attends Area Councillors' Committee, raising problems of lodging houses, FHA proposals, deterioration of shopping facilities, and a community building in Glodwick.
16 January 1975	Six-month experiment of GAG information centre operating as extension service of Oldham CAB begins.
12 February 1975	Plan of Waterloo Street Redevelopment phase 1B submitted to housing committee. Committee resolves 'that the proposals be approved in principle, subject to consultation with the Glodwick Action Group'.
17 February 1975	Further meeting with planning and architect's department to discuss amendments to plans for the phase one redevelopment. Some larger houses are now to be provided for large families, and the housing mix now accords precisely with the proportions of different sized households revealed by the group's survey of people wanting to move into the new development.
27 February 1975	Area Councillors' Committee meeting; subjects discussed are the inspection of shops in the area, procedure for demolition of property, various problems over the delay in re-letting some council-owned houses, the closure of a local baths complex, and the future of the Area Councillors' Committee structure.
12 March 1975	Housing committee agrees to three-year experiment with Oldham and Tameside Family Housing Association managing

council-owned re-lets in the later phases of the CPO.

2/6 April 1975   Glodwick Exhibition, organised jointly by CDP and the local authority, and showing local authority services in Glodwick and future plans for the area. Local authority departments mainly concerned are planning, housing, engineering, environmental health, education, social services, and solicitors. The Community Relations Council and the two community groups in Glodwick – GAG and the East Glodwick Group – also participate.

Chapter 5
Failsworth Community Association

Introduction

The Failsworth Community Association (FCA) was formed in 1973. It arose from the concern of some members of the Failsworth Amenity Society that views of Failsworth residents on issues important to them might receive less attention once the old Failsworth Urban District Council was dissolved in the local government reorganisation in April 1974, and the area came under administration of the new Oldham Metropolitan Borough. The association was largely concerned with physical planning, and health, welfare and social needs, but in general concerned itself with any proposals or needs in the area in which its members felt that Failsworth residents had an interest. The constituency of the association was the whole of the population of the former Failsworth Urban District.

To give an indication of the kinds of issue with which the association was concerned, at one executive committee meeting the topics discussed or reported on included a planning application for the building of a bungalow on green belt land, the fluoridisation of Failsworth's water supply, the possibility of a new circular bus service in the area, benches missing from a local park, the Greater Manchester Council structure plan and district plan, drainage from a pig farm, a home safety exhibition, and a report from a meeting of the Oldham and District Community Council (i.e. Council of Voluntary Service) which included mention both of a welfare rights campaign, and of the future of Urban Aid projects in the area.

The context

Failsworth is an area of about 22,000 people which lies between Oldham and central Manchester on the north-east side of the city. Before local government reorganisation in 1974 it was a separate urban district, but it became part of the Oldham Metropolitan Borough. Information from the 1971 census shows that the population of Failsworth has been growing gradually over the years, while Oldham's has been declining.[1] There is a noticeable difference in tenure patterns between the two areas, with Failsworth having more owner-occupation (67 per cent as compared with 47 per cent);[2] dwellings there also have a higher standard of amenities.[3] The census figures show that 27 per cent of economically active men in Failsworth in 1971 were in the Registrar General's non-manual class groups I, II and III, compared with 21 per cent in Oldham. These facts taken together suggest that Failsworth is a more suburban and middle-class area than the former Oldham County Borough.

The impetus behind the formation of the association came from some members of the Failsworth Amenity Society, an organisation established in 1970 to 'protect and improve the local environment'. The general issues in which the society was interested were:

> Pollution of local rivers, streams and canals; pollution of the air and land by harmful chemicals; the disappearance of open spaces and the green belt areas; wildlife conservation; unauthorised tipping in the district; the preservation of historical buildings and archaeological sites; the future of water supplies and refuse disposal; the protection of existing public rights of way; and the provision of adequate recreation and sports facilities in the area, including the provision of bridle paths.

The society described itself as 'a representative body of opinion, with an adequate voice in local affairs – non-political and having no connection with either statutory or secular bodies, but prepared to work with them towards a common cause'. The society 'has through its contact with the Civic Trust, the Civic Trust for the North-West, and the Medlock and Tame Valley Conservation Committee a most effective and democratic method of fighting indifference, apathy, and ill-informed criticism'.

The main project which seems to have been undertaken by the society was the cleaning up of a part of the disused Rochdale Canal running through Failsworth, which involved clearing it of rubbish, reeds, and undergrowth, and planting trees and shrubs donated by members of the public. When later pollution of the canal resulted in the death of many fish the society concerned itself with trying to find out who had been responsible for this and with restocking the canal with fish.

The society also compiled a list of buildings of historical and architectural interest and carried out various surveys in the area, one of derelict sites and plots of land, another of trees with a view to having a blanket Tree Preservation Order made, and one of public rights of way. In addition, the society presented objections to planning permission being granted in a number of cases, one where there was a proposal to tip industrial waste into the derelict Ashton Canal, another where a developer wanted to build 500 houses on green belt land, and a third where planning permission was sought to establish a commercial vehicle and plant auction business in a residential area.

The secretary of the amenity society also became the secretary of the Failsworth Community Association.

Formation of the group

The event which precipitated the formation of the Failsworth Community Association was the imminent reorganisation in 1973 of local government, and fears that, when Failsworth became part of the Oldham Metropolitan Borough, Failsworth issues would receive less attention than they had when the area had had its own urban district council. A further fear was, in the words of one member of the executive committee,

> 'that the former Oldham Borough had large debts and
> little finance coming in, because of the vast area of
> dereliction mainly due to the authority's policy over the
> city centre. Also, with the Manchester Outer Ring Road
> creating a physical barrier between Oldham and
> Failsworth, it would have been better for Failsworth to
> have been incorporated into the central Manchester city
> area. It is with this view of isolation that the association
> was formed, in an attempt to maintain standards and
> ensure that Failsworth received the benefits of a fair
> proportion of the finance raised in the area.'

The initiative in forming the association, as already mentioned, was taken by the Failsworth Amenity Society. The society called a public meeting in September 1972, and invited representatives from local voluntary groups as well as individuals to attend. At this meeting it was agreed to pursue further the idea of a community association. The annual report of the society, talking about the reasons for calling this public meeting, said that the new Oldham Metropolitan Borough Council

> will have 75 members responsible for policy concerning local authority services covering 44 square miles, and an estimated population of 277,000. Failsworth as part of this conurbation will have six councillors elected locally to represent 22,500 people. How well they represent us depends very largely on the attitude of all the elected representatives to each other, and the way they adjust themselves to their new role and responsibilities. The purpose of the meeting is to discuss how best we as a community can help and work together improving the town and ensuring that it does not fall below today's standards. Times are changing, and in some matters we have got to change with them; no longer can we continue to live as a community of individuals. In the past, only those connected with political associations or members of groups interested in the well-being of the town received information of some kind; very often it had to be sought, and was restricted to that particular group's activities. The rest of the community, if they were fortunate, received it second-hand, sometimes in casual conversation, or as a rumour. Lack of information at any level often leads to mistrust and misunderstanding. With this in mind, and should the new authority be prepared to implement the Skeffington Report or the proposed community councils, then as one executive committee of representatives, the voluntary bodies in Failsworth will represent a united front of public opinion.

The people who took the initiative towards forming the association were all local people who were already members of the Failsworth Amenity Society. No outside community workers were involved. The public meeting was attended by 40 people, and resulted in a steering committee being elected to prepare a draft constitution. This was circulated to those groups whose representatives had attended the meeting, and then went through a lengthy process of revision, re-revision and agreement before all the individual groups were satisfied. The secretary said that the most difficult part to get over to the groups was that they would lose none of their autonomy by becoming members of the association. A second public meeting (attended by 47 people) was held after the constitution had been agreed by each of the participating groups, and a permanent executive committee of representatives from voluntary organisations was ratified, and the officers elected.

While local government re-organisation appears to have been the most important factor in the formation of the association, this was reinforced by a considerable commitment to the idea of such an association by the secretary and perhaps also by other members of the Failsworth Amenity Society.

Objectives and general aims

The aim of the association was to bring together 'voluntary groups under a joint management committee of representatives from a number of voluntary organisations in the district, each group retaining its separate identity and functions, but meeting together as one executive to decide joint policies and share responsibility on sub-committees'. The association would be concerned, according to its constitution:

> To protect and preserve and stimulate public interest in the area comprising Failsworth; to promote high standards, and to protect the interests of the community, involving local authority services connected with the environment, education, health and welfare; to provide local information which would help the local elected representatives in the performance of their duties to the community; to undertake surveys in the district as and when required, and to collate this information on a statistical basis; to act as a lobby, and to provide a platform for public debate; to protect the environment against dereliction and bad planning; to make contacts with other voluntary groups in Oldham, and to include those in the Greater Manchester Metropolitan County; the group shall be non-political, and non-sectarian, bound together by mutual interest.

The primary aims of the association remained constant, but specific objectives waxed and waned over time. Issues with which the association was concerned included the production of a directory of welfare services in Failsworth, the provision of meeting places for the elderly, the accessibility and adequacy of services to be provided at a new health centre, bus-only lanes, neighbourhood councils, the provision of a new community centre, the Greater Manchester structure plan, and a planning application by the Territorial Army Volunteer Reserve to use a derelict quarry in the area for troop training with heavy earth-moving vehicles.

Organisation and development of the group

According to the association's constitution, membership was open 'to all who are interested in actively furthering the purposes of the committee', and any member of the constituency, that is any resident of Failsworth, could attend meetings of the executive committee of the association, express views, and indeed vote. Members of the association did not pay subscriptions, though the possibility was being considered by the association's finance sub-committee. The association's finance came from donations from members of the executive committee.

Since no subscriptions were levied it is difficult to identify members of the association, but the members who were readily identifiable were those forming the executive committee. This committee was made up of representatives nominated by their constituent organisations (generally two from each organisation). The constituent organisations included the Labour Party and Conservative Association (the Communist Party was also invited to participate in the association but did not do so), three churches (Roman Catholic, Anglican and Unitarian), two Owner-Occupier Associations, the Townswomen's Guild, Women's Royal Voluntary Service, Old People's Welfare Committee, Failsworth charities, NSPCC, and the local youth clubs. Usually about 18 of the total of 24 members attended executive committee meetings. There were three changes of membership of this committee, with one representative resigning for personal reasons, and two members resigning from a constituent organisation (the Old People's Welfare Committee) for health reasons and therefore having to be replaced on the executive committee by others nominated by the OPWC.

The secretary thought the only characteristic that members of the executive committee had in common was a concern about the area and that the services available within it before local government reorganisation did not further deteriorate. Because of the way the executive committee was composed, however, most members were by definition members of other voluntary associations and presumably of some standing in these organisations in order to act as their representatives on this committee. A significant proportion of the committee in fact were members of a number of voluntary organisations. Some were also magistrates and a number (and not just the representatives of the political parties) were ex-councillors.[4]

It was not possible to ascertain the core activists of the group, as the research worker's observation of the association was limited. If one were to assume, however, that the core activists were its office-holders, then they amounted to nine people: the chairman, vice-chairman, and honorary secretary of the executive committee, and the chairman and secretaries of its three sub-committees, welfare, planning and finance. Four of the nine office-holders were ex-councillors (existing councillors were not eligible to be officers of the association), and all four had been chairmen of committees of Failsworth UDC during their term of office. At least two were magistrates.[5]

At the time of the formation of the association it had been envisaged that there would be seven sub-committees concerned respectively with planning, welfare and personal social services, refuse collection, housing, health, education/recreation and finance, but in the event only three of these – planning, welfare services and finance – were established. In addition, after the formation of the association, another sub-committee, the Home Safety Committee, was set up. This committee was administered and serviced by the association by means of an annual grant from the Oldham Metropolitan Borough Environmental Health Committee. It was concerned with matters such as the prevention of accidents and poisoning in people's homes, and was one of seven home safety committees covering the Oldham Metropolitan District. The chairman/secretary of each HSC was co-opted on to the parent committee of the borough council.

The executive committee of the association met every six weeks, as did the welfare services sub-committee. Meetings of the planning sub-committee (which largely incorporated the work previously done by the Failsworth Amenity Society, although the society continued to exist as a separate entity) were, however, held fortnightly, shadowing those of the local authority planning committee, which also met every two weeks. Meetings were held at the former Failsworth Town Hall. The executive committee meeting attended by the research worker was formal in that there was an agenda and this was closely adhered to, but informal in the sense that the members seemed in general to be on easy terms with one another. Few decisions were actually made, as much of the business involved reporting back either from meetings of outside bodies or from sub-committees of the association. Where decisions were taken, they were made by agreement and without dissent. The secretary confirmed when interviewed that executive committee decisions were usually by consensus but might on rare occasions be decided by vote. He also said that there were no obvious splits or personality clashes within the executive committee.

The planning sub-committee had considerable delegated powers, as decisions often had to be made quickly about the association's response to planning applications. There was, however, provision for matters on which there was disagreement to be referred to the executive committee for decision. The welfare services sub-committee did not have such wide delegated powers. Each sub-committee reported on its proceedings at the executive committee meetings and decisions made by the sub-committees were discussed and then either approved or, if necessary, disputed there.

The association's expenditure was largely on administration; in its early days it was financed by voluntary donations from members of the executive committee and others interested in the association's work, although in November 1975 the executive committee decided to seek donations from local industrial firms. The secretary thought the association would in due course have to charge a subscription for membership, but said that one of the difficulties was that some of the member organisations were forbidden by their constitutions or terms of reference to make donations to other bodies. Tentative approaches had also been made to the local authority for some finance; but members were concerned how far such grant-aid might affect the group's independence.

Strategy

Efforts to attract general support for the association included public meetings and articles in the *Oldham Evening Chronicle* (the local daily evening paper), in the *Clarion*, a paper produced by local churches, and in *Contact*, the newsletter of the Civic Trust for the North-West. Support from participating groups was maintained by their representatives on the executive committee reporting back on the association's transactions; any matters on which there was then disagreement could be raised at the next meeting of the association.

The secretary said that in attempting to achieve its objectives the association acted through the 'normal channels of democratic protest', lobbying councillors, writing to MPs and Ministers, and giving evidence at Public Inquiries into planning matters, or registering objections on planning applications with the planning department. One of the two representatives on the executive committee from local owner-occupiers' associations had made himself an expert on planning objections, particularly those relating to Compulsory Purchase Orders, and was used by the association as its authority on the subject.

One of the features of the association was the promotion of links between itself and other local bodies by overlapping memberships. In an article about the association in the newsletter of the Civic Trust for the North-West the secretary said that

> Members are encouraged to take up commitments on outside bodies, by becoming more involved with the affairs of other local and national committees which cover a much wider range of interests and activities; their interest and personal experience help to influence the work and policy decisions. Smaller voluntary groups, if they are to remain effective, should become more involved in the work of others, and use this knowledge to further their own aims.

While the amenity society had been limited in its outlook, there were members of the community association on the Oldham and District Community Council, the Medlock and Tame Valley Conservation Committee, and the Oldham Community Health Council.

Two major issues which the association was involved in fighting were the provision of a community hall for Failsworth, and the proposal of the Territorial Army to use a local quarry for training. The history of the community hall issue was that before reorganisation was projected, Failsworth UDC had made plans for a new civic hall in a development which largely comprised a new Co-operative Society store; but after reorganisation the new Oldham Metropolitan Borough Council rejected the plan in one of its rounds of economic cuts. This rejection had important implications since under the original agreement the capital cost of the civic hall was to have been paid for largely out of the ground rent accruing to the council from the other occupier (the Co-operative Society) of the development over a period of 125 years, provided that the hall was built by the developer at the same time as the rest of the development; and the other building was already in progress. If, therefore, the hall was not proceeded with immediately these financial arrangements would lapse, and it was envisaged that Failsworth would have to wait indefinitely and compete against other demands in Oldham to get a community hall.

In July 1975 FCA took the initiative in setting up an *ad hoc* committee, inviting participation from the local Labour and Conservative parties and both existing and former councillors for the Failsworth area, which agreed to ask the Oldham council to reconsider its decision on the grounds both of the loss of amenity to Failsworth residents, and of the new Oldham council's 'constitutional commitment to honour the resolution made by the former Failsworth UDC', which it was revoking by its decision in this case. The *ad hoc* committee decided to send a deputation to press its case with the Oldham council; and subsequently a deputation of six from the community association had a meeting with the three leaders of the political parties forming the council (Conservative, Labour and Liberal), the chairmen of the Oldham Development Committee and the Arts and Recreation Committee, and various chief officers, in which they urged that the scheme should not be abandoned and that, although a civic hall was now inappropriate, a community hall at least should be built on the site. The matter was still unresolved when this case study was completed.

The other issue concerned a planning application by the Territorial Army Volunteer Reserve to use a derelict quarry in the Failsworth area to train their troops in the use of heavy earth-moving machinery. The planning sub-committee of the association co-operated in the collation of evidence from the Failsworth Amenity Society and the two Failsworth owner-occupiers' associations to object to the application. A local councillor acted as an intermediary to arrange a meeting between the association and the TAVR, but no agreement was reached. After an on-site demonstration by the Army the association reiterated its earlier objection to the Army's request to the planning committee for a change of use of the site, adding the additional objection that when the quarry had earlier been used as a dump for chemical waste a particularly poisonous substance had been deposited there and it was feared that disturbance of the soil could lead to its liberation. The TAVR subsequently abandoned its application, and the association claimed some credit for this.

Achievements and failures

The secretary considered that the main achievement of the association had been in getting the twenty-four local groups to associate themselves in one body; what still remained to be achieved, in his view, was the implementation of a system whereby a few local people with relevant interests could be co-opted to sit on local authority committees with councillors. He recognised that this would involve a change in legislation as well as in thinking.

The secretary found it hard to assess the impact of the association within the constituency. The association did not publicise its activities much because of lack of resources. There had been no radio or television coverage of the association's activities, and the secretary thought that public awareness of the association resulted mainly from personal contact with the local Citizens' Advice Bureau and other local organisations.

The secretary claimed that because of the number of ex-councillors on the executive committee the association had the ear of a number of serving councillors, and the local MP. In general he thought that the association's relationship with local councillors was good; as already mentioned, both the local Labour and Conservative organisations nominated representatives to the executive committee and the committee had on it a number of ex-councillors representing various local organisations. The secretary (himself an ex-councillor on the Failsworth UDC) said that the association saw part of its function as being to inform councillors about issues that were arising in the Failsworth area, and said that if the executive committee wished to discuss a certain issue with councillors they would invite them to a meeting.

He felt there might initially have been some degree of caution in the reactions of local authority officers to the association, although he also believed that the relationship was quick to improve. The officers soon became willing to accept information put forward by the association as reliable, and seemed more confident that the association was not seeking as a primary aim to embarrass them. The secretary increasingly felt able to get in touch direct with any of the chief officers about issues that arose. He mentioned in particular the good relationship that he felt the association had with the planning department; the Borough Architect, and Director of Planning, and a number of his staff had been found to be very approachable and helpful.

The future of the group

The secretary thought that the association could have an indefinite future provided it continued to be constituted and to operate in the same way. But it is clear that the association was performing functions which might elsewhere fall within the orbit of a neighbourhood council, and the secretary thought that if neighbourhood councils were set up on a formal basis in the Metropolitan Borough this might well mean the end of the association.[6] He feared that if neighbourhood councils were established with a formal election procedure then they might well be organised on party political lines and could become training grounds for future councillors. In his view the system should be designed to work in the opposite way; that not only should neighbourhood councils remain non-political but that they should provide a means by which members of the community with relevant interests could be found to sit alongside elected members on local authority committees.[7]

Chapter 6
The Joint Working Party on Vagrants

Introduction: an overview of the group's activities and main concerns

'In our town four convents provide 30 to 40 meals a day to vagrants, and, with that type of direct contact, we might find more out about them, it was said at a meeting of the Council of Churches last night.' So ran a report in the 11 December 1970 issue of the evening paper which serves the northern town in which the events described in this case study took place.[1] At that time, neither the Council of Churches nor any other organisation (apart from a private hostel, itself about to close down) knew 'more about them', still less made any provision to supplement the sisters' meals.

Both the Council of Churches and Council of Social Service set up vagrants' working parties at about that time. After several meetings and an exploratory study, the two organisations joined forces in July 1972 to form a 'joint working party' committed to follow-up action. Three months later, this body opened an experimental night shelter in a disused potato warehouse near the town centre. After considerable public and political controversy, through the second half of 1973, about this shelter, the local authority provided an alternative hostel in April 1974. This hostel was constructed, and predominantly funded, by the district council whose boundary coincided with that of the town. The voluntary organisation made up the financial difference in running costs, continued to provide volunteer manning on a shift rota basis, and had a minority representation on the Housing Services sub-committee specifically established to manage the shelter.

The context: the situation prior to the formation of the joint working party

The situation prior to the organisation's formation was that local provision of cheap overnight accommodation had declined to nothing, while the need for it had increased. In 1972 the Department of Health and Social Security estimated that there were 42 people with no fixed abode for every 100,000 of the population. The northern town concerned had a population of 105,000, with a further 50,000 in adjacent suburbs. By that reckoning, between 60 and 70 single people in the area had no overnight accommodation.

From the mid- to late-1960s, national bodies like the Simon Community and the Cyrenians had been sponsoring shelters in different parts of the country.[2] Others had arisen from independent local initiatives. A Department of Health and Social Security circular in the summer of 1972 also expressed concern, and encouraged the setting up of shelters. This read:

> The Secretary of State has been reviewing the ways in which more help can be given to single adults who are without a permanent home. Such people consist mainly of men without a settled way of life for whom specific provision is not at present made on a long-term basis and for whom local authorities have a responsibility to provide residential accommodation under Section 21 of the National Assistance Act, 1948. Authorities' ability to meet the full need will vary, but this should not deter any authority which sees and can create an opportunity to experiment from making a start in a modest way either directly or by mobilising or co-operating with voluntary effort.[3]

In the town concerned, an increase in the numbers of single homeless people had been noted by parish priests, some statutory social workers, in particular a medical social worker and a probation officer, and voluntary workers at the Citizens' Advice Bureau. These people communicated their concerns to the Council of Churches and Council of Social Service.

Formation of the group

These councils separately set up *ad hoc* working parties. Both were concerned that provision should be made for vagrants, but also felt that 'hard facts were a necessary basis for any approach'.[4] The resources for collecting the facts were found when the Council of Social Service obtained the help of a local post-graduate student. He conducted a survey during April 1972, and obtained information on 68 people. The most frequently expressed needs were for food, money and accommodation. The report on the study, submitted in July 1972, listed among its suggestions for action 'provision of shelter for the coming winter' and a 'co-ordinating group to enable agencies to work together closely'.

Perception of an apparent need (and the lack of actual or potential provision to meet it) had led to the setting up of the working parties. Their members, and in particular their secretaries, were strongly committed to the cause of single homeless people and pursued this concern persistently throughout the difficulties of, and delays in, acquiring reliable information. Their persistence resulted in an empirical enquiry, and the results of this sparked off the formation of the voluntary organisation.

Objectives and general aims

The co-ordinating group advocated by the report to the Council of Social Service was established immediately, adopting the title of the Council of Churches and Council of Social Service Joint Working Party on Vagrants. Its only formally ratified and recorded goals were decided some two years after inception (and after responsibility for the running of a shelter had been taken over by the local authority). These 'broad terms of reference' were: 'to maintain a general concern for homeless men in the town; to maintain contact with the national organisations concerned with the homeless; to assist with the running of the local authority shelter by providing volunteers, and in such other ways as are appropriate.' Similar objectives were implicit at the start of, and throughout, the working party's initiative.

In practice, at the outset of the venture, the most urgent priority was determined as the provision of shelter for single homeless men before the worst of the winter. Moreover, the working party became committed (not least after rebuffs from the local authority to requests that a central, council-owned, vacant property might be made available) to supplying such accommodation themselves, in order to ensure its early readiness. The immediate *de facto* primary task, therefore, was the establishment of a shelter. Subsequent overriding priorities were the development and administration of its service, and, later, the preservation of its existence when threatened by external pressures.

Organisation and development of the group

The structure of the working party was simple. The two sponsoring bodies appointed the committee. Its eight members comprised an equal number of representatives from each. The secretary of the Council of Churches became the chairman and treasurer of the joint working party, and the executive officer of the Council of Social Service became its secretary. Volunteers were co-ordinated by a secretarial member of the Council of Social Service staff. No constitution was drawn up. The committee (in practice often the officers) determined priorities and strategies, and took responsibility for ensuring financial liquidity. Volunteers sometimes met separately, mainly to discuss the day-to-day administration of the shelter, once it was established, and to organise work groups for the building's rehabilitation. A few general meetings between the committee and volunteers took place (there was in any case, at least initially, a large degree of overlap), but these were seen as advisory, rather than executive, by the committee. Later in the life of the project, volunteer representatives (at first one third, later 6 out of 14) acquired a minority place on the committee.

Tensions between the committee's and the volunteers' perspectives were a more or less permanent feature of the working party. These seldom came out into the open, however, mainly because the ninety-odd volunteers were demographically heterogeneous, operationally fragmented into different shifts, and internally divided in terms of the relative priority given to 'social-treatment-oriented practice' and 'social-change-oriented practice'.[5] In addition, names and numbers fluctuated considerably, and college vacations interfered with continuity.

One issue on which volunteers did independently organise in strength was the threatened closure of the shelter in November 1973. The local authority Development and Planning Committee had decided to recommend the town council to reject the renewal of planning permission for the shelter. The working party committee's response was deliberately restrained. Individuals and sympathetic organisations were merely encouraged to write letters of support to the town clerk.

This was not acceptable to the volunteers. At a standing-room-only meeting between the committee and volunteers, which took place only ten days before the crucial council meeting, they refused to accept the committee vice-chairman's verdict that there was 'no real chance' of saving the shelter. Effectively taking control of the organisation, the volunteers chose not to be diverted by suggestions of how the consequences of the shelter's closure might best be mitigated (seeing this as accepting defeat without putting up the kind of public fight waged by the shelter's opponents). They determined on action and the exertion of pressure to create the maximum chance of this eventuality being prevented. The result was a multi-faceted public campaign to save the shelter, leading one unsympathetic councillor to say 'they've organised a huge pressure group to keep it going and they've done it very successfully'.

Strategy

Three main priorities have already been attributed to the voluntary organisation during the first few months of its existence: the establishment of the shelter, the development of its service, and its maintenance in the face of external threats.

The action taken to establish a shelter fell into five successive, though overlapping, phases: (1) finding a suitable building; (2) obtaining planning permission for new use and a rental agreement; (3) the raising of funds and recruitment of voluntary helpers; (4) carrying out essential repair work on the building; (5) opening up the shelter. The first task was achieved in August 1972. The committee toured several possible sites, and decided that a disused potato warehouse near an old cattle market was the most suitable. Planning permission for change of use was sought and obtained in September. This came about partly through the oiling of council decision making wheels by a leading working party member who was also chairman of the local authority Development and Planning Committee; in part, too, it was because the application was only 'for a temporary period of six months so that assessment can be made of the value of this type of provision and of the need for its continuation'. The council's liability was thereby limited and recoverable. The building was owned by the corporation's Markets Committee, which agreed to its lease at a generously low rent. Money was raised largely through Council of Churches networks. Manpower came mainly from church congregations and from local college students. Rehabilitative work was carried out by volunteers, and the working party achieved its objective of providing a shelter before winter by opening the warehouse for this purpose on 30 October 1972.

The numbers using the accommodation quickly built up. With the evidence that the shelter was meeting a real need, both the committee and volunteers became preoccupied with further physical renovation and maintenance of the property, with working out the mechanics and ground-rules of internal administration, and with the development of relationships with 'the men'. These reflected the overall priority at this stage of service provision and improvement.

But the next stage of the shelter's development was entered soon after this, with the emergence of external pressures which threatened its future survival. The first was financial. The DHSS prevaricated for fifteen months when approached for a grant, eventually intimating that an award would be conditional on the voluntary organisation imposing a nightly accommodation charge. The organisation was therefore constantly stretched to raise financial resources, as well as subject to internal divisions over the charges issue. Considerable badgering by committee members of potential donors, and a series of fund-raising events organised mainly by volunteers, enabled the working party to remain solvent.

There was also pressure from the growing opposition of nearby residents. The light evenings of the early 1973 summer months increased the visibility and perceived nuisance of shelter users. Residents, and in particular a leading spokeswoman, wrote letters to the working party and to the local press, and collected 391 signatures for a petition urging the shelter's immediate closure. The working party had neglected to communicate with residents up to this time. They responded to the complaints by inviting residents' representatives to subsequent committee meetings and by drafting a circular letter, signed by the local spokeswoman, outlining proposed methods of curbing the nuisance. The working party took no action to counter the residents' petition.

It was in council circles that opposition to the shelter was next expressed. Of the three external threats, this was the most serious: the Damocles sword of renewal of planning permission hung over the shelter's future. Successive planning and markets committee and full council meetings from August to October 1973 debated the issue, and narrowly (once by a casting vote) voted either for a short-term reprieve or for a postponement of the decision.

The Development and Planning Committee called a public meeting about the shelter early in November. This was predictably stormy, and resulted in the committee's recommendation that the shelter should be closed. This was when the working party was most in need of public support. With volunteers taking an organisation lead, large numbers of letters were sent to the local press and Town Clerk, and all councillors were personally lobbied. Nearly 3,000 signatures (including a significant number from the residential area close to the shelter) were obtained for a petition 'urging the council to keep the Central Street Shelter open, until such time as alternative provision is made available for the homeless men'. Maximum publicity was obtained for the submission of the petition to the Town Clerk, and both local and national organisations were approached to give active support. The public controversy was further heightened by (and itself helped to spark off) letters and resolutions from several previously unconnected organisations and individuals. Arms of the Labour and Liberal parties issued public pleas for the shelter's maintenance. The influential Labour MP argued in a newspaper letter that 'it would be monstrous to close Central Street until an alternative is provided'. In addition, the local press gave considerable space to the issue in the run-up to the council debate, and included a feature article which concluded:

> It takes so much effort and organisation to give these men what most of us would regard as commonplace. But even these small acts may be stopped. The shelter isn't asking the council for much – just to stay open until somewhere else is found, and, failing that, until the warmer weather comes next spring. The decision is surely out of the realm of politics now and into the province of compassion.

Even though the final sentence was more an expression of hope than a description of reality, the article carried impact, and the shelter working party found a powerful ally in the local paper's staff.

This feature article was denounced at the council meeting, as were many of the letters which appeared in the press and were received by the Town Clerk. But the most powerful speeches in support of the shelter cited 'the evidence . . . proved by the correspondence in the press; the vast majority of the people in the town want the council to treat the issue as one of compassion'. 'By 32 votes to 11 . . . the council agreed . . . on a course of action which will allow the shelter to continue in the former potato warehouse until March 31 at the latest . . . that the Social Services Committee should give consideration to the problem and that the Markets Committee be instructed to take vacant possession of the Central Street premises not later than March 31.'

The working party's internal differences over political strategies persisted beyond this meeting. In broad terms, many volunteers were concerned to capitalise on the organisation's newly acquired position of public strength and support, believing that it should take the initiative in finding alternative premises and, more importantly, ensure that it secured maximum influence in any collaborative enterprise with the council. The committee, and in particular the officers, on the other hand, felt that the sooner the local authority took both the responsibility and the initiative for shelter provision the better. One reason was that such provision was now dependent on local authority sponsorship and involvement; this was a condition of future operations spelled out in the council debate. Another was that as soon as the 'reprieve' had been granted, decision making about the shelter returned to private domains, and the shelter officers set about re-establishing harmonious relations, and re-activating informal communications links with their erstwhile council friends. This reflected their general consensual perspectives and approaches. It was also designed to restore the tarnished collaborative and responsible image of the voluntary organisation, not to mention the images of its sponsoring bodies. In practice, it meant that minimal representations were made about alternative provision in the weeks following the council meeting.

In spite (or perhaps because) of this, early in 1974 the council appointed an 'action working party to set up a replacement for the Central Street Shelter'. This later gave way, for running purposes, to a Shelter Control Sub-committee of the Housing Services Committee on which the working party had a minority representation (composed of its three officers). Despite this collaborative machinery, and verbal commitment to joint decision making, the council unilaterally drew up a design for the replacement shelter, unilaterally determined the rules to be adhered to, took sole responsibility for appointing the warden, and unilaterally determined 'that the control of the shelter should be in the hands of the corporation assisted by volunteers'.

The working party committee made no objection to these moves by the council, partly because they were given little opportunity to do so, and partly through a concern to avoid jeopardising in any way the prospective provision. The establishment of the new shelter was being left late, and things had to happen fast if they were to happen at all. The committee anticipated that, by not rocking the boat before the replacement shelter was opened, they would be able to exert more influence for change afterwards.

The future of the group

This did not prove to be the case. The control sub-committee seldom met, and had little influence over finance or policy for future provision. Noises were made by the voluntary representatives, behind closed doors, about, for example, the need for informality in administration, and the urgency of extending the facilities. These apparently fell on deaf ears, however, and tended to pre-empt more public pressure.

Several alternatives were open to the voluntary organisation. It could continue in the position of having responsibility for doing, without any authority for deciding. It was argued by some members, in particular the officers, that this remained the only way of ensuring continued provision, that any other strategy would undermine the working party's credibility, that the organisation had not to mind its relative powerlessness in the interests of provision for its clients, and that its influence, in any case, would increase through a constructive long-term working relationship on the venture, and the improved mutual understanding with the council which this would promote.

Others felt that the deleterious effect on the organisation (for example, reduced morale and cohesion) of the present situation, the extent to which it had been co-opted by the local authority, and the, at least partial, achievement of its aims, justified pulling out of the so-called partnership, thereby releasing the additional resources both for alternative initiatives and for the more open exertion of pressure on the overall issue of homelessness and the need for more extensive facilities.

The first view prevailed, not least because many volunteers felt that pulling out would excessively jeopardise even the present provision. Elements of the other approach were broached by some volunteers at different stages. But the committee, as the working party members with the most direct dealings with the local authority, re-asserted its internal influence and ensured that criticisms and demands were properly expressed and channelled. Some of the more radical volunteers found their way into alternative initiatives, mainly of a general housing nature, and, although volunteer manning remained a persistent problem, they were largely replaced by others with a prime concern for the provision of a service. This was healthy for the shelter provision, and no reason was apparent why either that service or the statutory-voluntary relationship should break down. There remained the likelihood, however, that consolidation of what had been achieved would divert energies and attention from what still might be.

Achievements and failures

The working party could claim some solid achievements. Statutory provision of overnight accommodation for homeless individuals was promoted, and later established on a secure footing. A sensitive service was provided for those using the shelter, and in many cases this was extended to supplementary support in finding lodgings or negotiating with welfare benefits officials. In addition, the consciousness of many members of both the organisation and the public about such needs, and about the political difficulties in getting them met, was raised. Subsequent ventures in the town – for example, a Women's Aid Refuge for Battered Wives – tailored their campaigns to lessons learnt from the shelter experience. Other initiatives, like a Squatters' Association, developed partly as a result of the frustration experienced by early volunteers in dealing with local authority representatives through conventional channels. All these achievements (or, at least, effects) of the shelter venture were attributable to two main advances: the initial establishment of the shelter; and its maintenance in the face of political, and some public, opposition.

The first of these advances was promoted by the persistence and commitment of the two sponsoring organisations, and in particular of some individual members and officers. The prestige, and recognised good faith, of the Council of Churches and Council of Social Service also helped both in the fund-raising and negotiations with the town council. The working party vice-chairman's knowledge of, and involvement in, the decision making processes of the local authority facilitated this vital communication flow. In addition, a wide range of skills was available, when required, to carry out the renovation of the building, to raise large amounts of money, to administer the working party's affairs, and to promote a supportive atmosphere for the shelter's users. Above all, the survey gave the venture both legitimacy and purpose. This proved a difficult step to take; but its importance was highlighted by the action which it triggered off.

The maintenance of the shelter through the public campaign prior to the crucial council meeting was achieved through rather different (indeed, in part, contradictory) strengths. This depended on the high level of identification which volunteers felt towards the project, their realisation that confrontative tactics were the most appropriate in the prevailing political circumstances, and their refusal to take no for an answer to their demands for a public campaign. In addition, the issue was controversial because 'it touched upon fundamental beliefs about caring for the less fortunate' and, in terms of the decision to be taken, presented clear-cut alternatives. Concern among members of the public was further provoked by some bitterly cold weather and the approach of the Christmas season. The role of the local evening paper was significant. It promoted the issue as one of public concern through extensive coverage of the 'story'. The editorial and features staff expressly sympathised with the shelter cause; and, through providing a vehicle for public debate, demonstrated the direction and weight of popular opinion. Finally, the mobilisation of this public support by the shelter volunteers was the factor which proved crucial in influencing councillors to support the 'reprieve'.

Short-term achievements, therefore, were substantial. Progress toward longer-term aims was less impressive. This was partly because these were never clarified; the organisation did not determine targets designed to mobilise sustained action in their pursuit. Another problem was the organisation's chosen cause, the stigma attached to vagrants and the extra dimensions of fear and hostility which they aroused, not least among residents in any sort of proximity. In addition, short-term considerations tended to dominate the organisation's approach. No sooner was the shelter established than its very existence had to be fought for. Preoccupation with service provision along with crisis management were the perpetual orders of the day. All the resources available were needed for this service provision and maintenance. The organisation was forced by external circumstance into defence of its 'bird in the hand'. The organisation's long-term lack of progress was in part directly attributable to its short-term success.

The final reason for lack of such progress was the working party's dependence throughout on the local authority for the concession of planning permission, and its junior partner status in the later collaborative machinery. Possible developments had to be raised through these channels, thus pre-empting further independent initiatives and campaigns. When 'offered a token share of power, at the price of co-operation and acquiescence in a feeble response to its needs', the working party could have taken 'the power, but refused the co-operation, exploiting each concession to gain more'.[6] The organisation was, in practice, acquiescing in a response which, while a considerable advance on nothing, was feeble in relation to the scale and overall nature of the needs of local homeless people. The constraints outlined above, and the predominantly service-oriented rather than campaigning approaches of recently recruited volunteers, suggested that there was little likelihood of the campaigning side of the

organisation being revived or of comparable advances in provision for homeless people again being achieved.

Concluding comments

The working party was at its strongest when the service-oriented
and campaigning commitments of its volunteers were integrated
in particular initiatives. Such a coincidence triggered the organisational power, which, in different ways, both established the
shelter and maintained its existence through the exertion of
public pressure. The working party was most vulnerable when
these two elements conflicted, especially when the split was
between the committee and volunteers. As Seeley has shown,
'where opposing viewpoints cut across different statuses, the
organisation faces much less danger of internal disruption than
if the viewpoints separate the statuses'.[7] The conflicts, as in many
other organisations, predominantly focussed on strategies rather
than goals, on questions of how rather than of what or why. But
the general, open-ended, undeclared *raisons d'être* of the working party, while having the advantage of wide appeal, had left
open the possibility that joiners[8] would hold too divergent commitments to ensure a requisite degree of continuing consensus.

The joint working party in practice fell short of excessive
organisational disruption through internal dissension. But the
fact remains that the service-oriented and campaigning elements
were not held together, the latter largely dispersing in the later
stages. Many might interpret the voluntary service rump which
remained as a realistic use of available resources, relatively easy
and congenial and generally consistent with the working party's
fundamental commitments. But if the argument that strength
derived from a combination of service-oriented and campaigning
perspectives is correct, the organisation seemed condemned to
weakness and minimal future development.

The periods of organisational strength were associated with
three inter-related factors. First, the working party was on the
up, going places, and actively pursuing unrealised, but realisable,
goals; second, it was independent, pursuing self-determined
aspirations in an entrepreneurial manner; and third, all members
felt in it together, participating simultaneously in (or at least
identifying with) both policy making and its implementation.
The times of weakness were associated with the opposite: an
emphasis on keeping going what was – this was important in its
own terms, but not developmental or challenging; dependence
on external authorities, like the Department of Health and Social

Security and district council, for the future direction of the organisation; and fragmented or constricted commitments, and non-participative decision making.

In general, it seems probable (though hopefully not inevitable) that the more a community group participates with a political authority in making some provision, and the more its representatives take into account that authority's constraints and *modus operandi*, the more those representatives adopt one-dimensional, service- and short-term-oriented perspectives, the less they retain meaningful contact with other organisational members, and the greater become the pressures against internally participative processes of decision making. The more organisational leaders participate with external power-holders in reaching decisions (and such participation usually takes place through group representatives in some form or another), the less do members appear to have the opportunity to participate in their group's internal decision making.

Chronological summary of events: February 1971 – April 1974

17 February 1971   First meeting convened by the Council of Social Service following requests from agencies and individuals to consider the need for accommodation for single homeless men in the town.

9 March 1971   Second meeting, at which social workers' reports stress the need for a well-supervised, clean lodging house.

21 June 1971   Council of Churches working party agrees that the need for a hostel seems to exist, but that more facts should be acquired.

17 January 1972   Evening conference arranged by Council of Social Service resolves that a survey is needed to ascertain the number of vagrants.

April–May 1972   Survey conducted by local post-graduate student. Information collected on about 68 men.

July 1972   Report on survey submitted to Council of Social Service.

14 July 1972	Council of Social Service and Council of Churches set up a joint working party which agrees the need of a shelter.
28 July 1972	Survey report circulated to relevant agencies, together with notification of the working party's intention of establishing a shelter.
September 1972	Temporary planning permission for Central Street Shelter granted by town council for initial period of six months.
30 October 1972	Opening of shelter.
November onwards	Volunteer working parties rehabilitate building; and committee and general meetings discuss procedures and general approach to running the shelter.
6 February 1973	Request by working party for renewal of planning permission.
15 March 1973	Renewal of planning permission for further six months granted by Development and Planning Committee of the town council.
5 June 1973	Letter of opposition from local residents' spokeswoman to chairman of working party; beginning of campaign for the shelter's closure.
18 June 1973	Two shelter users convicted of behaviour likely to cause a breach of the peace for an incident near the shelter.
	Letter sent to residents' spokeswoman expressing the working party committee's concern about the developing situation, and inviting residents to its next meeting.
First week in July 1973	Residents' petition, signed by 391 people for the closure of the shelter, presented to the council.
10 July 1973	Meeting between committee and volunteers. No residents attend.
23 July 1973	Letter in local evening paper from residents' spokeswoman complaining

about the harassment of residents by vagrants.

30 July 1973	Application submitted by working party for further renewal of planning permission.
2 August 1973	Warning given at Development and Planning Committee meeting that 'the controversial Central Street Shelter might be extended'.
3 August 1973	Circular letter from residents' spokeswoman (drafted by the working party's secretary) distributed round the area, containing proposals for joint action and a further invitation to residents to attend the working party's committee meetings.
30 August 1973	Vote of 5–4 at Development and Planning Committee meeting in favour of an eight-week reprieve for the shelter, 'to give the shelter organisers time to seek ways of controlling the nuisance'.
10 September 1973	This recommendation endorsed by six-vote majority at full council meeting.
20 September 1973	Meeting between the working party committee and representatives of statutory bodies about the problem of alcoholism among vagrants.
18 October 1973	Application by working party for further extension of planning permission.
25 October 1973	Development and Planning Committee postpones decision on this application until next meeting and calls a public meeting in the meantime to consult residents.
8 November 1973	Angry threats made by local residents against the shelter at the public meeting.
12 November 1973	Development and Planning Committee decides to recommend rejection of the working party's application for extended

	planning permission to the full council meeting in three weeks' time.
15 November 1973	Working party committee decides on 'line of restraint' over threatened closure.
21 November 1973	Council of Social Service Executive Committee endorses working party's tactics.
23 November 1973	General meeting of working party committee and volunteers at which the organisation of a public campaign to save the shelter is agreed.
29 November 1973	Pro-shelter petition with over 2,000 signatures presented to the council (several hundred more were collected between the presentation and the council meeting).
3 December 1973	Full council gives the shelter a further reprieve of four months.
7 January 1974	Finance Committee of the town council sets up an 'action working party' to oversee the building of the replacement shelter.
14 February 1974	Development and Planning Committee decides the site of the replacement shelter.
25 February 1974	The District Council Policy and Resources Sub-committee about Shelter for Vagrants decides the ground-rules for the future operation of the replacement shelters.
7 March 1974	Meeting between district council and working party representatives at which the council side presents these rules as a *fait accompli*.
18 March 1974	Results of this meeting reported to general meeting of committee and volunteers.
1 April	Replacement shelter opens under the control of a sub-committee of the Housing Services Committee of the new district council.

Part three
Thematic commentary and analysis

Chapter 7
Groups and their environment

Case studies contain interest, and help to develop insights, in their own right. But a major aim of this book is to generate grounded propositions about community groups in action from detailed examination of empirical case material. In the early stages of our thinking we tentatively established as pertinent topic headings: goals and goal achievement, organisation, group strategies, and worker roles. But it soon became clear that if such an undertaking was to be tackled with coherence and economy then some initial conceptual ground clearing was essential; if we could employ a common terminology and, better still, a common approach to the way we wished to order our data then we would stand a greater chance of discerning systematic relations and obvious contradictions between any generalisations which we might eventually formulate. We were mindful of Merton's clear statement concerning the need for a system of concepts:

> It is only when . . . concepts are inter-related in the form of a scheme that a theory begins to emerge. Concepts, then, constitute the definitions (or prescriptions) of what is to be observed; they are the variables between which empirical relationships are to be sought.[1]

In short, we felt increasingly constrained to attempt an identification of those key variables and dimensions along which the case study material could be analysed.

Community organisation practice: the Rothman typology

Contemporary community work literature is not short of books and articles claiming to systematise and conceptualise community group practice at the local level.[2] Though providing a rich source of insights, for a variety of reasons we found these attempts

139

inadequate for our own purposes. A brief discussion of one of the best known attempts to conceptualise community organisation practice, that of Rothman, will highlight some of the difficulties we encountered in trying to utilise existing schemes. Rothman's threefold typology of community organisation practice – designated as locality development, social planning and social action – immediately confirms the diversity of that practice. The three models, or ideal types, are differentiated on each of twelve dimensions including goals, assumptions concerning problems, orientation towards the power structure, and conception of the client being served. In outlining the essential characteristics of each of Rothman's three models of community organisation practice we can hardly do better than quote Perlman and Gurin's succinct summary:

> *Locality development and organisation:* The goal is self-help and the integration of community groups. The target is the total community, regardless of class cleavages. It is assumed that there are common interests among the different groups and the strategy is directed toward achieving communication and consensus among them. The practitioner serves as an enabler, catalyst, co-ordinator and educator. The community is, however, self-determining.

> *Community planning:* The focus of this model is on problem solving in regard to substantive social problems. The practitioner serves as expert, fact-finder and analyst, and as a program implementer and facilitator. His clientele is made up of consumers or recipients of services. Either consensus or conflict may be employed as a strategy. A basic assumption is that change can be brought about through rational decision making.

> *Social action:* The goal is a change in power relationships and resources. The clientele are disadvantaged segments of the community and the practice is one of helping them to become organised, to crystallise action issues, and to engage in conflict-oriented action against the power structure.[3]

At first glance the utility of this scheme would appear obvious. At the simplest level it seems to provide a series of conceptual boxes, neatly labelled, to which the case study groups can be assigned. The twelve dimensions offer a vocabulary in terms of which it becomes possible to look for relationships and to develop generalisations. Nevertheless – and this is in no way a criticism of Rothman's stimulating and suggestive analysis – this kind of formulation is deficient for our purposes. In the first place, it is practice orientated rather than group orientated. That is to say, it focusses on the goals, strategies, conception of the client being served and other variables, from the vantage point of the practitioner or change agent. In some instances this is unimportant: concepts and tentative generalisations can be reworded to apply as well to an organisation or group as to a worker. Members of a social action group, for instance, may indeed perceive community structures as 'comprised of a hier-archy of privilege and power (in which) there exist islands of oppressed, deprived, ignored, or powerless populations suffering social injustice or exploitation at the hands of the oppressors such as the "power structure", big government, corporations, or the society at large'.[4] However, in other cases general statements are made which have little meaning divorced from the practi-tioner perspective. Rothman tells us, for example, that 'process goals' receive heavy emphasis in locality development, and that these are goals 'concerned with a generalised or gross capacity of the community to function over time . . . with aims such as establishing co-operative working relationships among groups in the community, creating self-maintaining community problem solving structures, improving the power base of the community, stimulating wide interest and participation in community affairs, fostering collaborative attitudes and practices, and increasing indigenous leadership'.[5]

This is the language of the professional change agent; such goals are unlikely to be an important element in the thinking of an indigenous activist or grass-roots member of a community group. Our argument is not that some (probably the vast major-ity) of community groups and organisations operate without professional help: the difficulty with the Rothman approach (and with so many others devised by professionals for other profes-sionals) is their worker perspective. We have tried, in our own case studies, to examine goals, strategies, and other factors, from the point of view of the group or organisation itself, and have made the assumption that any attempt we make at conceptualis-ation and generalisation must be congruent with this basic approach.

A second difficulty in may typologies and schemes is a relative neglect of self-help, mutual aid or service strategies and goals. Too often these concerns are treated in a rather partial or dis-missive fashion. But if our case study groups are at all represen-tative, then service and self-help activities can be taken to constitute central and time-consuming group operations. Rothman cannot be accused of ignoring service approaches, but he does pigeon-hole them within his locality development category, thereby subsuming them within a wholly co-operative and consensual set of approaches. He quotes Warren to help to underline the importance of 'co-operative, inclusive techniques for the practice we are designating as locality development':

> Because it seeks to organise people to express their own needs, and to consider action alternatives with respect to them, the term has been applied to the organisation of social action groups of the poor. However, such usage is misleading, since the organisation of one segment of the population in a contest relationship to the other segments which have not been brought into the process violates the major tenet of inclusiveness in community (locality) development principles. This passes no judgment on its desirability or feasibility, but simply indicates that in the commonly accepted sense of the term, it is not community (locality) development.[6]

Thus service and self-help approaches become labelled and delimited, and the range of service approaches adopted by groups gets overlooked. It is clear, for example, that when a community group sets out to run an advocacy orientated advice service it anticipates engagement in contest strategies – and yet it is at the same time providing a service. Similarly, the pensioners' household goods club in Cleator Moor constituted an (albeit small-scale) alternative to existing commercial distribution networks and, as such, involved the pensioners' group in conflict with other vested interests. In short, we would argue that service strategies can engender dissension and conflict in much the same way as campaign and pressure activity directed at external targets. It is unhelpful to place all service strategies under the locality development label.

The treatment of self-help by writers like Rothman is but one illustration of our third criticism of existing conceptualisations: that the typologies tend to make use of composite or omnibus concepts with the effect of imposing a premature straitjacket upon analysis of empirical variability. It is extremely difficult to label a group as being of a particular type. It may at first sight appear helpful to see WCAC as an example of a social action group, and to see the Failsworth and SCAG organisations more in the locality development mould; but ultimately the range of goals, strategies and tactics pursued by each organisation render such characterisations too simplistic. We believe that it makes more sense to focus on particular action systems; i.e., the relatively discrete complexes of goals, strategies and structures that characterise elements of group activities at particular times. To meet this need we found ourselves forced back to a reliance upon simpler, more primitive, uni-dimensional concepts. Such concepts have enabled us more readily to encompass, chart and analyse the real-world complexity discernible in our case studies without in any way preventing us from using them in particular combinations to signify the more commonly found group types and regularities. It is to a brief discussion and clarification of some of these first order building block concepts that we now turn.

Group–environment exchanges

A basic question confronting community groups relates to how they attain and deploy resources in order to realise their aims and objectives. Attaining and deploying resources gives rise to a variety of group-environment exchanges. All of the groups studied engaged in a number of such exchanges: with the press, the general public, local authorities, planning inquiry bodies and (when providing a service to non-group members, as in the case of the Joint Working Party) clients.

The groups we have described adopted one of two basic approaches to the question of resource deployment. Either they opted to use their own resources (for example, their skills, numbers, members' time and motivation, and contacts) to tackle a problem directly via self-help or voluntary service; or they decided that their goals were more likely to be realised by deploying their own resources in attempts to modify the performance of wider resource allocation systems (through lobbying and protest). Some groups are almost wholly externally orientated, their internal organisation being but a means to pursuing the end of effective influence on external targets. Other groups, while in no sense able to divorce themselves from their environment, exist almost entirely to meet members' (or clients') needs through the organisation of their own internal resources.

Two riders must be made at this point. First, we do not intend to imply that group resources are fixed. Group activity is often orientated to securing a balance of resources to enable effective goal achievement; for example, securing volunteers in the case of the Joint Working Party and the Senior Citizens Action Group, and securing an understanding of local government power and responsibilities in the cases of Glodwick Action

Group and West Cumberland Action Committee. This illustrates a point made above: that even when a group employs a self-help approach it is nevertheless impelled to engage in extensive inter-action with external organisations and groups. Second, we in no way wish to make the mistake of prematurely characterising particular groups as internally or externally orientated. There will be pure cases; but only in the case of the WCAC did we find a fairly unambiguous approach to the question of resource deployment among our own study groups. In the other four groups the messy reality was that each had multiple concerns and, appropriately enough, adopted a mixture of internal and external approaches. Thus we return to a point made earlier, that it is often unhelpful to attempt holistic comparisons; it is generally more fruitful to concentrate on examining and com-paring action systems. By 'action system' we refer to a sub-system within a group or organisation orientated to a particular issue or activity. Thus in SCAG there was a sub-group of people concerned with running the household goods club; this sub-group had its own aims, internal organisation and overall strategy. The notion of action system is inevitably somewhat abstract, as there is considerable overlap between the members of this sub-group and the people involved in other group activities and action systems; for example, helping to organise the socials, and engag-ing in pressure group activities.

The relationship between a group, or action system, and the beneficiaries of its activities provides a further useful distinguish-ing factor. An action system may be working to meet a need or tackle a problem that is confronting its own group members, or it may be concerned to take action on behalf of another (pre-sumably more disadvantaged) group or population segment. Combining this latter distinction with the internal/external dimension already discussed (and ignoring mixed cases) gener-ates four key models of action system-environment relationships. These are represented diagrammatically in Figure 2, with exam-ples from our case studies noted for illustrative purposes. For the sake of simplicity external targets of group activity have been represented as resource providers in these examples.

One of the key problems confronting groups that adopt exter-nally orientated approaches is related to the choice of influence strategy, and one of the key problems confronting groups that adopt internal orientated approaches is related to the choice of service strategy. The strategies pursued by our case study groups will be examined and analysed in detail in Chapter 10; the task here is a more limited one, to explore strategy in relation to action system-environment exchanges.

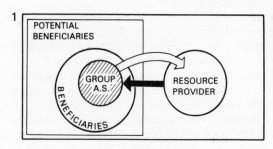

1. Beneficiaries attempt to influence resource provider on own behalf
   e.g. WCAC
        Failsworth
        Glodwick

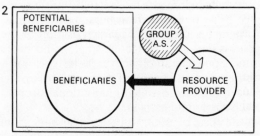

2. Concerned pressure group attempts to influence resource provider on behalf of disadvantaged population segment
   e.g. later Joint
        Working Party

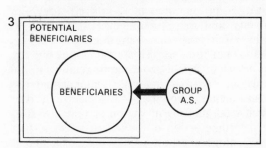

3. Service provision by interested outsiders
   e.g. early Joint
        Working Party

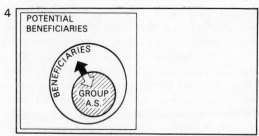

4. Group provides services for its own members
   e.g. SCAG

KEY:

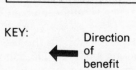 Direction of benefit

 Direction of influence

Group A.S. = Group Action System

Figure 2 Models of action system-environment relationships.

Influence strategy

The case studies report a host of techniques and tactics used by the five groups to influence external targets. These include deputations, lobbying, presenting evidence to public inquiries, encouraging media publicity, petitions, marches, rallies, leafleting and surveys. The fact that groups have multiple goals has implications for discussions of strategy: it is unhelpful to talk about group strategy in a blanket fashion. Different strategies were tried at different times in pursuit of the same goal. In discussing influence strategies, therefore, it is wise to illustrate points with reference to strategies used in pursuit of particular goals, rather than attempt a premature characterisation of the group as a whole. This is not to pre-judge the single-mindedness with which some groups pursued an objective or strategy; nor is it to detract from those observations noted in the Joint Working Party case study concerning the possible organisational strength that accompanies such single-mindedness.

There has been no shortage of attempts to distinguish the main types of influence strategies open to community groups and organisations.[7] In proposing our own three-fold typology – of collaborative, campaign and coercive influence strategies – we draw upon these previous attempts in varying degree. We assume that the three types do not refer to discrete categories but represent points on a continuum, this continuum relating to the degree of consensus seen to exist between action and target systems over ends and means. The types of strategy, then, refer to the stance implicitly adopted by an action system towards a target system.

Collaborative strategy
Action and target systems may be at one in acknowledging the existence of a particular problem and in agreeing that genuine efforts must be made to tackle it. At the same time, however, there may remain ignorance about the incidence of the problem in certain quarters, or differing views about the most effective means of confronting it. A group adopting a collaborative strategy would set about obtaining evidence to show that existing solutions were ineffective, or were failing to reach legitimate potential beneficiaries. In the end the debate and disagreement would be about technical matters, about means rather than ends.

Campaign strategy
This is seen as an appropriate form of action when it is clear that debate, influence and pressure must move beyond the technical

to consideration of the legitimacy and salience of the problem or issue itself. The legitimacy of the target system to make the relevant resource allocation decisions is not questioned, though the justice of particular decisions may be hotly disputed. Action system strategy will be directed toward heightening awareness of particular problems, ensuring that they receive attention as legitimate public issues, and attempting to ensure that such problems receive the highest possible priority on public resource allocation agendas. The range of tactics subsumed under this heading is very large, and can include disruptive tactics when these are used for demonstration and publicity purposes.

Coercive strategy
This third type of strategy will be pursued in situations where the action system disputes the target system's legitimacy to make particular resource allocation decisions. While campaign strategies are pursued within an agreed set of ground-rules, coercion is seen as the only available option when the ground-rules themselves are disputed. Coercion implies a power struggle between action and target system, the action system attempting to force the target system to meet its demands; or, in more extreme cases, the action system's ultimate goal is the destruction of the target system. It is tempting to hypothesise that the adoption of more extreme coercive strategies, in particular those directed towards destruction of a target system, will involve a degree of organisational and ideological sophistication perhaps more characteristic of some kinds of social movement than of community groups. Interesting parallels are to be drawn betwen radical community groups and certain types of social movement and, indeed, on some dimensions the two forms of collectivity merge one into the other.

It is important to stress that the distinctions we have drawn between collaborative, campaign and coercive strategies relate to the perceptions and understandings of activists working within particular community groups. The significance of this point becomes clear when we attempt to examine specific tactics. For example, members of the West Cumberland Action Committee decided to encourage people to board school buses and refuse to pay the fare: only when we know the meaning of this disruptive tactic to the participants concerned can we say whether it represented an element in a campaign strategy or a coercive strategy. It is also as well to bear in mind that there may not be consensus within groups concerning such meanings. Individuals or sub-groups within a community organisation may invest different meanings in the same action (with varying consequences

Examples of action system tactics	Action system strategy	Perception of target system by action system	Related practice concepts		
			Implicit view of political sub-system		*Broad practice label at different levels of operation*
			Level		*Practice label*
Surveys, collection and presentation of information	COLLABORATIVE	Target seen to have right to make resource allocation decisions. Broad consensus over importance and definition of issue; dispute over technical matters.	Consensus	National — Local — Grass-roots	Social planning / Service development / Community development
Writing to MPs, ministers; lobbying					
Deputations					
Advocacy at Public Inquiries		Target system seen to have right to make resource allocation decisions. Conflict over importance/definition of particular issues.	Pluralist	National — Local — Grass-roots	Community organisation
Petitions	CAMPAIGN				
Mass letter-writing					
Rallies					
Marches		Right of target system to make resource allocation decisions disputed.	Structural Conflict	National — Local — Grass-roots	Direct action
Picketing	COERCIVE				
Striking (rent strikes, etc.)					
Other direct action					

Figure 3 The links between strategies and tactics at national, local and grass-roots levels

for organisational strength and effectiveness in goal achievement); and external audiences, including the members of target
systems, may construe and react to particular group initiatives
in ways quite unanticipated by group members themselves.

Our five case study groups illustrate strategies and tactics at
a number of target levels, and Figure 3 both illustrates some of
the linkages we see between strategy and tactics and incorporates
a useful distinction made in an NCDP Inter-Project Report
between grass-roots, local and national target levels.[8] While it is
an over-simplification to talk in terms of three levels only, this
is a useful dimension to bear in mind when analysing group
activity.

Finally, it will be seen that the figure incorporates a further
set of distinctions noted by CDP workers: in their view community group strategies embody within themselves (implicitly or
explicitly) divergent views concerning the operation of the wider
political system. For example coercive strategies are deemed to
be congruent with a structural-conflict perspective on socio-pol-
itical organisation. To point out such linkages is useful, providing
two qualifications are kept firmly in mind. First, our own work
has impressed upon us the ease with which community organisations can incorporate members with divergent views concerning
the realities of power distribution in society. Agreement can be
found for the pursuit of particular courses of action, without
there being any substantial consensus about the workings of the
wider political system. Only properly mounted comparative research will be able to determine in what ways, and under what circumstances, heterogeneity in member belief systems influences
effective goal achievement and other features of group life. Second, it is also as well to recognise that group members do, to a
greater or lesser extent, accept ambiguities and contradictions in
their own thinking – that a rationale which an individual provides
for supporting a particular initiative may, at the level of implicit
assumptions, run counter to the rationale used to reject some
other kind of initiative. With such reservations in mind, we do,
nevertheless, believe that the 'structural-conflict', 'pluralist' and
'consensus' distinctions made by the CDP workers are valuable,
and have incorporated their terminology accordingly.

Service strategies

Except for the West Cumberland Action Committee each of the
community groups we studied became involved with internally
orientated activity designed to meet need through the deploy-

ment of the groups' own resources. The Failsworth Association
produced a local directory of welfare services, the Glodwick
Action Group provided an information service, the Senior Citizens Action Group ran a food co-operative and a variety of
social events, and the Joint Working Party ran a refuge for single
homeless people. There have been exceptionally few efforts to
order and classify the great variety of internally oriented group
strategies in the way that influence strategies have been discussed
and classified in the literature. It is possible to talk about collaborative, campaign and coercive influence strategies with some
degree of confidence because a host of writers has typified group
activities in somewhat similar ways before. Internally orientated
strategies tend to get lumped together as self-help, as something
that groups habitually get involved with, but which is of little
intrinsic interest. This is unfortunate, particularly as so many
community groups do engage in such activities. An attempt to
modify this situation must acknowledge that groups often have
multiple internal strategies; and so it is, once again, better to
examine particular action systems rather than attempt a premature characterisation of a group as a whole: it seems likely that
action systems, concerned with different goals and internal strategies, will encounter different problems with respect to internal
organisation and structure and relations with external systems.

It is by no means an easy matter to isolate the most significant
dimension(s) along which internal strategies range. Reverting
for a moment to influence strategies, these seemed to range
along a dimension concerned with 'the degree of threat to established practices of external systems'. This is, perhaps, a rather
too functionalist formulation; but it is only a short step to acknowledge that external systems serve particular interests and that
different influence strategies therefore pose variable degrees of
threat to established sectional interests in a community or
society.

In similar vein we feel that it is analytically useful to see the
content of internal strategies as varying in the degree to which
they pose a threat to external systems or interests. The Senior
Citizens Action Group's 'tea and crack' clearly posed no threat
to any external system; to provide a pleasant social afternoon
for persons of retirement age is seen as a worthwhile objective
by most people and, in SCAG's case, this indeed received support from the statutory social services. The household goods
club, on the other hand, was rather more threatening: whereas
the 'tea and crack' augmented or complemented existing provision, the food and household goods co-operative was designed
as a (partial) alternative to established retail distribution systems.

The history of the latter venture, including the protest by local traders when the scheme first got under way, indicates that it was seen as some sort of threat by particular sectional interests. The internal strategies adopted by four of the five of our study groups fall into one or other of these categories – what we shall call 'complementary' or 'alternative' strategies. These seem to parallel (in terms of degree of threat) collaborative and campaign influence strategies. We have chosen to call the third, and most threatening, type of internal strategy a 'substitute' strategy; in this case the organisation attempts to move beyond provision of an alternative to existing forms or provision and accomplish the more ambitious goal of providing a replacement or substitute form of provision. Organisations offering radically different forms of therapy to the mentally ill or to the drug addict constitute an example of what we have in mind.

To be rather more precise and formal concerning our service strategies: *Complementary strategies* are those designed to duplicate or augment existing services, perhaps exploring technically better ways of meeting needs. External systems recognise the need that the group is attempting to meet and view its approaches to meeting the need as unexceptionable. *Alternative strategies* offer beneficiaries a choice between different ways of meeting the need(s). The need is acknowledged by external systems, and external systems do, indeed, meet the needs in their own way. In offering an alternative form of provision the group does, however, pose a threat to established practices, values or interests. *Substitute strategies* pose the greatest threat to established values and interests in that they are either directed at the replacement of existing methods of meeting needs, or orientated to meeting needs the legitimacy of which is not generally accepted or recognised.

Interesting, if somewhat extreme, examples of substitute strategies are to be found in the various types of ideological communities and communes that have existed for many years and which, of late, have enjoyed a revival of interest. Clearly of a rather different order to the organisations treated in this volume (while some can be seen as voluntary organisations, others are better viewed as part of a social movement[9]), such limiting cases serve, nevertheless to highlight the fact that self-help concerns can be just as conflictual and radical in their approach as some of the more conflict-orientated action groups that are prepared to employ coercive strategies. This is clearly brought out in Thorn's comparative examination of ideological communities. He noted that such communities are created outside the 'public' system of planning and development by those who accept alternative values to those predominant in the society. This means that they are very often in conflict with the rest of the society in which they are situated. For example, the history of the Hutterite development in North America has been marked by conflicts between them and the local American population, these conflicts arising out of their distinctive values, dress and behaviour.[10]

Although our treatment of self-help and service strategies in many ways parallels the approach we have used in analysing influence strategies, we do not yet feel able to articulate the links between strategy, tactics, practice label and other factors in the way that we have attempted to do for influence strategies in Figure 3. This is largely attributable to the fact that an appropriate terminology does not exist (due, in turn, to the relative lack of attention paid to self-help groups by writers on community organisation). A number of dimensions along which service tactics could be analysed do, nevertheless, suggest themselves. For example, we would guess that groups orientated to complementary strategies are likely to enjoy more permeable organisational boundaries than those endeavouring to offer alternative or substitute services to their members. As boundaries become more impermeable we would expect to see, first of all, the introduction of more stringent membership criteria; second, the imposition of more rigorous socialisation (and even *rite de passage*) procedures, and third, tactics to maintain and enhance ideological purity and conformity to group norms. All this must remain, unfortunately, speculative. Neither our own case study data, nor other published material on self-help groups, permits us to refine and develop these ideas further in a systematic way.

Chapter 8
Goals and goal achievement

At first glance it would appear that the goal of a community group is easily defined; it is surely the 'end state towards which the organisation is striving'. Although writers on organisations have tended to find this form of definition too simplistic for worthwhile analytical purposes (and we will illustrate in a moment why this holds as true for community groups as for other types of organisation) the notion of goals is, nevertheless, a useful one. In the first place, it provides a yardstick against which to assess the impact and effectiveness of group activity. Second, an organisation's goals comprise an important factor influencing, and influenced by, other features of group structure and development; goals can be viewed as both dependent and independent variables, helpful in explaining and understanding features of group structure and strategy as well as being in turn shaped by them. In this chapter we attempt to clarify some of the factors which contribute to an understanding of these inter-relationships.

We start by examining the process of a group's initial goal setting, and then offer some comments about the role of conflict in goal formulation. After an assessment of how far the case study groups were successful or unsuccessful in achieving their operative task goals we continue with a review of goal change, succession and displacement. Finally, an attempt is made to pull together and summarise the most significant factors in the overall goal determination process.

Clarification of terms

First we must be clear about terms. It was suggested that to view group goals simply as organisational 'end states' may be crude and unhelpful. Difficulties spring from the fact that different actors (both leaders and rank and file members within groups, as well as external beneficiaries and constituents) are likely to perceive goals in different ways. Further, goals characteristically take a number of different forms, for example 'task' and 'group maintenance'. Such a definition is likely to lead us to overlook the fact that goal change and flux are often the rule rather than the exception where group objectives are concerned. Our case study material amply demonstrates that the distinctions between different kinds of goal made by students of formal organisations have equal applicability to community groups.[1]

Multiple goals and focal goals

Rothman's generalisation that 'organisations typically pursue a set of multiple goals when examined behaviourally',[2] receives considerable confirmation from our case study material. The range of aims and activities pursued by both the pensioners' group and the Failsworth Association provide the best illustrations of diversity in goals. Groups do not, of course, simultaneously pursue all goals with equal vigour. As expressed in the Failsworth study, specific objectives 'waxed and waned' over time. The concept of focal goals is therefore helpful in highlighting those goals receiving particular attention or priority at particular times.

Task goals and system maintenance goals

While system goals relate to an organisation's efforts to maintain its own equilibrium and stability, task or substantive goals refer to the desired end product of group effort and activity. According to the Failsworth study one of the main achievements of that organisation was in the field of system maintenance: getting the 24 constituent organisations to associate themselves in one grouping. This achievement is to be distinguished from the number of task objectives, relating to environmental improvement and civic amenities, held by the Failsworth Community Association.

Official and operative goals

The Failsworth and SCAG case studies also provide illustrations of a further useful distinction, that between the official aim of a body written into its charter or constitution, and what its members actually set out to achieve. The Failsworth constitution encompassed a broad range of concerns, expressed in the rather vague and high-sounding language that characterises such pronouncements. The association outlined its aims as follows:

To protect and preserve and stimulate public interest in

the area comprising Failsworth . . .; to promote high
standards, and to protect the interests of the
community . . .; to provide local information which
would help the local elected representatives in the
performance of their duties to the community; to
undertake surveys in the district as and when required,
and to collate this information . . .; to act as a lobby and
to provide a platform for public debate; to protect the
environment against dereliction and bad planning.

In operative terms, however, the organisation was concerned
with, for instance, producing a directory of local welfare services,
providing a community centre, making representations on bus
lanes, and establishing a meeting place for the elderly.

Similarly, when SCAG eventually drew up a constitution,
some two years after the inception of the group, members committed themselves to pursuing the social welfare of local pensioners. Such all-embracing formal statements should not be seen
as indications of overweening arrogance on the part of those
who draft and ratify them. It may be that all-inclusiveness and
even ambiguity can be beneficial; it can hold disparate elements
together by playing down differences and helping to ensure
organisational continuity. These are not unalloyed benefits;
open-ended constitutions may encourage the persistence of
organisations, through goal displacement and goal succession,
long after their useful life is over.

Changes of goal: goal displacement and goal succession
We have already alluded to the fact that change, at least at the
operative level, tends to be more characteristic of community
groups' goals than stability and continuity. Even though the case
studies cover a relatively short period of time it is nevertheless
possible to see significant changes in the operative goals of all
five groups. Only in the case of the WCAC is there evidence of
concerted commitment to goals yet to be attained; but even in
this case we see that the committee made efforts to re-define for
itself a role as a local transport policy watchdog.

Two notions are of particular use in making sense of the
process of goal change. The first is the concept of goal displacement, which refers to situations in which relatively minor or
system maintenance goals come to assume greater operative
importance than key task goals. We have already noted that a
significant accomplishment of the Failsworth Association was
getting its 24 constituent organisations to associate themselves
into one cohesive body. The secretary's inclination to put more

weight on this achievement than on critically reviewing the degree to which official or operative task goals had been achieved provides an example of goal displacement. According to writers following Michels,[3] goal displacement is most likely to occur in organisations with a high degree of bureaucratisation. It is perhaps no accident that it is from the case study of the Failsworth Community Association, the most formally organised of our case study groups, that an example of goal displacement springs most readily to mind.

The more likely phenomenon in less bureaucratically organised community groups is goal succession. The replacement of one operative goal by another will occur either when the original goal has been achieved, when there has been a failure to achieve it, or when it has become irrelevant in a changed environment. The case studies are rich in examples of goal succession, and we will return to this topic later on.

If the goals of community organisations are to be characterised in terms of their development, evolution and replacement, it makes sense to treat goal determination and change as a process. Perlman and Gurin note that 'setting a goal or choosing a policy is not an event. It is a process of making a series of decisions'.[4] We begin our substantive analysis with an examination of initial goal setting.

Initial goal setting

All five case study groups were externally orientated in their early stages. None of them started out with clear proposals for self-help or service action systems, though it is clear that SCAG's concern with small jobs quickly developed a mixed influence/ service orientation, and the Joint Working Party soon found itself making plans to run a shelter. However, SCAG at no time saw itself providing an odd job service, and although the working party did very quickly organise to provide a direct service, its initial goals emphasised issue-raising, co-ordination and influence. In the case of the Glodwick, WCAC and Failsworth organisations the original external orientation and goals were clear. With Glodwick it was to prepare a case for the impending CPO public inquiry; with WCAC it was to secure a change in the allocation of scholars' bus passes; and in the Failsworth case it was to ensure that voluntary organisations, by speaking with one voice, could influence the decisions of local government policy makers.

It is worth noting that all initial goals must have been seen as broadly legitimate by those target organisations that the groups set out to influence. Government reports and circulars had sanctioned the setting up of shelters for homeless people, and had encouraged the search for machinery to secure greater grassroots participation in planning and local government decision making. Similarly, helping pensioners to get odd jobs done and schoolchildren to obtain free passes were fairly unexceptionable aims of group activity. Perhaps resistance could be expected (relating to technical problems of implementation or financial priorities), but on the whole the initial goals were conventional and respectable.

No less can be said about the later goals that groups set themselves. While on a few occasions group strategy and tactics posed a threat to established organisations or interests (though coercive or substitute strategies were never used) the goals to which these strategies were directed were fairly traditional. Leaving aside the rhetoric of formal or public relations statements, we feel able to echo Turner's observations about 'community self-help organisations' in the USA, that the bulk of organisations (included in his study) were concerned with: '(1) expansion of services, (2) changes in patterns of implementation, (3) increasing citizen involvement with respect to policy and implementation'.[5] Our findings confirm his conclusion that objectives were generally 'focussed on how to make existing community service programmes work better rather than on designing new alternatives to existing problems'.[6]

Conflict over goals and the goal formulation process

Community groups, like other organisations, can be usefully viewed as coalitions, with the interests and preferences of individual members, sub-groups, sponsors and constituents coming into conflict to a greater or lesser extent. Goals become formulated as a result of argument, negotiation and power struggles between the interested parties. Our case study material provides evidence of such conflicts and of different ways of coping with them.

In some cases coalitions were manifest. In the Failsworth Association it was clear from the beginning that members had come together as representatives of sectional interests. The likelihood of conflict and disagreement was acknowledged and confronted from the start; from the very inception of the group a great deal of time was spent hammering out a constitution acceptable to all parties. This, among other things, attempted to

set out agreed goals. As already noted, goals written into constitutions are often rather abstract and all-embracing. Certainly
in the Failsworth case the constitution specified only very broad
aims and objectives. These gave general guidelines in terms of
which the organisation could proceed. Such guidelines do, nevertheless, provide a minimum basis for agreement, in that those
unable to work within them presumably cease to be members.
Conflicts and differences are likely to remain, but at the level of
interpreting and operationalising the formal goals. Other methods must be found to resolve or accommodate remaining conflicts of view. Examples of divergent approaches are evident in
the case studies.

One way of accommodating conflicting interest and facilitating
the pursuit of a number of focal goals at the same time (without
the necessity of deciding priorities between them) is through the
use of sub-groups and sub-committees. These offer the possibility
of providing some satisfaction to different parties and interests
at the same time. It is clear that the evolution of sub-groups in
the pensioners' organisation helped both to strengthen the organisation and to minimise destructive conflict over goals.

Another way to avoid rancorous and debilitating conflict over
aims and objectives is to focus quite consciously and deliberately
on an area of maximum common concern. In the case of the
Glodwick group, attempts at self-help and other activities failed
mainly because of racial and other conflicts. Mutual concern
over the CPO was left as the surviving basis for group continuity;
the CPO was the only issue sharp enough to overshadow
entrenched differences, barriers and hostilities; 'bury the hatchet
in order that we can deal with the enemies outside' was the
sentiment expressed.

The study of the Joint Working Party provides an illuminating
example of an organisation subject to fairly clear-cut conflicts
which, unresolved in the long term by the techniques illustrated
above, resulted in a persistent power struggle. Differences
between the committee's and the volunteers' perspectives
became a 'more or less permanent feature of the working party'.
The conflict reached a head when the very existence of the
shelter was threatened. While the volunteers pressed for a public
campaign to save the shelter, the committee believed that there
was no real chance of saving it and proposed only a 'line of
restraint'. The volunteers won that particular argument; they
also managed to gain minority representation on the working
party committee. But their different backgrounds, operational
fragmentation and internal divisions between the 'social treatment orientated' and 'social change orientated' factions pre-

vented them from gaining a firm grip on the continuing process of goal determination.

It is difficult to move beyond speculation in considering the variables that might account for the type and intensity of conflict over goals, or how and why different approaches to their resolution come to be adopted. Such conflicts are clearly a reflection of different interests and perceptions; but it is just as clear that such interests and perceptions are neither free-floating nor absolute. They will in their turn be influenced by other factors; and one of these, the availability of resources, comes through clearly from the case studies. A later chapter on strategy, tactics and resources indicates how the type and availability of resources helped to channel considerations about action plans and strategy. The studies bring out no less clearly the importance of resource availability in the determination of goals themselves. For example, the expertise and skills of the community worker were an important resource in the Glodwick group's early days. He helped the group to define and focus on its two primary concerns, to force the council to take into account the residents' wishes, and to improve their part of Oldham.

If a community worker was an influential external resource in helping the CPO group to formulate its goals, then the influence of CDP resources on goal formulation was even more clearly brought out in the SCAG study. The story is related of the group member who was able to divulge that CDP pump-priming coffers were far from empty, going on to urge SCAG to think up useful schemes on which the money could be spent.

Goals and goal achievement

The achievements, total, partial or negligible, of objectives that a community group sets itself constitute an important variable in the goal determination process. At the same time, the degree of success that community groups have, together with the larger question of their organisational effectiveness, are clearly of immediate practical concern to all those people engaged in trying to promote social change at the local level.

It has been argued that assessments of goal achievements are of limited value in coming to conclusions about overall organisational effectiveness.[7] It is suggested that for various reasons most formal organisations are found to be very ineffective when actual achievements are measured against objectives. Comparative assessment is advocated as a better approach, involving the study of the relative achievements of organisations of a similar type.

Although this is a persuasive suggestion, it is not one which we feel able to adopt, partly because of the limited number of groups for which we have gathered systematic and comparable data, but also because of the enormous variability, in structure, membership, resources and other characteristics exhibited even within these five organisations. We are forced, therefore, to examine the groups' accomplishments in terms of goal achievement, trying to avoid the worst pitfalls of the goal model by limiting our evaluations to achievements of operative goals. It is clear that the groups studied have substantial achievements to their credit, though it is also important to bear in mind the point made earlier, that the groups' objectives were generally fairly conventional and non-threatening to established interests.

In terms of self-help and voluntary service, the main achievements of the Joint Working Party included the provision of overnight accommodation for homeless individuals, the sensitive delivery of this service, and additional personal support like help with finding lodgings and negotiation over welfare benefits. The pensioners' action group in Cleator Moor provided companionship and enjoyment through their regular socials, trips and entertainments; and, through the household goods club, a range of basic food and cleaning items were made available at reduced prices.

Turning to groups concerned with influencing the behaviour of external target systems, GAG secured the ear of those decision makers and administrators with responsibility for the local CPO area, and achieved certain programme modifications in the light of local feelings and needs. The Failsworth Association persuaded a variety of statutory and other decision makers to recognise their organisation as a legitimate and consolidated voice for the many local interest groups in the area. The WCAC helped to generate and sustain awareness of school bus travel as a public issue.

It is by no means easy to move from a description of what the groups achieved to explaining or accounting for those achievements. This difficulty stems partly from the relative paucity of empirically tested propositions about community groups against which we might have examined and interpreted our case study data. Moreover, the limited number of our studies, the range of types of organised activity they encompass, and the variety of geographical and cultural settings from which they are drawn makes us hesitant about embarking upon such an interpretation. In addition, although each case study writer followed the checklist, the accounts nevertheless differ in the emphasis or depth given to discussion of particular features and variables. For example, the study of the Joint Working Party provides substantial data on internal organisational structures and processes. The SCAG study, on the other hand, emphasises the crucial role played by resource availability in a pensioners' organisation. How far these different emphases reflect differences in the interest, focus and approach of the respective research workers, and how far they reflect real differences in the importance of these factors to an understanding of the groups, is difficult to determine.

This is not a complete list of the pitfalls and difficulties that confront any attempt to account for particular achievements. However, the topic is clearly an important one and, without trying to identify recipes for successful community action, we can draw up a tentative listing of some of the ingredients.

Membership
Whether concerned to exert some influence on external decision makers, or to organise for service delivery, the corpus of skills, knowledge and motivation contained within a group's active membership clearly represents a significant organisational resource. The importance of specifically organisational experience and skill comes across clearly from the case studies. The pensioners' group surmounted some not insignificant organisational problems, and this was probably facilitated by the fact that it numbered an ex-councillor, a trade unionist, a retired store manager and others with organisational experience among its core members. The Joint Working Party included officers from the Council of Churches and the Council of Social Service among its members. About half of the core membership of the WCAC had experience of voluntary organisations or community self-help initiatives, and the Failsworth Association consisted wholly of representatives with experience in its constituent organisations. Finally, in the Glodwick group there was a fair amount and diversity of organisational experience, a factor which was thought to have contributed to the group's effectiveness.

While organisational experience and skills can be a valuable resource that members contribute to a group, the previous affiliations (or contemporary overlapping memberships) that generate this experience may lead to relationships and commitments inimical to adoption of particular types of strategy, and thus in turn, goal achievement. The SCAG case study provides an example of these limiting and constraining consequences of organisational experience. Some of the group's members had known, and worked in voluntary associations with, councillors and other local decision makers for some time. This had the

effect of inhibiting direct criticism of council action and a reluctance to employ strong pressure.

Besides providing organisational knowhow (narrowly defined
in the sense of how to run and contribute fruitfully to meetings
and decision making, and how to keep accounts and write
minutes), previous organisational experience also brings other
useful skills and knowledge. The Joint Working Party could draw
on administrative and other skills 'to raise large amounts of
money, to administer working party affairs and promote a supportive atmosphere'. The working party also had a member who
was well versed in the technicalities of securing local planning
permission. In the Failsworth case, on the other hand, a member
made it his business to become the organisation's expert in this
field. The pensioners' group provides other examples: the ex-
store manager became a lynchpin in the household goods venture, a number of members had experience of fund-raising, and
an ex-employee of the local bus company contributed valuable
background information on transport issues. Finally, it is interesting to note that a central role performed by the community
workers associated with the Glodwick group and the WCAC was
in the area of 'making good' knowledge areas which were central
to group goal achievement yet unavailable within the
membership.

It is clear from the case studies that a high level of motivation
and commitment was another important membership factor in
goal achievement. The groups were not fly-by-night organisations and most of their initiatives demanded hard work over
substantial periods of time. The Joint Working Party study draws
attention to the persistence and commitment of the two sponsoring organisations and mentions in particular the effort and
energy maintained by some individual members and officers.
Again, the example quoted in the SCAG study does not seem
unrepresentative; seven months to get a small odd jobs scheme
under way, seven months of negotiating, planning, decision making, thinking and organising.

The studies bring out the significance of particular membership
characteristics. The housewives in the WCAC and the pensioners
in SCAG were well pleased to contribute time and effort to
daytime activities, from organising afternoon socials to attending
important meetings with transport officials.

External resources
In noting that a community worker may augment a group's
internal resources we began to focus on external resources and
their significance to goal achievement. Groups are only rarely

self-sufficient, and they may of necessity have to draw important resources to themselves if they are to be effective.

There is a distinction to be made between service resources (duplicating facilities, access to poster making or printing facilities) and material resources (grants of money, buildings and equipment). Two generalisations seem fairly clear: organisations that embark on mutual aid and service initiatives are the most voracious users of resources, and they tend to make particular demands on resources of a material kind. The Joint Working Party had to raise considerable sums of money in order to rehabilitate and run the shelter, first from fund-raising activities through the Council of Churches networks and then with a retrospective DHSS grant to cover debit balances. SCAG, similarly, required funds to translate its ideas into action, and it obtained a number of grants from the CDP-sponsored pump-priming committee. In addition it made extensive use of the minibus and other CDP financed 'hardware'. Although the pensioners' group did run a number of fund-raising ventures the case study notes that 'in so far as service initiatives remain central, the continued existence of CDP-instituted organisations (like its community resource centre) and funds will remain important influences upon goal achievement'.

The pursuit of influence strategies seems to involve a lower level of external resource use, as well as a difference in kind. While it is true that the WCAC did, for example, make use of the resource centre minibus to transport members for lobbies and delegations, influence-orientated action systems are much more likely to generate a need for secretarial and related services. The bus fares protest group, for example, made a 'heavy and continuous use of CDP resources: typing, copying and poster-making facilities'. Similarly, the Failsworth Association's expenditure was largely on administrative items.

The group and its potential beneficiaries
All five case study groups recognised a commitment to the interests of people – 'beneficiaries', 'consumers', or 'constituents' – outside their own membership. While group members themselves might often have stood to gain from the achievement of objectives pursued by their organisation (benefits, for example, from a sought-for change in policy, or making use of a service organised by the group) none of the initiatives taken by any of the five groups were taken up with the interests of members only in mind. The groups either spoke for a population whose boundaries extended beyond their membership, or provided a service to a population different from the membership. The case study

data seems to indicate, further, that the ways in which groups related to wider beneficiaries was an important factor in helping to account for goal achievement.

In the case of service initiatives, the respective action systems were compelled to provide a minimally relevant and acceptable service if take-up and usage were to be assured. There can be little doubt that this happened: the shelter was used by homeless men; and SCAG pensioners 'praised the trips, raffles, household goods club and bring-and-buy'. Different approaches to ensuring a minimum of service relevance are illustrated. The pensioners' socials, trips and suppers were an established and traditional response to the perceived needs of this age-group in Cleator Moor; SCAG members recognised such needs and had an intuitive grasp of what would 'work'. Other ventures invited a somewhat different approach: the household goods club and the shelter were both new to their respective organisers and localities; and partly because of this a survey to gauge needs was seen as an appropriate way of establishing demand in both cases. A continuing sensitivity to needs, along with the most appropriate ways of meeting them, was buttressed in the Joint Working Party by the high level of identification felt by the volunteers and the 'fundamental beliefs about caring' held by members of the committee.

If sensitivity to needs and an awareness of what constitutes an appropriate form of provision to beneficiaries is a *sine qua non* of an effective approach to self-help and voluntary service, then an influence strategy would, similarly, seem to require of its organisers sensitivity to the needs, views and aspirations of those they purport to represent. Such sensitivity serves a dual function: it increases the likelihood of generating support (and thus of building a powerful organisation); and, in so far as this can be demonstrated to the targets of group pressure, the group is perceived as a force to be reckoned with. This latter point is well illustrated from the study of the CPO group. The Glodwick Action Group organised a door-to-door survey among local people and, on the basis of the views gathered, came to insist that they represented the views of all residents. The target system was, it seems, impressed that the group could legitimately speak for the 'wishes, needs and preferences' of all the people in the CPO area. The right of the WCAC and the Failsworth Association to speak for their respective constituents was established in somewhat different ways; as far as the WCAC was concerned, the strength of popular feeling about the school bus fares issue was demonstrated through the early marches and petition. The Failsworth Association, on the other hand, could claim, by virtue of its composition, to represent its member organisations on issues of common concern.

The local social system

The case studies provide a wealth of information about groups' interaction with their social environment, and how this interaction sometimes inhibited successful achievement of goals and at other times facilitated it.

The Glodwick, SCAG and WCAC material provides examples of how the respective local social systems (networks of social relationships, permeated with reciprocal rights and obligations) served to influence the extent and type of collective action. In the Glodwick study the lack of any tradition of organised activity was seen to have acted as a brake on community action – as was the long-standing loyalty of many local residents to the Labour movement. This latter point is interesting; it was suggested that such an affiliation instilled in people a reluctance to challenge or attack council decisions and policies. In the SCAG case it was the integration of local councillors into the close-knit local networks that seemed to inhibit certain kinds of action. To take a critical and abrasive stance towards local councillors in their official capacity could clearly generate an element of uncomfortable role strain if one also associated with them in the pub, sports club and pigeon society. In SCAG's case it is suggested that role conflicts of this kind encouraged self-help activities at the expense of influence-exertion strategies.

In West Cumbria, unlike Glodwick, lack of tradition of community action did not extend to the self-help field; it was not so much history as contemporary social networks that inhibited certain kinds of action. It can be argued that this is only half of the story. In the two Cleator Moor studies it was noted that SCAG and WCAC did indeed secure considerable support from local councillors. The support was, however, in areas unlikely to exacerbate role strain. Two councillors were influential in helping to overcome some of the sponsorship problems associated with the small jobs scheme, and a number took the role of advocate for the group in cases where criticism was directed towards decision making bodies other than their own council. That is to say, councillors made representations to the Community Health Council over the chiropody issue and let themselves become associated with protests to the Northern Traffic Commissioners.

Basic social fragmentation within the community from which groups draw their members seems to be another contextual factor with an important bearing on group effectiveness. In the

Glodwick case racial tensions inhibited local action on all fronts except the common CPO issue. In Cleator Moor, religious dif- ferences and divisions stood out as a potential threat to united action. Potential conflicts and differences were also noted in connection with the WCAC and the Failsworth Association. In the latter case there were clear differences in value and interest stemming from the conflicting perspectives and priorities of the constituent organisations, whereas in the former case accidents of geography generated certain conflicts of interest and prompted differences in choice of operative goals.

It is in the Joint Working Party case study, however, that differences in perspective and outlook are most clearly discerned and the damaging consequences most clearly discussed. Here the major division between the committee members and the volun- teers was exaggerated and sharpened because the 'service' versus 'campaign' conflict coincided with, and overlay, the organisa- tional division.

Interaction with the power structure and other organised interests

We have observed that few organisations can maintain for long a significant detachment from their social environment. In the case of those groups setting out to influence the policy or practice of a target system the organisation's very *raison d'être* impels them to enter into a variety of exchanges with their environment. Service organisations, leaving aside their need to negotiate resources, may well find that their initiatives evoke a (sometimes hostile) reaction from established interests which, in turn, demands a response. The manner in which a group manages these organisation-environment exchanges can have an import- ant impact on goal achievement.

Taking service activities first, we saw that for the bulk of SCAG's self-help initiatives, the reaction of local organisations and interests was benign. The reasons are not difficult to discern. Old people are regarded as a good cause, a section of the popu- lation fully deserving of help. In providing opportunities for companionship and entertainment the group was providing a culturally acceptable outlet for voluntary effort and at the same time complementing existing social welfare provision. The pen- sioners' household goods club and the joint committee's shelter evoked rather more hostile and critical reactions, in both cases because the service provision fuelled certain conflicts of interest. Cleator Moor traders were alarmed that pensioners' bulk buying would constitute an element of unfair competition; and people living close to the shelter found the proximity of vagrants a public nuisance.

The pensioners' group chose to respond to traders' criticisms by maintaining a low profile, avoiding public exposure and press coverage, and running their service as best they could until offended interests could see the real (i.e. small) dimensions of the threat. The Joint Working Party responded to residents' pressure, directed at preventing the renewal of planning permission for the shelter, in a more direct way. A public campaign was mounted in which a petition was organised, sympathetic press coverage achieved, and influential people (MP, local councillors) successfully lobbied into pledging public support for the continuation of the venture. The campaign was helped by the fact that the particular service, though new as far as the town was concerned, was essentially a complementary form of provision. It was a service which could quite properly have been, and later was, provided by the local authority.

The influence strategies utilised by our case study groups are best viewed as largely collaborative, with the exception of aspects of the WCAC's activities which reflected a campaign strategy approach. In seeking changes from external target systems a variety of (more or less successful) group-environment exchanges are recorded in the case studies.

The Failsworth Association, for example, helped to create a situation in which it was well placed to pursue shifts in local policy and practice: an important element was the degree of overlap between its own membership and the membership of other key decision making forums. In an important sense it could work from the inside, bringing a direct and unmediated influence to bear in a way which did not have a direct parallel in the approach adopted by the other groups. The potential opportunities of the insider approach were multiplied through the association's tactic of encouraging members to pursue an activist role in other bodies and organisations, thereby increasing their influence through 'interest and personal experience'.

For the Glodwick Action Group the infiltration of interlocking local élites was not a feasible approach. Two tactics that did help the group to gain some leverage in the fight for the interests of residents were, first, the building of a strong and representative base from which to speak and, second, the provision to a key local target, the local authority, of information that was of interest and use to them. In other words, GAG secured for itself a base from which to negotiate. Its survey work played an important part in creating this base, enabling the group to legitimately represent the views of many more residents than actually became group activists; and the range of preferences and demands revealed was in itself information of use to the council.

Two other features of Failsworth's and Glodwick's interactions with the power structure deserve mention. Both of these groups clearly identified and engaged with appropriate intervention targets, and, linked to this, both organisations concerned themselves with issues that came within the sphere of responsibility of local decision makers. The experience of the WCAC over scholars' passes, and the pensioners' group over pedestrian safety and chiropody services, were less happy: these groups' failure to identify appropriate targets undoubtedly goes some way towards explaining their failure to achieve particular goals. Both WCAC and SCAG took up issues, the solutions to which were not (in full at least) the responsibility of local decision makers. Social or policy change that would have fully met the concerns of these groups would have involved movement in central government departments with responsibilities in the health, transport and environmental fields. Groups drawn from, and with a brief to speak only on behalf of, closely circumscribed geographical areas are not well placed to pursue shifts in central government policy. To encourage the growth, or forge links with, national pressure groups, or to work with organised political parties and trade unions, are options open to groups that wish to continue to pursue issues at a national level. They are clearly not easy options to take; and, equally clearly, WCAC and SCAG failed to come close to doing so.

Goal change

The time scale covered by our case studies was modest. Yet within a span of two to three years quite significant changes in goals were discernible. Two processes seemed to be at work: in the first place there was a cyclical movement in the emphasis placed on particular goals; secondly there was evidence of goal succession and goal displacement.

Just as the groups usually had multiple objectives, so the popularity of particular goals tended to increase and decrease over time. In the Failsworth case study 'specific objectives waxed and waned over time'. Similarly, in the case of the pensioners' group it was clear that goals relating to pedestrian safety, chiropody services and other issues tended to command primary attention in turn. This was not merely a reflection of increased activity as the phases in group strategy called forth more or less member involvement; there seemed to be a genuine ebb and flow in the interest, and therefore the priority, accorded to particular goals.

Where changes were more linear we can see examples of goal succession and goal displacement. An example of the former process – where a goal once actively pursued is abandoned in favour of a new goal – is seen in the study of the Glodwick Action Group. This group started out wanting to secure information about the council's clearance plans; later organisational goals became more concerned with attempts to exert influence over the shape and quality of those plans. The group went on to perform a watchdog role, in which a major goal became that of monitoring the way that the local authority managed the re-housing programme. The first goal of the organisation concerned with the plight of homeless single men was to secure some form of provision; from this members moved on to a preoccupation with running the hostel they had helped to establish; and finally, when external pressures began to present a real threat to the hostel's existence, the organisation adopted defensive, preser-vationist goals.

It might be objected that in these two examples we have been concerned only with identifying a succession of tasks. This is not so: each of the goals mentioned could well have provided a community organisation with its total *raison d'être*. Clearly there are often good reasons why, once an organisation has success-fully achieved one important goal, it should continue in existence to pursue a further, related, objective. However, the reasons for this will be contingent, not necessary.

Finally, we can identify goal displacement as a third type of goal change. The concept is a well known one and, as noted above, we see an example of the process at work in the Fails-worth Community Association; its secretary attached consider-ably more importance to the fact that 24 organisations had come together in one association than he did to the achievement of any of its particular task goals.

How do we begin to account for these observed changes? Hall's[8] analysis offers a useful interpretative framework. In his review of goal change in formal organisations he suggests that three sets of variables may have explanatory value: in the first place, significant changes in the relationships which any one organisation has with outside bodies (he categorises these rela-tionships as competition, bargaining, co-operation and coalition) can have a marked effect on goals; second, changes internal to the group (alterations in membership or modification in the system of power relations, for example) can be significant; and third, general environmental change (changes in local economic conditions, or the general cultural or political climate) can also have repercussions for the pursuit of particular goals.

The case studies certainly pinpoint the importance of environmental change as a relevant factor, and in particular the way in which groups were constrained to re-formulate their goals in response to environmental changes which they themselves helped to bring about. The examples of goal succession in GAG and the Joint Working Party case studies, which we drew attention to above, are cases in point: the successful outcome of early strategies had wrought a change in the organisational environment which, in turn, evoked a new response.

This process need not necessarily be so direct. For example, some success in achieving initial goals can help to encourage confidence among group members, and serve to raise expectations. These internal changes can then contribute to a modification of goals. There was some evidence that a process like this was at work in SCAG. Demonstrated ability to organise the Wednesday afternoon socials helped to give members the confidence to embark upon organising the food and household goods co-operative; similarly, some success in negotiating with the local council and other outside agencies in connection with the small jobs scheme seemed to encourage people to tackle the bus company over the issue of discretionary passes, and the health authorities over inadequacies in chiropody services. Here we are focussing upon what Hall calls 'internal' changes: changes in expectations or aspirations, evoked in this case by past activity.

The SCAG study also illustrates a further way in which internal changes stimulate goal change: the pursuit of one objective can help to highlight new needs, or lead to the recruitment of new members, and both of these can encourage a re-formulation of objectives. In distributing HELP cards, members of SCAG became impressed with the extent of social isolation among elderly people in the town. 'Tea and crack' was the result; this in turn brought an expanded membership, vocal about the inadequacies in chiropody provision.

Two examples of co-option, one actual and one anticipated, provide illustrations of the third cause of goal change identified by Hall: modifications in the inter-organisational relations sustained by groups. The Glodwick group successfully demonstrated the need for an information and complaints service for local people; this objective was partially lost when the service was taken over by Oldham CAB. In this case co-option was actively encouraged by the local action group. It is perhaps more usual to view co-option in a negative light, as part of a process of incorporation by established interests that serves to emasculate locally generated initiatives; the Failsworth Association, for example, viewed with some trepidation the possible introduction of neighbourhood councils in the Greater Manchester area. The independence and viability of their own association would be put at risk, and the secretary foresaw that the association would probably be 'taken over' in such an eventuality.

With only a restricted number of action systems to generalise from, and case study material that covers only a limited time period, we are prevented from drawing conclusions of a quantitative type. It is impossible to venture a view about the most likely types of goal change in voluntary community groups, or advance an opinion about the most likely causes. However, it has been possible to utilise a general classification of the sources of goal change developed in the organisational sociology literature and to illustrate some of the underlying processes at work. It is clear that goal change is a common phenomenon associated with community groups, one that is the outcome of a complex interaction of internal and external factors.

Summary and conclusions

Throughout this chapter we have focussed on process, on the inter-related factors that affect goal setting, goal achievement and goal change. It is worth reiterating a point made earlier: care must be taken in putting too much weight on generalisations derived from such a limited number of case studies. Nevertheless, our tentative propositions about the influence of group-environment relationships, member characteristics and resource attainment should at least provide a point of departure for future thinking and enquiry.

A crucial question here concerns the representativeness of our sample. All our study groups were externally orientated at their inception. Is this reflective of community groups in general, or is such a generalisation peculiar to our particular sample? Similarly, we concluded that the aims and goals of the action systems examined were relatively modest, indeed generally unexceptionable, in their aspirations, and we went on to suggest that one reason for this might be the fact that the groups studied were most appropriately seen as coalitions of somewhat divergent interests. Common observation would suggest that our groups were not unusual in this respect.

Our evidence also suggested that community groups attempt to cope with internal conflict over goal priorities in a variety of ways: by adopting all-embracing constitutions, by recognising the freedom of sub-groups to pursue divergent focal goals, by consciously choosing to work towards goals that command maximum consensus. The small number of groups studied prevents us from even speculating on the reasons for choosing between these different strategies. Besides an answer to that question we would also like to know of other types of organisational strategy used by community groups as a solution to this problem.

Goal achievements were modest. The overall commitment and organisational experience of group members came through as an important factor in accounting for success, as did the ability of the particular action systems concerned to attract the resources necessary to mount a successful campaign or offer a viable service. Both mutual aid initiatives and advocacy orientated campaigns had to demonstrate a minimal level of relevance to be successful; and the skill with which groups managed important organisational-environment exchanges seemed to be a further crucial factor in accounting for successful goal achievement.

Inter-organisational relations and general environmental change were also seen to be important factors in accounting for goal change: goal displacement, goal succession, and cyclical change in emphasis placed upon multiple goals were identified as discrete and significant processes. Overall, goal change rather than goal stability seemed, from our evidence, to be a particular feature of the community group scene. Again, we must return to question how far this generalisation has a validity that extends beyond our five study groups, but we would be surprised if it did not.

In any event, our conclusions about the factors and processes that influence determination, achievement and change in goals do seem to hang together in a coherent way. The voluntary nature of group membership helps to account for the observed plurality of interest and aspiration, which in turn gives rise to conflicts, conflicts that must find an acceptable organisational resolution if even modest achievements are to be made. The permeability of group boundaries, which is linked to the voluntary character of the organisations studied, provides a general explanation of our recurrent identification of organisational-environment exchanges as important elements in analysis. Finally, these cross-boundary problems are also reflective of the resource problems faced by voluntary organisations. While membership constitutes a vital resource, it is rarely possible for a group to achieve its goals without external aid; but the acquisition of this runs up against the ever present danger of co-option by outside bodies, an outcome liable in turn to weaken groups' independence and political strength.

Chapter 9
Organisation: process and structure

Community groups are formed and kept in being both because certain individuals wish to do something about aspects of their or others' lives, and because they believe that this is best done by collaborating with those who share the same concerns. Additional factors, like the personal support derived from belonging, spur many both to join and to remain involved in groups; but our main perspective in this book is that 'an organisation . . . is the outcome of the interaction of motivated people attempting to resolve problems'.[1] We will focus on organisation as the medium between intention and action, and as the mechanism for converting individuals' aspirations into practical collective initiatives.

Organisation is necessary for community groups to take action; if the Glodwick Action Group, the Senior Citizens Action Group and our other study groups had not developed, no collective promotion of their members' concerns and interests would have occurred; and little, if any, notice would have been taken of these concerns by outside bodies. Furthermore, human skills and energies were the primary resource available to the groups; as in most community situations money, buildings, access to decision makers and other non-human resources were in short supply. Organisation is required to ensure that individuals' potential contributions are both realised and integrated in the most effective ways. As Dickinson has said, 'organisation is one of the most important and difficult areas in voluntary action. The form your organisation takes, and the way it is seen by the people involved, are both crucial to the continued existence and effectiveness of your group'.[2]

This centrality of organisation to groups' practice is not reflected in its coverage by research and evaluative studies. Bryant's comment in 1972 that, among social scientists, 'comparatively little attention has been paid to documenting and examining the processes through which local groups engage in organised action' remains true.[3] Our case studies set out to document some of these organisational processes in the five groups studied. This chapter aims to examine them.

After briefly discussing the meaning of the term 'organisation', we will first explore factors which lead to the instigation of community groups; we will then consider stages involved in groups' formation, and aspects of this formation process which seem critical to the successful establishment of groups; we will go on to review the dynamics of leadership in groups; and will then explore the development of their organisational structures.

Broad definition of organisation

> 'Now', said Rabbit, 'this is a search and I've organised it.' 'Done what to it?' said Pooh. 'Organised it, which means – well, it's what you do to a search when you don't all look in the same place at once. So I want you, Pooh, to search by the Six Pine Trees first, and then work your way towards Owl's house; and look out for me there. Do you see?' 'No', said Pooh, 'What – ' 'Then I'll see you at Owl's house in about an hour's time.' 'Is Piglet organdised too?' 'We all are,' said Rabbit, and off he went.[4]

That is one very dynamic definition, not to mention demonstration, of organisation. More soberly, it has been described by Hall as 'a collectivity with relatively identifiable boundary, a normative order . . . communication systems and membership co-ordinating systems; this collectivity exists on a relatively continuous basis in an environment and engages in activities that are usually related to a goal or set of goals'.[5]

This is not the place to discuss the details of semantic distinctions. These quotations seem to provide an adequate basis for a common understanding of the term. Moreover, they are complementary in their different emphases. Milne makes it clear that to Rabbit organisation is a happening, and a highly frenetic one at that, while Hall views it more as a psychophysical phenomenon, embodying a clear form and momentum over time. Rabbit sees it as a verb, as the doing of something. Hall sees it more as a noun, as the something done.

These two aspects of organisations, traditionally termed their process and structure, have often been separated in studies and discussions of organisational issues. Indeed, this was our original intention for this chapter. But the case study data did not allow it. Process and structure seemed to be constantly inter-weaving, in a state of continuous inter-dependent flux; although less tidy, therefore, we will discuss the groups' organisational processes and structures in the dynamic way in which they developed.[6]

Factors leading to the instigation of community groups

Community groups do not just happen. As Hill and Issacharoff have pointed out, even 'the occurrence of a crisis or issue need not necessarily induce co-operation';[7] and, in spite of claims by newspapers, like the one which reported the West Cumberland Bus Fares issue, that the recent decade has been 'the age of protest', in many communities organised collective action remains the exception rather than the rule.

Nevertheless, one factor which can be confidently hypothesised as likely to be significant to a group's formation is suggested by Hill and Issacharoff's reference to a 'crisis or issue'.[8] This is the existence in, or introduction into, people's life situations of a threat or shortcoming liable to provoke a concerted response. These threats or shortcomings arise independently of prospective group members' choice or own creation; though, as discussed later, they do have to be perceived as issues by prospective group members for organisation to occur. As Glaser and Sills have put it, 'every association obtains . . . its originating stimuli . . . from a larger social system';[9] in the case of the kinds of community group with which we are concerned (where a social change perspective and the exertion of pressure through influence strategies often play a central part) the stimuli can be expected to arise particularly from the political, or related public serving, elements of that larger system.

Eckstein has said of the national political scene that:

> The activities of governments are the most obvious determinants of their (pressure groups') entrance into politics. We may regard political systems as amalgams of potential and actual pressure groups: groups which from a political standpoint are merely 'categoric' groups and groups which have actually been drawn into politics, chiefly through the impact of public policies.[10]

By the same token it seems likely that, in local situations, community groups both form and enter politics chiefly through the impact of local public policies.

Two of the case study groups were formed in response to specific decisions made by public authorities: Glodwick Action

Group to the imposition of a Compulsory Purchase Order by the council, and West Cumberland Action Committee (or, more accurately, the parents' protest groups which later merged to form WCAC) to the raising of school bus fares by the county motor services company. Two other groups formed because of needs or shortcomings which they perceived and which seemed unlikely to be resolved by relevant statutory bodies. The Joint Working Party arose from concern about the scale of need for, and deficiency in provision of, shelter for homeless men and from the local authority's unwillingness to do anything to help. The Senior Citizens Action Group focussed on the need among elderly people for assistance with small-scale repairs and odd jobs, and the failure of any outside body to provide a relevant service.

The fifth group, Failsworth Community Association, also came together in response to a public policy, though of a different kind. Its formation stemmed from Parliament's decision to re-organise local government, and the implications which this had for the Failsworth area. The locus of council decision making in relation to Failsworth was to be transferred to comparatively remote departments with a broader geographical scope than before, which was seen as a threat to effective representation of the area's interests. This presented a challenge to local groups to coalesce into a 'united front of opinion' in order to ensure that equitable levels of public resources were allocated to the area in the future. Failsworth Community Association therefore came about in response to a public policy, but one whose object and effect was to alter the structures and processes through which public policies would be locally determined in the future.

So far, so good. The activities of governments have been demonstrated as important influences on groups' entrance into politics. We have also suggested that there are different kinds of such public policy: (1) specific, concrete threats, as with GAG and the bus fares groups; this is the kind referred to by Hill and Issacharoff as a crisis or issue; (2) long-term dispositions of disinterest and negligence towards the meeting of needs, as with SCAG and the Joint Working Party; and (3) changes in the structures and processes through which decisions relevant to localities or other 'categoric' groups in communities are made.

But is this the whole story? We think not, and suggest that, while these 'stimuli from the larger social system', or provocative factors as we will call them, are clearly significant to a group's formation they are not the only, or necessarily the main, determinants. Other variables (in particular those that we will term 'promotional' and 'facilitative') seem important in the stages between the manifestation of provocative external stimuli and the organisational initiation of community groups. These additional factors will be examined in detail following a summary of the stages which, from the evidence of our study groups, appear to be involved in groups' formation.

The stages involved in the formation of community groups

Issue recognition
The first stage leading to collective action is perception by at least some of those on the receiving end (or others, in our cases professionally, interested in their welfare) of one or more provocative stimuli as an unresolved threat or unmet need which constitutes a cause for concern; the perception that a decision, long-term disposition, organisational change or other output from a public authority can and should be seen as an issue to be taken up and pursued. This first stage of perception and recognition of a provocative factor as an issue was fulfilled respectively by West Cumberland mothers; Glodwick residents and the CDP employed community worker; members of the Companions Club in Cleator Moor with the catalytic help of the community worker; professionals and parish priests who came across single homeless men in the course of duty; and the officers of the Failsworth Amenity Society.

Development of the appreciation that organised action is both possible and likely to be productive
Further developments in consciousness and conviction are then necessary: that without an independent intervention, improvement in the situation is improbable and deterioration likely (this step is usually taken readily, indeed implicitly, in response to specific decisions like those which provoked the formation of GAG and the constituent groups of WCAC); that resources available are sufficient to ensure sustained organisational action over time; and that such action stands some chance of being productive, in the sense of benefits outweighing costs, effort and difficulties being justified by results. SCAG provides a good example of a number of people, who had previously gone no further than recognition of an issue, gradually coming to see that, by organising a group, common concerns could usefully be taken up.

Development of the collective will to act
A further stage in group formation is the collectivisation of this will to act. This may be developed collectively anyway, as happened in the case of SCAG; but when it is not, as with Failsworth Community Association and Glodwick Action Group, the two initial steps need to be repeated by those convinced of the value of organised action as an educational process with others who might also develop a similar commitment.

Organisational mobilisation of potential members
Education about the possibility and likely advantages of organised action needs to mushroom in this way. So, in complementary fashion, does mobilisation of potential members. This happened in our groups through the identification of likely key members by the main organisers (for instance, the community worker in Glodwick), the establishment of steering or working groups (for example FCA, GAG and the Joint Working Party), the discussion and negotiation of the prospective group's organisational form (FCA), and the holding of open or public meetings (for instance GAG, FCA, WCAC).

Collection of information about the issue, the target, and likely resources available
An additional stage (though not necessarily sequentially following the others) is often collection of information about the issue (for instance, about Compulsory Purchase Orders) or need (for example, about numbers of single homeless men). This can be used to promote greater awareness of the problem and commitment to its resolution, and to strengthen further the group's capacity for taking action.

All these stages were involved in the formation of our groups. Their order and the degree to which they involved formal planning varied. So did the identity of the stage(s) which were particularly critical: for example, SCAG's breakthrough was the realisation of the possibility of organised intervention, while the Joint Working Party's was the impetus given by the survey report. But in all cases the process was hazardous, and in some it was long-drawn-out. It seems apparent that more than just provocative stimuli are necessary for groups to form.

Factors which seem critical to the successful establishment of groups

The formation of a community group apparently requires not

just provocation by external factors but also 'promotional' inputs in terms of organisational and financial backing, and 'facilitative' help of administrative and process-oriented (developing and structuring inter-personal relationships) kinds. Over and above the efforts of prospective group members in providing such inputs, the promotional boosts can come from already existing voluntary organisations or community development agencies, and the facilitative tasks can be performed by members (usually holders of official positions – indeed, in our cases, predominantly the secretary) of the already existing organisations or agency employed community workers.

In our case studies there are two examples of the promotional and facilitative roles both being performed by already existing organisations (the Joint Working Party and Failsworth Community Association and their officers), one where both were performed by CDP and one of its community workers (GAG), and two where the promotional task was shared between already existing organisations and the CDP, with the facilitative work carried out mainly by CDP workers (WCAC and SCAG).

The Joint Working Party was particularly dependent for its instigation on already well-established bodies. The two voluntary councils nursed the project from the idea to the reality stage, providing a promotional impetus by making available or raising the finance necessary to cover initiating costs and by embodying the organisational strength and prestige sufficient to promote confidence in, and commitment to, the project's eventual success. The councils established the 'co-ordinating group' as a consortium, retaining their 'parental' interests and appointing their own officers and executive members to the new organisation's committee. The councils also provided or raised the manpower to carry out the facilitative tasks of providing administrative back-up, conducting a survey, seeking out possible premises, and inter-personal and inter-organisational liaison.

Failsworth Community Association was similarly piloted into existence by an already active body, Failsworth Amenity Society. Although the latter was more influential than others both in the formation of FCA and in its representation on the committee that was eventually elected, the relationship between the two organisations was less tightly meshed than in the Joint Working Party case. Failsworth Amenity Society took the initiative in collectivising the will to act; but as soon as a conglomerate body was becoming an embryonic reality, an autonomous multi-representative steering committee was formed. Both on that and on the Association, the Amenity Society formally had the same status and voting rights as other members. As well as providing the promotional boosts and backing, the Society also, through its officers and in particular its secretary, carried out the back-room facilitative work of administration and general servicing of the project's development. As suggested above, it is no mean task to create a new group from scratch, and the success of the two voluntary councils and of Failsworth Amenity Society is a measure of the organisational resources (for example, adminis-trative skills and knowledge, finance, and personnel with time and expertise to offer) at their disposal.

In terms of its initial promotional process WCAC was similar to FCA; one of several complementary groups took the initiative in forming a federal committee to co-ordinate the representation of interests. Some of its members played leading roles in facili-tating the new organisation's establishment. The embryonic WCAC, however, also drew on financial sponsorship from the CDP, and on a background facilitative function performed by a CDP worker.

SCAG also arose out of an already existing organisation. In this case the Companions Club acted more as a convenient back-drop, and source of membership recruitment, for SCAG; and, apart from the enthusiasm and energy of its own prospective members, it was the CDP which offered the little organisational and financial backing required, and one of its community work-ers who took the facilitative initiatives of suggesting the possi-bilities of organisation, and initially leading the group, on its formation, as chairman.

The group which is significantly different in the context of this discussion is Glodwick Action Group. There had been no self-starting initiatives in response to the CPO because the scale and complexity of both the issue and the decision making processes from which it emanated were felt by the residents to be beyond their power to tackle. Nor were there any existing organisations with sufficient concern for the area to act. This unpromising situation required a major promotional effort, for which the worker time and other necessary resources were possible only through a sponsoring organisation like the CDP. It also required the unremitting facilitative work entailed in the strong and initially directive intervention of the community worker.

The common experiences of the groups suggest that promo-tional and facilitative factors are significant in groups' formation. But some of the differences between the groups' histories raise questions about the relative influence of provocative, promo-tional and facilitative factors in different situations. Sills has said of provocative outputs from the political system that:

Organisational response is more likely: to specific decisions rather than to priority sets; the more threatening decisions are likely to be to individuals' and communities' ways of life; the more concrete and immediate the threat presented; the more clear-cut the issues involved, and the more directly implicating they are for natural collectivities with the potential for organisation.[11]

The development of the WCAC constituent groups, and indeed the drive to set up the federative body, confirm these suggestions; the Glodwick experience, for reasons already outlined, does not.

A further development of this hypothesis is that the more a prospective group is formed in relation to a long-term disposition, rather than specific decision, of political authorities the more important to a successful outcome are promotional factors. The Joint Working Party and FCA, for instance, would not have happened without their 'parent' organisations; nor would SCAG, GAG, and possibly WCAC, without the sponsorship of CDPs. Indeed in the cases of SCAG and GAG particularly it was not only this sponsorship and provision of resources which made the difference. It was also the community worker. When political outputs are insufficient to promote new organisation, and when already existing organisations do not compensate (as was the case particularly in Glodwick), both an alternative sponsoring body and an actively committed worker seem to be required to stimulate organisation. Each group therefore arose from a mixture of provocative, promotional and facilitative factors. But different factors were critical in each case. For WCAC it was the provocative issue; other factors were helpful but probably not vital. For FCA and the Joint Working Party the critical factor was the promotional support of already existing organisations. This was also partly true of SCAG (both in terms of the Companions Club and CDP), but on balance the operational facilitation of the community worker was probably most crucial; and such facilitation was indisputably essential for GAG.

We conclude this discussion of groups' formation by summarising the propositions developed:

1   The initial stimulus to the formation of community groups is a threat or shortcoming in people's life situations liable to provoke a concerted response.
2   This can be one or more of three kinds of public policy: a specific concrete decision by a local political authority or other public serving body; a long-term

disposition of negligence towards the meeting of a need; or a policy to change the ways in which future policies will be made.

3   The original provocative factor(s) need to be perceived as issues or needs sufficient to cause concern by consumers, sufferers or others in a position to act on their behalf.

4   In addition to issue recognition the stages involved in the formation of community groups include a development of the appreciation that organised action is both possible and likely to be productive; the development of a collective will to act; organisational mobilisation of prospective members; and an action-orientated knowledge base, concerning the issue, the target system and available resources.

5   Promotional and facilitative inputs seem to be required to convert the idea of possible action into the reality of organisation. In addition to the contribution of prospective members,[12] these can be provided respectively by already existing voluntary organisations or community development agencies and by members, usually officials, of the voluntary organisations or agency employed community workers.

6   All three factors seem necessary to groups' formation, but their relative importance varies in different situations. On the whole, the more provocative factors are of a specific, threatening kind the more likely is a group to form in response; the more the provocative factor is a generalised disposition, the more significant are promotional inputs; and when either of these are weak or insufficient a facilitative community work role seems indispensable.

The dynamics of leadership in the groups

Many community groups tend to reject traditional assumptions about the value of, or need for, leadership roles and positions. They question traditional beliefs that certain people are likely to be blessed with leadership characteristics while others are not. If any members become designated as leaders, it is assumed, then all should have equal and frequent opportunity to attain such positions. These seem unexceptionable aspirations; but how do the dynamics of groups' leadership work out in practice?

The performance of leadership roles has been seen to be a crucial factor throughout the process of formation of our groups. Initial leadership was undertaken in each group by one or a few individuals:

GAG	the community worker
SCAG	the community worker
WCAC	the leaders of the Cleator Moor bus fares protest group and the community worker
FCA	the officers of FAS
Joint Working Party	the officers of the Council of Social Service and Council of Churches

The next stage in each case was the widening of the lead-taking group. The community workers involved with GAG and SCAG identified potential leaders and called meetings of steering groups. The committees of Failsworth Amenity Society and the two voluntary councils similarly promoted or formed working parties to take their initiatives further. The Cleator Moor protest group and community worker, because of the pressure of time, decided to organise an immediate public meeting, and it was at this that the committee, the leading group from then on, was formed.

Leadership roles were then consolidated in different ways. The GAG steering committee and community worker organised a public meeting at which the Action Group was formed and a committee elected. The SCAG activists remained the core group, of which in the early stages the community worker was a part; later, formal elections to officer positions were held. The FAS-promoted steering committee carried out important groundwork in clarifying, and gaining the agreement of all parties, to the detailed constitution of the Association. This was then ratified at a public meeting and a committee elected. The voluntary councils' working parties similarly promoted the survey which elicited the degree of need among homeless men, and arranged between them the operational basis of the 'co-ordinating group'.

In all the groups except the Joint Working Party, those performing the community work role (and this is illustrated particularly in the GAG and SCAG cases) were concerned to identify, nurture and train a cadre of indigenous leaders who would assume ever-increasing responsibility for groups' activities and affairs. Kahn, from his experience of working with poor people's organisations, has said that:

The process of developing leadership is mostly one of involving others in the process of planning and decision making. The organiser should take pains to involve potential leaders in this process whenever possible. Whenever he is making contacts, visiting agencies or attending meetings one or more of these people should go with him. As they begin to develop an understanding of what the organiser is doing, they should be given the chance to try out these skills themselves; to make rounds in the community, to go . . . to visit agencies, to conduct meetings, to plan strategy, to negotiate. As they gain skill and confidence their dependence on the organiser must decrease.[13]

The leadership of four out of five of our groups was developed along these lines: but with what result? The Failsworth Community Association was run predominantly by the officers of the separate body (FAS) which had promoted its formation. FCA paid particular attention in its early stages to the form of its organisational structure, partly because members were concerned to provide in advance the mechanisms for resolution of conflict between different parties about policy or leadership. In spite of this scrupulous exercise and the formal openness of the leadership positions to all comers, those elected were those already holding the reins. They were also people with considerable experience of positions of responsibility and had a high standing in the community. At the time of the writing up of the case study no change had occurred in the officer positions, and only three out of the 24 executive committee members had 'turned over', all for extrinsic personal reasons.

FCA might be expected to have élitist tendencies, as it is the most formal body of our five. But variations on the same theme appear in the other three groups whose leadership was developed along the lines recommended by Kahn. Members of the steering group in Glodwick became members of the CPO Committee. This in turn was cohesive and 'formed the backbone of the group as a whole'. The six members had more than average experience of organisational affairs and held jobs which were prestigious in relation to those of other residents in the area. They worked together for fourteen months, and those who resigned did so only for personal reasons; the second chairman was chosen from among the remaining three, and these three continued to be the prime movers of the group.

In WCAC, the leading members of the Cleator Moor Group took the initiative in suggesting and facilitating the formation of the organisation, and 'came to be' the leaders and spokesmen of the federated body. Within their own protest group these individuals had above average experience of belonging to other groups in the area. Those with strong personalities and organisational experience from the Whitehaven and Workington groups made an impact at committee meetings, but the support from areas other than Cleator Moor gradually dissipated. As the numbers attending fell from 28 to 10 in a year the Cleator Moor mothers were left as a leadership rump. This was further reinforced by the chosen targets and strategies, in pursuit of which involvement with the original constituency (and therefore the possibility of widening access to leadership positions) was whittled away.

SCAG was probably the least élitist of the groups. Regular election of officers was provided for, leadership tasks were devolved, and there were several cross-cutting lines of conflict in the group. Only a minority (a third) of the original group remained core members. Nevertheless, this core group did persist and provided long-term leadership, bolstering their positions through experience of organisational leadership as well as through the carry-over of informal status networks into the group's affairs. For all its saving graces 'leadership both formal and informal is more or less co-extensive with membership of the core group'.

The picture from these four groups, therefore, is one of: continuity and constancy of leadership through different stages of organisational development (including pre-formation); a tendency for those who were already in leadership positions in other organisations, and who enjoyed the prestige in the community attached to such positions, to become leaders in the new bodies; the recruitment of little new blood and attrition through insufficient informal involvement of some of the old (in particular in WCAC); in summary, for an élite to set the organisational ball rolling in the first instance, and for more or less the same élite both to become the group's initial leaders at its formation and to maintain this leadership role over time.

The case of the Joint Working Party puts many of these factors into stark relief, providing the most blatant example among our case studies of leadership self-perpetuation. The two sponsoring bodies established their own leaders as the office-holders of their joint non-autonomous outgrowth (significantly not offshoot!). The officers remained the same for the period covered by the case study, and no formal machinery existed for any challenge. The numerical dominance of the committee by representatives of the two sponsoring bodies was also maintained even in the face of challenge from dissident volunteers who gained agreement to first four, and then six, representative places on the committee. This challenge from the shelter volunteers is significant because it provides the only example in our case studies of an organised resistance to the formal leadership. In the early days of the project the formal leadership had been accepted by group members; as in the other groups most of the time, formal and informal, task-oriented and socio-emotional, leadership coincided. But this soon dissipated as the gap developed between deciders and doers, and differences arose in their perspectives and priorities. Alternative spokesmen for the volunteers emerged; they sniped at the leadership, for instance on the charges issue, and gained some concessions. But they held no power of decision themselves, being able only to request a hearing from the formal leaders. Indeed this lack of openness by the formal leadership in part accounted for the confrontation between the two sides over the handling of the shelter closure issue. On this occasion the volunteers, through force of numbers, argument and the power accruing to them as front-line workers, operationally took the organisation over for the duration of the campaign. It was a ten-day revolution, however, not followed through or consolidated in terms of changes in leadership positions or in constitutional arrangements making them more accessible. The campaign over, the latent power of the formal leaders was retrieved. The most entrenched leadership in our five groups therefore received the most vigorous challenge. The loss of face over the closure issue was real but short-term; and the leaders' rapid retrenchment and re-establishment of internal 'them and us' relationships further confirmed the degree of their earlier, and persisting, entrenchment.

Michels's 'iron law of oligarchy' –

> that it is organisation which gives birth to the domination of the elected over the electors, of the mandatories over the mandators, of the delegates over the delegators. Who says organisation says oligarchy. . . . It is an essential characteristic of all human aggregates to constitute cliques and sub-classes[14]

– seems from this evidence to hold for community groups as much as for political parties.

Its force is probably regretted by most readers. So why does it happen, and does it have any mitigating aspects? The reasons for community group élitism in particular cases would seem from our evidence likely to be one or more of the following:

1   the power of leader appointment being retained by sponsoring bodies.
2   the extra cachet that accrues in organisations to individuals and groups who take the initiative in setting them up (similar to the aura which surrounds founders or founder-members in many more traditional bodies).
3   the consolidation of position possible from representation of a group to outside, and not least target, bodies; the group is reliant on the leader(s) to 'tell it how it is' – which can never be more objective than how he, she or they choose to present it to the group.
4   the input of a disproportionate amount of any necessary resources by the leaders, including in the case of FCA money, but more usually technical expertise and organisational experience.
5   the interplay between wider social and internal organisational status patterns and reinforcement of the latter by the former; this is particularly so when also inter-linked with friendship networks. Although we feel Freeman overstates the case in relation to our groups (she was discussing groups in the women's liberation movement), nevertheless her very overstatement makes this point:

> Elites are not conspiracies. Very seldom does a small group of people get together and deliberately try to take over a larger group for its own ends. Elites are nothing more, and nothing less, than groups of friends who happen to participate in the same political activities. They would probably maintain their friendship whether or not they were involved in political activities; they would probably be involved in political activities whether or not they maintained their friendships. It is the coincidence of these two phenomena which creates élites in any group and makes them so difficult to break.[15]

6   when leaders and friends converge, particularly in relatively informal groups, the friendship network creates a further dimension of exclusiveness by providing informal channels of communication through which, inevitably, items of group business pass. By such processes the select get sealed off. Insulation becomes complete.

Although this scenario looks bleak, some positive points can be made. First, some continuity in organisational membership and leadership between different stages of a group's development (for example, steering group and established committee) is likely to promote consistency in choices of goals and strategies. Second, at the *putsch* stage of formation and early development a core reservoir of energy and effort is indispensable. Third, it is often suggested that centralised leadership (and, best of all, a committee of one!) is the most efficient. It may be that at certain stages and for certain purposes it is advisable for a group to adopt such leadership forms, even though this may temporarily preempt other virtues of organisational behaviour. Fourth, in none of the groups, except perhaps the Joint Working Party, was the élite monolithic. In most, different members had different skills and expertise and the *de facto* leadership was both group-based and oscillated between individuals depending on respective relevance to the tasks in hand or strategies being considered. Fifth, there is only evidence in one out of our five groups of active dissatisfaction on the part of the underdogs with their treatment by the overdogs; and it may not be coincidental that the three groups in which no dissatisfaction is recorded, FCA, GAG and SCAG, are those which had most fully developed the organisational mechanisms for promoting change in the leadership if and when the members at large felt this to be necessary.

Oligarchy may not therefore be an unmitigated disaster; indeed for certain critical periods, particularly in task-orientated groups, it may be requisite. But many community group members might be keen to counter the tendency. The question arises, how? This question leads directly on to consideration of the development of community groups' organisational structures.

The development of organisational structures

Several possibilities are open to community groups concerned to restrict oligarchic tendencies; and it has already been shown how the least élitist of our groups, SCAG, developed a range of organisational devices to try to keep it that way. The possibilities include:

1   An awareness of the perennial possibility of élitism, as well as, more generally, of the importance to a group's effectiveness of its organisational forms; a commitment to considering and planning structures carefully, explicitly, and not until a stage has been reached when newly joined up members are sufficiently confident in themselves and each other to

make an equal (or, in each individual's terms, a full)
contribution to the debate and decision.

2   Leadership positions might be formally renounced or
kept in reserve, and the different roles (for instance,
chairing of meetings) rotated informally and regularly.
If leadership positions are established, there might be
more rather than fewer, elections might be held
regularly and frequently (for example, at least
annually), and some limit placed on the opportunity
for office-holders to stand for re-election; as Grusky
has observed, 'forms of rotation . . . weaken personal
executive power and encourage the development of a
general orientation toward organisational authority'.[16]
This in turn implies sufficient numbers of prospective
leaders and places an onus on continuous recruitment
of new members and the development of their skills
and knowledge so that they are seen as eligible for
leadership positions.

3   Such organisational or group authority might be
further promoted through leadership being located as
widely as possible in the group, that is in a group of
officers or committee members rather than one or
two, and still more in genuinely participative decision
making meetings open to all members, in relation to
which executive committees and officers perform
literally executive functions. Within limits agreed to
be consistent with this collective responsibility for
decision making, particular tasks might be devolved to
sub-committees or working parties.

How do our study groups shape up when viewed in the light
of these possibilities? In terms of the first suggestion, two of the
groups (the Joint Working Party and WCAC) never seriously
considered their structure; two (GAG and SCAG) did so some
time after their formation; while the prospective members of
Failsworth Community Association took great pains to get it as
right as possible before the organisational launch. In the Joint
Working Party, the sponsoring bodies' self-appointed leaders
pre-empted the setting up of procedures for widening access to
leadership roles, putting the protection of their parent bodies'
interests before the promotion of the working party's. They kept
a grip on power by discouraging and parrying any attempts to
loosen it and also by deflecting, or straightforwardly rejecting,
any suggestions that power distribution in the organisation
should be substantively discussed. At one point the dissolution

of the organisation through withdrawal of the sponsoring bodies was threatened in response to volunteers' moves to broaden the committee's base so that it was more representative of all members. The leaders used the power which they had initially given themselves to ensure that 'non-decision making' prevailed in the organisation;[17] the structuring of leadership roles did not make the agenda of any open discussion meetings.

WCAC, at the other end of the formal-informal spectrum, also never got round to structural considerations. The heat was on from the start and the members had to respond. Consideration of the niceties of internal organisational relationships was by-passed until forced on the group by the need to open a bank account. Positions were then created and duly filled by the informal leaders. This did not represent a serious attempt 'to structure the committee's roles', but rather a stage in the process of the initial leaders reinforcing their leadership positions in almost as thoroughgoing a fashion as those in the Joint Working Party. This might have appeared to 'just happen', and in terms of these individuals' conscious intentions probably did; the process can, but does not have to be, conspiratorial.

Glodwick Action Group and SCAG both considered their organisational arrangements some time after their formation, mainly because task-orientated commitments had previously preoccupied members' attention but also, from the workers' point of view, because this provided a period for members to shake down and get to know each others' strengths.

Failsworth Community Association, by contrast, only became a possibility after a multi-representative steering group had taken a great deal of trouble to work out a generally acceptable constitution. This was partly because the constituent parts were heterogeneous and themselves discrete entities with interests to protect (a consideration which WCAC neglected at a price). In addition, setting up a viable representative structure was in some ways the organisation's *raison d'être* and 'getting it right' was therefore of consummate concern.

In terms of the second set of possibilities for restricting oligarchic tendencies, the creation or not of leadership positions and of rules to ensure accountability and restricted tenure, WCAC had no officers except to satisfy the bank manager's requirements; and the Joint Working Party had a chairman, secretary and treasurer more or less in perpetuity to satisfy the sponsoring bodies' requirements.

Each of the three groups which explicitly worked out their organisational arrangements made provision for officer positions. SCAG created six: chairman, deputy chairman, secretary, assist-

ant secretary, treasurer and assistant treasurer. These were all
subject to annual election. In addition SCAG went to greater
lengths than any other group to ensure maintenance of membership levels and a flow of possible candidates for leadership
positions. Personal invitations to the weekly socials and other
group activities, and notices of meetings posted in the local
Action Centre's window, were designed to attract new members.
These efforts seem to have been repaid in greater turnover of,
and recruitment of new, leaders than in the other four groups.
GAG also provided for officer positions subject to regular elections, but apart from initial efforts to attract support through
newsletters and public meetings did not set out as deliberately
as SCAG to gain recruits and develop prospective leaders. Failsworth Community Association allowed for the equal representation on the executive committee of interested parties, made
officer positions subject to annual election on both the executive
and sub-committees, and enjoyed a possible source of new committee members through the incentive to constituent groups to
send representatives.

The third suggested set of defences against élitist tendencies
in groups concerns the location of authority in the group, rather
than its officers, and the diversification of responsibilities to sub-
groups. WCAC held monthly meetings at which anyone could
contribute. But these were so open that they tended to be incon-
clusive 'free-for-alls', with decisions largely being made between
times by the informal leaders. The Joint Working Party had no
general decision making meetings. Those open meetings that
were held were seen by the officers as advisory. Sub-groups were
set up, but these were for tasks like knocking the warehouse into
shape and fund-raising, rather than policy making. GAG embodied a collective focus in its leadership approach, not least in
representations to outside bodies, and attempted, though never
very successfully, to operate through sub-committees.

The two groups which most closely approximated to the suggested guidelines were FCA and SCAG. FCA, the most federative and formalised of our groups, nevertheless put its executive
committee rather than its officers at the centre of the decision
making stage. It set considerable store by reaching decisions on
the basis of a consensus among all parties. Indeed, it went further
than this in trying to ensure a broad endorsement for organisational policies: first, membership was deemed to be uncondition-
ally open to all Failsworth residents; and second, any 'member'
had the right to attend, address and vote at executive committee
meetings. FCA also made provision for six sub-committees; and
one in particular, the planning committee, was made up of mem-

bers with specialist knowledge and enjoyed considerable autonomy because it needed to act on behalf of the Association more
frequently and flexibly than it was practicable for this to be
collectively endorsed. SCAG, similarly, reached decisions by
consensus, promoted multiple leadership by drawing on different
members' skills and experience, treated meetings as open houses
and allocated several tasks to sub-groups. SCAG had a simpler
structure than FCA – its membership was made up only of
individuals, rather than individuals and interested organisations
– and operated less formally. But the group was equally careful
to design and maintain its structure along collective and decentralised lines; and, probably because it was able to be less formalised than FCA, it was in fact the least oligarchic of our five
study groups; its degree of operational informality meant that its
formal provisions for openness and member participation went
a considerable way towards promoting the practical realities.

Conclusion

Maximising member participation in community groups is not
the only requirement which their structures need to fulfil. Nevertheless, this is important to many community group members
both for its own sake and in order to demonstrate that alternatives to the bureaucratic structures which tend to characterise
target systems are possible. It would also seem to be inter-related
with other structural requirements such as integration of individuals' contributions, accountability not only of leaders to members but also of members to leaders for the tasks which they
have undertaken to perform, and the provision of collective
mechanisms for making effective representations to outside
bodies.

The comparative inadequacy of the Joint Working Party's and
WCAC's structures in promoting member participation is mirrored in relation to these other criteria. It is probably not coincidental that in the more deficient groups organisational planning
was, on the one hand, manipulated by self-appointed leaders to
satisfy extrinsic pressures and, on the other, went by default.
The evidence of our case studies suggests the validity of Brager
and Specht's claim that 'although there is truth in the maxim
that "in unity there is strength", strength is unlikely to be
realised without a structural framework'.[18] Happy accidents may
occur through a *laissez faire* approach to organisation; but
unhappy outcomes seem more probable. Inappropriate, if not
detrimental, organisational structures are less likely if carefully

planned. FCA provides a model of a formalised approach to such careful planning. GAG, and particularly SCAG, show that such planning can be undertaken seriously without either the process or the resulting structures being so formal. Either way, organisational planning seems conducive to the development of a group's cohesion and collective strength.

Chapter 10
Strategy, tactics and resources

The word strategy was originally essentially military, being derived from the roots of 'an army' and 'to lead'; from this the word has been generalised and is now used in non-military situations to mean 'the art of conducting a campaign'. In Chapter 7 it was suggested that a basic question for community groups is 'how they attain and deploy resources in order to realise their aims and objectives'; it is this process which we should like to define as strategy.

To evaluate the strategy followed in a certain situation one needs to know first of all the aims and objectives which the group was trying to pursue, so that the results can be judged against the goal they were striving for, and also the resources available and the ways in which these were used. In simple terms, the relevant questions in considering strategy seem to be: What did the group want? What resources were available? And how were these resources used to try to achieve their goal? The separate components of the group's overall strategy are their tactics, the 'nuts and bolts' of action taken in pursuing individual objectives.

Chapter 8 draws the distinction between task and system maintenance or process goals. The pursuit of process goals is more likely to be implicit rather than actually stated among a group's formal objectives, but clearly some of a group's effort must be devoted to its own maintenance if it is to pursue its formally stated objectives. In this way one could include a group's structure, financing and membership as part of its strategy. This chapter, however, will focus on a group's strategy in relation to its formally stated objectives – the cause or causes for which the group was formed or which it has subsequently taken up.

In Chapter 7 we pointed out some of the difficulties that arise in trying to define a group's overall strategy (for example as confrontative or consensual), because methods of approach often vary according to the different objectives being tackled. For this reason the idea of looking at individual issues and action systems was suggested, and this is taken up here.

This chapter looks at the strategies adopted by the groups in relation to the 18 different action systems which can be identified from the five case studies, and differentiates between those which relate to services provided by the groups and those where the groups sought to bring influence to bear on other bodies. Both groups of action systems are then related to the resources used, tactics employed, and the success or otherwise of the outcome, in order to establish some working hypotheses.

Service strategies and influence strategies

We have already suggested that our case studies show two different attitudes to resource deployment; that in particular instances groups either opt to use their resources to tackle a problem directly with a self-help or voluntary service scheme (the Senior Citizens Action Group's food and household goods club, for example), or use these resources to modify the performance of larger resource allocation systems (which, in our case studies, were usually local authorities; the Glodwick Action Group's evidence to the public inquiry is an example). The first instance, the self-help approach, is called for our purpose a 'service strategy', and the latter, where a group attempts to bear upon other resource holders, is called an 'influence strategy'.

These two approaches are not necessarily exclusive but may be combined or succeed one another. An example is the campaign to set up the Central Street Shelter, which was pursued first by an influence and then by a service strategy. Here speed was the crucial factor as the shelter was needed before winter came, and the group, in an unconscious cost-benefit exercise, opted for establishing the shelter itself to get it into operation in the time available.

The 18 action systems which can be identified from the case studies are listed in Table 1. This categorisation shows that all the groups engaged in influence issues, and three in both influence and service issues. The last column in the Table classifies the issues in accordance with the divisions suggested in Chapter 7: that is, by the degree of threat presented to outside bodies by the group's pursuit of an issue.

TABLE 1 The 18 action systems in the five study groups

Group	Issue focus of action system	Service or influence	Type of strategy
Joint Working Party	Setting up shelter	S and I	Complementary/ collaborative
Joint Working Party	Threat to close shelter	I	Campaign
Failsworth Community Association	Provision of community hall	I	Campaign
FCA	Territorial Army's application to use quarry for training	I	Campaign
Glodwick Action Group	Information and advice service	S	Complementary/ alternative
GAG	Survey and evidence to public inquiry	I	Campaign
GAG	Issues arising from public inquiry	I	Collaborative
GAG	Re-letting of council-owned empty houses in good condition, managed by FHA	I	Campaign
Senior Citizens Action Group	Social activities	S	Complementary
SCAG	Welfare rights course	S	Complementary/ alternative
SCAG	Food and household goods club	S	Alternative
SCAG	HELP cards	S	Complementary
SCAG	Small jobs scheme	S and I	Alternative/ collaborative
SCAG	Improving chiropody service	I	Collaborative
SCAG	Bus pass issues	I	Collaborative
SCAG	Pedestrian safety	I	Collaborative
West Cumberland Action Committee	Children's bus passes – local issues	I	Campaign
WCAC	Public transport – national issues	I	Campaign

Service strategies

We have identified three types of service strategy: complementary, alternative, and substitute. Analysis of the case studies reveals seven service issues, two of which (the SCAG small jobs scheme and the working party's establishment of the Central Street shelter), are both service and influence.

Complementary service strategies

These are those which augment or complement existing services without threatening other people or bodies.

Two of the service issues, SCAG's social activities and its HELP cards scheme, are clearly complementary in that they were additional services to those already offered to the elderly in the area and were not in conflict with the aims or interests of other bodies. A third, the Joint Working Party's setting up of the shelter (in its service aspect) seems to come within the complementary category also, although the categorisation here is not easy; the proposal to set up the shelter was seen to threaten some people in the town, particularly those with tourism interests, but was complementary in the sense of there being no body which already provided a similar service.

Alternative service strategies

These are those which offer an alternative service and thus to a mild extent challenge, or at least compete with, an existing service.

Two issues or action systems, the SCAG food and household goods club and the SCAG small jobs scheme (in its service aspect) are both alternative in that they posed some threat, albeit very mild, to retailers and small builders in the area respectively.

The remaining two issues – the GAG information and advice service and the SCAG welfare rights course – contain elements of both complementary and alternative strategies. The SCAG scheme was alternative in its implication that the Department of Health and Social Security was not already doing as much as possible to see that its elderly claimants, usually assumed to be its most favoured clients, were receiving maximum benefits. The GAG information service is complementary in that it augmented the existing Citizens' Advice Bureau service in the town, but alternative in that by providing a service for Asian residents with translation facilities it was to some extent a threat to the CAB and the Community Relations Council. Both these organisations considered that their services covered the needs of Asian residents but neither could offer the combination of a comprehensive information system and Asian-speaking advisers or translators.

Substitute service strategies

These are those which are intended to replace existing methods of meeting needs or to meet needs the legitimacy of which is not generally recognised, and thus provide a major threat to existing interests.

From our case studies we are unable to classify any of the service action systems as being substitute. Nevertheless some do occur in community action activities; for example, the setting up of free schools.

Influence strategies

The initial breakdown provides a group of thirteen influence issues mentioned in the case studies, including the two which can be described as both influence and service. Again these issues can be sub-divided into three categories[1] according to the degree of threat they present to other groups or agencies: collaborative, campaign and coercive.

Collaborative influence strategies

These are those where both the group and the target system agree about the necessity of providing for a particular need, but the group seeks to show that existing services do not meet it and that further action or resources are needed.

From the evidence in the case studies, we would suggest that of the thirteen influence issues five can be described as collaborative: the setting up of the Central Street shelter, the SCAG small jobs scheme, and its pursuit of the chiropody, bus passes, and pedestrian safety issues. The Glodwick Action Group's taking up of issues from the public inquiry to some extent implied a threat to the local authority, but in general the council's willingness to meet most of the group's requests seems to place this set of issues more fairly in the collaborative than in the campaign category.

Campaign influence strategies

These are cases where a group attempts to influence the allocation of the target system's resources in favour of people with a particular need, the legitimacy of whose claim has not so far been recognised.

The remaining seven issues all seem to have involved campaign strategies; these were the possibility of closure of the Central Street shelter, the Failsworth Community Association's community hall campaign and its opposition to the Territorial Army's proposed use of a local quarry for training, the Glodwick Action Group's survey and evidence to the public inquiry, the GAG Family Housing Association scheme, and the West Cumberland Action Committee's local and national transport policy campaigns. All these involved threats to other bodies, as can be seen in Table 3. Most often it was the local authority which was challenged, but other groups threatened included local retailers and tradesmen, tourist interests, and also national bodies such as the Department of Education and Science and the Territorial Army.

Coercive influence strategies

These are those where a group attempts to force a target system to meet a particular need, or indeed to destroy the target system as a means to this end.

As with the service strategies, there seems to be no example in our case studies of the most extreme category of a coercive or confrontative strategy, although there is an example of a confrontative tactic being used by the West Cumberland Action Committee, when it organised its members into boarding buses and then refusing to pay the fares.

Strategy and resources

As was mentioned above, the acquisition and deployment of resources, which encompass help and support of various kinds as well as money and material resources, seem to be integral to a consideration of strategy. Various writers have categorised lists of resources available to pressure groups. A study of five[2] of these suggests various attributes of groups which may be important resources: cohesion/solidarity/commitment (mentioned by all 5 writers); size of group (mentioned by 4); prestige (4); material resources (4); access to or control of media (4); members in influential positions, access to community leaders, influence on councillors, party leaders, others in power structure (3); skills of leadership and political skills (2); ability to rally support from, or control, other organisations (2); technical competence and knowledge (2); control over values (2), pull from electoral votes, right to vote (2). It is worth noting that since these relate to a wide range of pressure groups they do not necessarily include resources of importance to local community groups or to those

TABLE 2 The prime resources used by the 18 action systems

Group	Issue focus of action system	Service or influence	Type of strategy	Prime resources							Successful or unsuccessful
				Material resources	Effective internal organisation	Power base	Public opinion	Access to influentials	Information, knowledge and expertise	Ideology	
SCAG	Social activities	S	Complementary	°P.CDP	°						S
SCAG	HELP cards	S	Complementary	°CDP	°						S
GAG	Information and advice	S	Complementary/alternative	°CDP					°P.CDP		S
SCAG	Welfare rights course	S	Complementary/alternative	°CDP	°				°		S
SCAG	Food and household goods club	S	Alternative	°CDP	°				°		S
Joint Working Party	Setting up of shelter	S/I	Complementary/collaborative	°	°	°		°	°	°	S
SCAG	Small jobs scheme	S/I	Alternative/collaborative	°CDP	°	°		°	°		S
GAG	Issues from public inquiry	I	Collaborative	°CDP				°	°	°P.CDP	S
SCAG	Chiropody issue	I	Collaborative					°			S

TABLE 2 (cont)

Group	Issue focus of action system	Service or influence	Type of strategy	Material resources	Effective internal organisation	Power base	Public opinion	Access to influentials	Information, knowledge and expertise	Ideology	Successful or unsuccessful
				Prime resources							
SCAG	Bus passes	I	Collaborative					○			U
SCAG	Pedestrian issues	I	Collaborative					○			PS
Joint Working Party	Threat to close shelter	I	Campaign	○	○	○	○	○	○	○	S
FCA	Community hall	I	Campaign			○		○	○		U
FCA	Territorial Army's use of quarry	I	Campaign			○		○			PS
GAG	Survey and evidence for public inquiry	I	Campaign	○ CDP		○		○	○ CDP		S
GAG	Family Housing Association scheme	I	Campaign					○	○ P.CDP		S
WCAC	Local issues	I	Campaign	○ CDP		○		○	○ CDP	○	LS
WCAC	National issues	I	Campaign	○ CDP				○	○ CDP		U

PS = partial success   LS = limited success
CDP = resource provided by CDP   P.CDP = resource partially provided by CDP

providing services. For this reason some of these attributes apply to the action systems in our groups and some do not, but in any case it is important to say that we did not start from a pre-determined list such as the one above but began with the case studies and built up the categories of resources used by the groups from the material in them.

In this way seven main categories emerged (which are not listed in order of importance):

1   Material resources: finance, secretarial assistance, transport, etc.
2   Effective internal organisation: that is, membership, decision making ability, group structure, etc., which enable the group to carry through particular courses of action. In general, of course, any group has to have some internal organisation, no matter how rudimentary or haphazard. The term used here, effective internal organisation, is meant to denote something more than this, an example from our case studies being the SCAG food and household goods club, which could not have operated without something more than a minimum degree of planning and preparation by group members.
3   Power base: support from members, potential beneficiaries, or others, which could be used, for example, either to participate in demonstrations of strength (such as petitions or marches) or to lend weight to arguments.
4   Supportive public opinion.
5   Access to appropriate influentials: 'the ability of a group to put its views directly to those responsible for making the decision it wants'.[3]
6   Information, knowledge, or expertise, which might either be available from the members themselves or from outside sources (often, in the case of CDP groups, from the CDP community worker).
7   Ideology: belief systems which sustain and motivate group members, particularly at times when there is opposition or resistance from people or bodies that the group is trying to act upon.

An analysis of the resources used by the 18 action systems is shown in Table 2. (More detail of the resources used by the groups as described in the case studies is given in the Appendix.)

Service strategies and resources

Looking first at the service-only issues and action systems, all used either two or three resources, one of which in all cases was material aid. The next most important resource was effective internal organisation, crucial in four of the five action systems; and the remaining one (the GAG information and advice service) was heavily reliant on the community worker for organisational skill in its early stages, in calling meetings, writing the minutes, and helping the groups with their surveys. However, some caution is needed in drawing any general conclusions about service action systems and the resources required, not only because there are only five examples but because four of them relate to the same group, and therefore what could appear to be prime resources needed for service strategies may merely reflect characteristics of this one group or its method of operation.

The two service/influence action systems also utilised both material resources and effective internal organisation, and in this respect were like the service-only action systems. The chief difference was that both these action systems made use of access to influentials, as one might have expected because of their influence component. The Joint Working Party's scheme to set up the shelter stands out among the service and service/influence issues because it utilised six resources, and in this respect resembles some of the influence-only action systems.

Looking at the seven action systems together there appears to be no great difference in the resources used by those with a complementary and those with an alternative type of strategy, except for a tendency for information, knowledge and expertise to be more used by those action systems with an alternative aspect.

Influence strategies and resources

In considering the influence action systems, the first differences one notices are that effective internal organisation was a resource perceived to be significant in only one case, and material resources were used in only half the cases. The crucial resource in influence action systems, from Table 2, appears to be access to influentials, which was used in all the cases. This indeed is an outcome one might have predicted; influence strategies are directed towards decision makers in order to affect policies or practices, and therefore by their very nature one would anticipate access to such people to be a primary and essential element in these strategies.

The other most often used resources appear in these action systems to be information, knowledge and expertise, used in seven of the eleven cases, and a power base, used in six. Again these are results which might have been anticipated, and the heavy employment of the latter resource contrasts with an almost total lack of its use in the service and service/influence ones, with the exception of the Joint Working Party's initial campaign.

Overall there is a tendency for a more variable number of resources to be employed in fighting influence and service/influence issues, although one can only suggest rather than declare a relationship in view of the small numbers involved.

As can be seen from Table 2, eleven of the fourteen action systems in CDP-supported groups used some resources supplied by CDP[4]. Six action systems used one CDP-provided (or partially provided) resource, and five used two. The most commonly used were material resources (ten instances), and in all other cases information, knowledge and expertise (six instances).

Provisional hypotheses about the relationship between strategies and resources

We are now in a position to put forward some tentative conclusions about strategy and resources in the action systems described here. We present them as hypotheses which we hope will be tested and developed by other research workers analysing similar case study material.

1   Service action systems seem to need and use a fairly narrow range of two or three resources, while the number required by influence action systems varies more widely.

2   Material resources and effective internal organisation seem to be crucial to service-only issues.

3   Service/influence issues also require material resources and effective internal organisation.

4   Looking at the sub-divisions of complementary and alternative service and service/influence action systems, there appear to be no obvious differences in the number or type of resources used, except that access to influentials was used only by the two service/influence systems.

5   Material resources and effective internal organisation

seem to be less crucial in influence than in service and service/influence action systems.

6   An essential resource in influence and service/influence action systems is access to influential people or bodies.

7   Also important, but not necessarily essential, resources for influence and service/influence action systems are a power base, and information, knowledge and expertise. The former does not appear to be an important resource for service issues.

8   Ideology and a power base seem to be important in influence and service/influence issues but not in service-only ones.

9   The main resources supplied by CDPs to CDP-aided groups studied were material resources, and information, knowledge and expertise. These are consistent with the promotional and facilitative requirements of groups already mentioned in the chapter on organisation.

Strategy, resources and success

At this point it seems appropriate to add a further aspect of the issues pursued by the groups, which is whether or not they were successful. A judgment of their success, at least in the short term, has been made from the details given in the case studies, and a brief description of the reason for each decision is given in the list below:

SCAG social activities: successful; activities run.
SCAG HELP cards; successful; scheme set up.
GAG information and advice service: successful; service set up.
SCAG welfare rights course: successful; course run.
SCAG food and household goods club: successful; scheme came into being.
The setting up of the Central Street Shelter: successful; shelter established.
SCAG small jobs scheme: successful; scheme came into operation.
GAG issues from public inquiry: successful; achieved four main requests.
SCAG chiropody issue: successful; service reinstated.
SCAG restrictions on use of bus passes: unsuccessful.

SCAG pedestrian safety: partially successful; more police to be in Market Square.

The threat to close the Central Street Shelter: successful; shelter not closed.

FCA community hall: unsuccessful.

FCA opposition to Territorial Army's proposed use of local quarry: successful in that planning application refused, but not necessarily as a result of the Association's campaign.

GAG survey and evidence to public inquiry: successful; residents' wishes taken into consideration.

GAG Family Housing Association scheme: successful; scheme implemented.

WCAC local issues: limited success in getting sympathetic consideration from Education Department, and more consistent opposition to fare increases from local authorities, but no actual changes.

WCAC national issues: unsuccessful.

It is clear from Table 2 that the service and service/influence action systems were all successful, at least in the short term. Of the eleven influence-only action systems only five can be described as successful, three were unsuccessful, and three had partial or limited successes. Attempts to relate success to resources used in these cases are not very fruitful, though in general the successful action systems used somewhat more resources than those with limited or partial success, and more again than the unsuccessful.

Opposition to issues pursued by the groups

The differences between the success of the influence and service action systems raises an aspect which has not so far been touched on in this chapter, and yet is crucial to any consideration of the success or lack of it by community groups in pursuing their causes: the strength of opposition they encounter. Dearlove says that:

> To assess and adequately explain the influence which interest groups have in the making of public policy, we must not only study the groups doing the talking, 'taking for granted the persons they press upon' . . . but we must also actively study 'who is listening' . . . in order to understand better the basis on which they selectively respond to group demands.[5]

Resources are, of course, only one aspect of strategy, and indeed may in this case be seen as the 'pros' which are pitted against 'cons' such as vested interests, the economic situation, and the tendency towards conservation in a bureaucracy. Ham asks:

> What determines the strength of group pressure? To begin with, there are the resources a group possesses. These indicate an organisation's potential for power. . . . But this only refers to potential for power and, in practice, a group may not utilise all of its resources or it may use them inefficiently. . . . The outcome of any conflict between a pressure group and the decision makers depends on the relative position of the two sides.

He goes on to present in tabular form the likely outcomes of the different combinations of weak, medium and strong pressure groups when they come into conflict with weak, medium and strong government attitudes. His table refers to national pressure groups and central government, but its conclusions are adaptable also to the local as well as the national context.[6]

It is an acknowledged limitation of our research that no attempt has been made to assess the strength of the attitudes and organisations on which the groups had to bear in the issues described in the case studies. This omission arises in the main from the fact that the checklist as we originally devised it did not contain a section on the strength and other attributes of the people or organisations community groups come up against. This is an illustration of the fact that in this study we were at times learning as we went along, and is something which, with hindsight, we would now add into the checklist. However, in the next section some effort is made to look at whether particular campaigns presented threats to other bodies and at the tactics used to overcome these.

Tactics

So far this chapter has been concerned with strategy in relation to resources, or, in terms of the original question: What resources did the campaigners have available to them? We are left then with the questions: How did they use these resources to try to achieve their goals? What were their tactics, the detailed components of their overall strategy?

Again an inductive approach has been taken in our delineation of tactics, the starting point being not a theoretical list of possible

TABLE 3 The threats presented by the action systems

Group	Issue	S or I	Type of Strategy	Threat?	To whom?
SCAG	Social activities	S	Complementary	No	
SCAG	HELP cards	S	Complementary	No	
GAG	Information and advice	S	Complementary/ alternative	Yes	Councillors
SCAG	Welfare rights course	S	Complementary/ alternative	No	
SCAG	Food and household goods club	S	Alternative	Yes	Local traders
Joint Working Party	Setting up of the shelter	S/I	Complementary/ collaborative	Partial	Tourist interests
SCAG	Small jobs scheme	S/I	Alternative/ collaborative	Yes	Local plumbers, joiners, etc.
GAG	Issues from the public inquiry	I	Collaborative	Yes	Local authority
SCAG	Chiropody issue	I	Collaborative	No	
SCAG	Bus passes	I	Collaborative	No	
SCAG	Pedestrian issues	I	Collaborative	No	
Joint Working Party	Threat to close the shelter	I	Campaign	Yes	Residents and thus local authority
FCA	Community hall	I	Campaign	Yes	Local authority
FCA	Territorial Army's use of quarry	I	Campaign	Yes	Territorial Army Volunteer Reserve
GAG	Survey and evidence for public inquiry	I	Campaign	Yes	Local authority
GAG	Family Housing Association scheme	I	Campaign	No,	but opposition from local councillors
WCAC	Local issues	I	Campaign	Yes	Local authority
WCAC	National issues	I	Campaign	Yes	Department of Education and Science

tactics, but the ones which were adopted by the groups described in the case studies.

Tactics involve contact and often contrast with other people and groups, and Table 3 shows the service and influence action systems together with the extent to which their aims presented a threat to any outside group. The case studies gave various examples of the type of action taken by the groups when seeking to influence other bodies, ranging from carrying out surveys to, in the case of the West Cumberland Action Committee, holding rallies and marches and refusing to pay bus fares. In most of the service action systems such tactics were not employed, because the influencing of other people was only an aim in those cases where an action system presented a threat to people outside the group.

Table 4 shows the different tactics used in each influence issue. While it is not possible to plot the tactics in an obvious sequence on a continuum which goes from persuasion to force (nor, for example, by the degree of personal contact between group and target system), nevertheless their positions on such a continuum can be roughly indicated as shown below, and the overlap of categories from collaborative and campaign, through campaign only to coercive tactics can be seen:

Surveys, collection and presentation of
  evidence
Petitions
Lobbying local government officers
Lobbying councillors
Lobbying MPs, Ministers, government
  departments   collaborative
Lobbying others who are decision   or
  makers   campaign
Presenting evidence at a public inquiry
Mass letter-writing
On-site discussion and demonstration
Fighting individual cases
Deputations
Sustained maximum publicity
Rallies   campaign
Marches
Refusal to pay fares   coercive

If one were to attempt to draw any general conclusions about the type of overall strategy the five groups tended towards in their different influence campaigns as shown by the tactics they used, then looking at Table 4 one would suggest that the Senior

TABLE 4 Influence tactics used by the action systems

Group	Issue	Surveys and other evidence	Petitions	Lobbying local govt officers	Lobbying councillors	Lobbying MPs, Ministers, etc.	Lobbying others	Evidence to public inquiry	Mass letter-writing	On-site discussion	Fighting individual cases	Deputations	Sustained maximum publicity	Rallies	Marches	Refusal to pay fares
SCAG	Social activities															
SCAG	HELP cards															
GAG	Information and advice				○											
SCAG	Welfare rights course															
SCAG	Food and household goods club						○									
Joint Working Party	Setting up of the shelter	○														
SCAG	Small jobs scheme			○												
GAG	Issues from the Public Inquiry	○		○	○											
SCAG	Chiropody issue				○	○	○									
SCAG	Bus passes			○	○		○									
SCAG	Pedestrian issues				○	○										
Joint Working Party	Threat to close the shelter			○	○	○			○				○			
FCA	Community hall			○	○	○						○	○			
FCA	Territorial Army's use of quarry			○	○	○				○						
GAG	Survey and evidence for public inquiry	○				○										
GAG	Family Housing Association scheme	○	○		○											
WCAC	Local issues		○	○	○	○					○	○	○	○	○	○
WCAC	National issues		○		○	○								○	○	○

Citizens Action Group and the Glodwick Action Group (at least after its public inquiry campaign) would be at the collaborative end, and the West Cumberland Action Committee at the other, with the Failsworth Community Association and the Joint Working Party in between. It does not appear possible at this stage, at least from the material available from our groups, to define tactics definitively as collaborative, campaign or coercive; nor, therefore, to label their strategies in similar ways. Further studies over a wider range of community groups with more disparate aims might well, however, enable a more reliable continuum to be composed.

Tactics of service issues

Since the tactical approaches already described seem to refer in the main to influence issues, there remains the problem of trying to identify the tactics of service issues. If one returns to the question of how the groups used their resources to try to achieve their goals, then a different typology of tactics can be seen. Table 5 shows how the groups either mobilised their own or used outside resources to achieve their ends.

Attempts were made to relate Table 5 to resources used and the success of the campaigns but they did not prove fruitful, since all the services were successfully set up and in many cases similar resources were used. One could speculate that in general it is easier to predict the success or failure of a proposed service than of a proposed influence campaign, particularly because the former is usually, though not invariably, less likely to arouse opposition.

Possibly, too, a crucial difference is that it is easier to know exactly which resources are needed in service strategies, and plans do not go beyond the discussion stage if an essential resource is lacking. Here one might draw on an example mentioned only incidentally in the case study, but concerning the Glodwick Action Group. At one point one member of the group became keen on the idea of a multi-racial playgroup being set up under the group's auspices. A series of meetings were held at which it was established that there were residents interested in using and running such a playgroup. In addition, it seemed possible that CDP would be prepared to fund the venture, and technical advice was likely to be available from the local pre-school playgroups organiser. However, despite repeated efforts and approaches by the group member and the community worker, no suitable premises which could be made available to

TABLE 5 The tactics of the service action systems

Group	Issue	Provided service for members	Provided service for certain sections of population	Provided service for population generally	Financial help service	Physical help service	Information service	Social activities service
SCAG	Social activities	o						o
SCAG	HELP cards		o			o		
GAG	Information and advice			o			o	
SCAG	Welfare rights	o			o		o	
SCAG	Food and household goods club	o						
Joint Working Party	Setting up of the shelter		o			o		
SCAG	Small jobs scheme		o			o		

the group were found in the area, and so the playgroup never came into being.

Conclusion

This chapter has attempted to explore the nature of the strategies utilised by the various community groups described in the case studies, and by employing various breakdowns and cross-tabulations some hypotheses, particularly relating strategy to resources, have been suggested. These, subject to the caveats about the small number of action systems and even smaller number of groups involved, seem valid for our material, but now need testing out in relation to other case studies. Whether further work could ever produce material which could be used for practical or predictive purposes may be doubtful, but certainly further analytical work would be interesting, particularly if material were to be collected on the lines of our suggested checklist.

There is also much scope for relating this approach to work which analyses the other essential dimension to the whole subject of strategy: the effects of community groups on the bodies whom they seek to influence, of which some interesting studies in the CDP context already exist.[7]

Chapter 11
The role of the community worker

Community workers are not free agents. The very title 'community worker' immediately suggests someone whose actions are accountable to an employer. So long as the services provided through the labour of a community worker are seen as valuable, an employer is likely to maintain him on the staffing list. Once his services cease to be relevant or worthwhile, the community worker is heading for redundancy. The job title also implies that a worker's activity involves him in relationships within or between communities. Whatever 'community' is taken to mean, whether it be a neighbourhood, an estate, or a section of the population defined by commonly held characteristics (for example, the deprived, ethnic groups, or consumers of public services) this determines the scope of a worker's activity and affects the kinds of role he performs. This is simplistic, but it illustrates that community workers are subject to constraints which directly influence their role performance.

Earlier chapters have discussed the significance of key variables in the development of community groups. In this chapter, the community worker is the independent variable. The argument is developed that a worker cannot merely be a channel for the expression of the needs of a 'client' group. Not only is he constrained by his position in an employing organisation, and by relationships which he is likely to have with other resource providing bodies, but his own ideology is also significant. As the Association of Community Workers asserts:

> even when the community worker's stated objective is to realise the ideological objectives of his 'clients', his own ideology and/or that of his agency will obtrude on such things as which group he chooses to work with, how vigorously he supports certain acts, ideas, strategies, and when and why he withdraws his support.[1]

The case studies include three groups – Glodwick Action Group, the Senior Citizens Action Group and West Cumberland Action Committee – which were aided by community workers employed by the CDPs in Oldham and Cumbria. The case studies describe the community workers' role specifically in terms of their association with these groups. We will not be evaluating the operational effectiveness of these particular workers; but, as in previous chapters, will attempt to draw out general guidelines and hypotheses concerning community workers' role performance.

We will start by outlining various perspectives on the practice of community work, and will then suggest a typology of community worker roles. This typology will form the basis of detailed analysis of factors which influence the functioning of workers. This analysis will focus particularly on community groups and their target systems; the managers, sponsors and colleagues of a community worker, and their goals and resources; and the community worker's own personal attributes.

Perspectives on community work

Paid community workers find themselves in a variety of employment situations. They are increasingly employed in both statutory and voluntary organisations; for example, local authority social services and education departments, adult education centres, councils of voluntary service, community arts centres, and occasionally by community groups themselves.

The very variety of employment situations, and hence different client/community populations whom community workers hope their actions will benefit, tends to obscure the key dimensions of community work practice. Community work has gained a reputation for its vagueness. At present, available literature seems to oscillate between two levels: one concerns practical organising methods in the community (for example, how to run a community newspaper or set up a playgroup); the other valiantly attempts to constrain community work within neat classificatory models. Our starting point is the statement of the Association of Community Workers that the role of the community worker is

> to help organisations and groups within the community
> (geographical community or community of interest) to
> identify their own needs and their own interests, and to
> act in consort to influence policy and get resources to
> meet those needs and to develop the confidence and skill
> to achieve their own interests is a way that will lead to
> the improvement and greater fulfilment in life for
> themselves and for other members of their community.[2]

This is a relatively clear and concise summary of the two key elements that relate to the social change ambitions of community work. As an organiser encouraging people to act, the worker aims both to change people's assumptions and expectations of themselves and their social relationships with others, and partly through this re-ordering of relationships, to promote action which improves the social environment. In clarifying different perspectives on the purposes and processes of community work, the work of Perlman and Gurin is valuable. They suggest that there are four major purposes of community work practice:

1 *Strengthening community participation and integration*: The main concerns of this kind of practice are to encourage the expression of views from all groups in the community and to achieve interaction among them, leading toward agreement on how to improve their common environment. Adjustment among groups and organisations and facilitation of co-operative relationships are important objectives. . . .

2 *Enhancing coping capacities*: This can be considered a variation of the first type. The concentration, however, is on improving means of communication and interaction in order to build up the ability of a community (or some segment of it) to cope with its environment and with change. . . .

3 *Improving social conditions and services*: The central goal here is to identify needs and deficiencies and to develop effective provisions and methods for solving or preventing social problems. This includes setting specific goals and mobilising resources to achieve them. . . .

4 *Advancing the interests of disadvantaged groups*: In sharp contrast with the first type, the primary purpose here is to promote the interests of particular groups of increasing their power, their participation in community decision making, and their status.[3]

These approaches to community work are distinct; different values and assumptions are implicit in each. The first approach is concerned that the use of resources should be equally of benefit to the whole community, while the fourth approach asserts that resources should be deployed primarily for the benefit of particular segments within the community. Values thus help to identify the focus and direction of work; they also relate to the actual worth of the change that is being sought. Thus it may be seen as desirable for people to form co-operative relationships, or that people be helped to compete with other groups in terms of power sharing. In one way or another, all approaches emphasise the common value and assumption that people should be encouraged to participate in the making of decisions which affect their lives within the community. Perlman and Gurin's four approaches can also be distinguished in terms of the differing emphasis given by community workers to social relationship and social environment goals. The approaches can be located on a continuum:

Emphasis on			
High . . . . Social Relationships Goals . . . . Low			

Approach 1	Approach 2	Approach 4	Approach 3
Strengthening community participation	Enhancing coping capacities	Advancing interests of disadvantaged groups	Improving social conditions and services

Emphasis on			
Low . . . . Social Environment Goals . . . . High			

A typology of community work roles

With this continuum it is possible to look at the activity of community workers from a broad perspective. Few community workers operate exclusively at one end of the continuum, though different employment situations are likely to lead to one approach being emphasised more than others. The co-ordinator of a council of voluntary service, for example, might be primarily involved in strengthening community participation by supporting the development of voluntary organisations and promoting volunteer schemes. Yet the same worker might also become involved in a campaign to retain a local health clinic threatened with closure, or carry out research and produce a report on the need for more communal meeting premises. Such a range of activities involves the community worker in adopting differing roles, each employing a variety of skills and areas of knowledge, in different settings.

Several writers in the community work field have attempted to categorise such roles.[4] Rothman provides a typical example in his delineation of 'three models of community organisation practice.'[5] He suggests that the community worker engaged in locality development adopts the roles of enabler, catalyst, co-ordinator and educator; in the community planning mode the emphasis is on the roles of expert, fact-finder and analyst, and programme implementer and facilitator; whilst in the social action mode, the worker is described as an organiser and crystalliser of action issues. We have already pointed out some of the limitations of Rothman's schema for our analytical purposes, including its specific worker perspective (which in this chapter is not too much of a difficulty!). A further criticism is that the assignment of discrete roles to different 'models' of community work may well overstate the boundaries of practice and the actual role sets that workers adopt. However, we should note that Rothman was more concerned with outlining the parameters of community organisation practice as a profession than with the analysis of the roles actually performed by workers, which is our prime focus.

We have drawn on the work of Rothman, Barr[6] and Grosser[7] in identifying four broad categories of community work role. Like Rothman we are not arguing for the pre-eminence of any one role over another but see them as sets of associated skills and techniques that can be applied in a variety of situations. Using Grosser's terms, we summarise them as follows:

Enabler: the worker is skilled in the development and promotion of co-operative relationships, aiding people in groups to identify common needs and implement strategies to resolve problems and issues; the worker lays great store on the process of problem solving, including the framework for community involvement; this process becomes the purpose of his association with the group.

Broker: the worker acts as a support for the group and an intermediary when conflict occurs either between individuals within the group or between the group and other organisations, including resource-providing agencies. He may act as an interpreter for both the community group and the resource provider to create clear and understood communications between the parties.

Advocate: the worker acts as a support and representative of the groups' interests in both formal situations (for example, public inquiries) and more informal settings (for instance, acquiring information from local authority officials). He uses his skills to advocate on the group's behalf, and, as with the 'broker', the worker's interests are subservient to those of the group, or indeed of the action system on whose behalf he may be advocating within the whole group.

Activist: the worker is totally committed to the cause or interests of the group participants with whom he shares agreed goals. This distinguishes him from the agitator or manipulator who attempts to achieve goals determined by himself alone at the expense of a group's own interests. His prime concern is to seek redress of grievances, a change in policy, or the establishment of a service as a specific goal: he is less concerned with the process than with concrete results and tends to involve himself directly in a wide variety of tactics, including some which are visibly abrasive (for example, rent strikes and sit-ins). His job is to organise.

From this discussion it is clear that we are not talking about a single community work role but the multiplicity of roles which necessarily form part of community work practice. Community workers, like groups themselves, adopt a range of different strategies in operationalising their role set. On some occasions a worker might act directively, and on others non-directively,[8] he may base his actions on intuitive knowledge and experience, or on rational criteria; at one time the focus might be on the development of group processes (social relationship goals), at another, more explicitly on facilitating task achievement (social environment goals); he might adopt a provocative style or move towards smoothing tensions over and resolving conflict. His justification for involvement might rest on a radical political perspective which views collective action as tackling deficiencies in the 'system', or on a more conservative welfare perspective which expresses a general concern for people and how they can effectively adjust to the ever-prevailing changes in a modern industrial society.[9] It is to the consideration of how community workers act in reality and, particularly, the factors which guide or constrain their role performance that we now turn in our analysis of the work of the three community workers associated with our case study groups.

The groups and their target systems

Our earlier focus on the goals, organisation and the strategy and resources of the case study groups provides a general framework for analysing the enabler, broker, advocate and activist roles of the community workers. In Chapter 9 we outlined the process through which community groups pass in becoming mobilised. The case study groups can be seen as organisational vehicles through which members address problems, formulate goals and carry out a variety of strategies to implement plans. The community worker can help to facilitate these activities and indeed has been described as an agent assisting in the 'problem solving process'.[10]

We now explore the worker's role in respect of the tasks performed in each of the following stages of this problem solving process:

1. Defining the problem(s) to be addressed and the nature of his association with the social change process
2. Aiding the formulation of group goals
3. Supporting or building an organisational structure that is suitable for tackling the problem(s).
4. Aiding the group's selection of strategies and use of resources in implementing plans.
5. Monitoring and helping the group to evaluate the impact of its activities and, in the light of this, to revise plans for future actions.

Such a chronological evolution of worker tasks through stages of the problem solving process rarely occurs in reality. There is considerable blurring and overlap between each of the stages; for example, the GAG worker spent a great deal of time developing the organisational form of the group (from an umbrella group to a single issue CPO Committee) while simultaneously advising on its strategies and tactics.

We analysed each of the three case studies and drew up a list of the workers' tasks.[11] We now summarise these under each of the five stages.

Defining the problem(s)

Most neighbourhood-based community workers spend some time in initial contact-making in their patch and in carrying out an assessment of needs and resources. This involves both the building of relationships and the undertaking of analytical tasks. In more detail, we can see from our case studies that the following tasks were performed: completion of a community profile; clarifying areas and groups in greatest need; interpreting agency objectives in relation to proposed involvement with groups; monitoring policies of the local authority and/or relevant local enterprises; finding ways through local government procedure; making contacts with residents; and clarifying values in relation to the likely roles.

The GAG and SCAG community workers carried out these tasks both in terms of their brief from the CDP and in relation to the goal of facilitating group action. Thus the collection of information about the Glodwick area and about the needs of the elderly in Cleator Moor was performed in the context of general CDP objectives. As such the information was utilised in designing research programmes, in setting up demonstration projects such as an Information and Action Centre, as well as in providing a backcloth against which the workers could gear their actions with neighbourhood groups. Both the GAG and SCAG community workers also expended considerable effort in stimulating a collective awareness of common problems. In Glodwick this was necessary because of the pervasive conflict between different ethnic groups which inhibited community co-operation. Only when it was suggested that group action could be an effective means of achieving individual goals was such action possible. The work was also being undertaken in a neighbourhood where community organising had not been the norm (though some compensation for this was provided by the resident who was aware of the successes of community groups' action around similar issues in other parts of the country). The SCAG study suggests that in West Cumbria there were also certain community factors that inhibited group action. First, there were institutionalised conflicts between religious minorities; second, local decision makers (councillors) tended to be well known locally, and this deterred group members from adopting campaign strategies in respect of the chiropody and pedestrian safety issues.

It is clear, therefore, that the GAG and SCAG community workers carried out tasks appropriate to the facilitation of collective action. Indeed they verged on the performance of a direct activist role. Haggstromm[12] has described the community worker at the inception of a neighbourhood group as an agitator, adopting skills and resources to foster awareness and motivate people to take collective action. The SCAG and GAG workers followed this pattern.

By contrast, the WCAC worker was less active in carrying out a community profile and in contacting local individuals. Her actions were a direct result of the request for support from the already established Cleator Moor Bus Fares Group; thus her role was not thought through in advance but immediately assumed that of an enabler, helping the group to consider both organisational and strategic choices.

Goal formulation

Goals and goal definition at the embryo stage of group development were as important for the workers as for the groups themselves. Even though the SCAG and GAG workers were the initiators of group action, it was vital that the groups should be helped to formulate goals which would provide a rationale for the decision to act collectively. For example, the GAG worker was unwilling to do more than reinterpret the aims and objectives of the group once it was accepted both that the local authority should take the wishes of residents into account and that the group should strive for the physical improvement of the area.

All three community workers adopted enabling roles in goal formulation both at the groups' inception and throughout the period of their activities covered in the case studies. The WCAC worker, for example, was instrumental in helping each of the local bus fares action groups to accommodate their local transport concerns within the broad objective of opposing any fare increases or extensions in bus pass mileage limits for children travelling to school.

Finally, we should note that the availability of resources to the workers (by virtue of their attachment to CDP) was an influence in determining goals. The SCAG case study notes the reluctance of the group to identify targets outside the immediate vicinity and members' preference for attempting local solutions. Resources from CDP (finance and expertise) facilitated the persistence of this tendency to define goals at a parochial level. Both the SCAG and GAG workers acted as brokers between CDP and their respective groups.

Creation of organisational structures

From the case studies we can identify the following tasks performed by the three workers: helping the groups to develop structures on the basis of different action systems; helping members to make use of their own skills and resources; supporting members in their roles; helping to resolve internal conflict; encouraging the recruitment of new members; facilitating links between the groups and other organisations; helping the groups to develop relationships with their beneficiaries.

The SCAG worker, having been instrumental in the group's formation, attempted to help group members to consider the value of a secure organisational base. He was not involved in actually recruiting new members for the group. He acted as a continuing support and, after the initial meetings, resisted adopting any official role within the group.

One of the GAG worker's stated achievements was to 'hold the group together'; unlike the SCAG worker, he adopted a broker role and advocated that the Environment Committee should hold its meetings with the CPO Committee; he hoped this would act as a model for the way meetings could be run. In particular he hoped that the Environment Committee meetings would become less like grumble sessions, and that the business-like approach of the CPO Committee would rub off on them.

The federated structure of WCAC was clearly a result of geographic factors and an attempt to galvanise a West Cumbrian based strategy. Whilst local differences in respect of objectives were subsumed under all-embracing goals, this did not relieve organisational tensions within the group. Consequently, the worker was led to adopt the official secretarial role for most of WCAC's life. She became an activist within the organisation as a means to mediate conflict within the group. This meant that a proportion of her time was spent arranging the meetings of the group (carried out by group members in SCAG and GAG) and hiring minibuses to take members to the venues. In addition she played an important role in giving socio-emotional support to those women unused to participating in community affairs. She also helped to forge links with other organisations, while the GAG and SCAG workers merely encouraged their groups to consider this possibility.

Implementation of strategies

Worker tasks associated with strategic implementation included: locating resources for use by the group; providing, and advising on the use of, technical information; assistance in executing tactics, including letter-writing, organising public meetings and representing groups' interests.

Both the GAG and WCAC workers performed these tasks with greater frequency than the SCAG worker. The SCAG worker was particularly loath to help the group in implementing its tactics, to represent or speak on behalf of the group, or to act as a professional support in members' dealing with decision makers. The worker's involvement with carrying out tactics was most significant in the early days of the group's existence. The worker helped to obtain information and advice on the best means of establishing the odd jobs scheme and of pursuing the pedestrian crossing issue. Gradually, as the group developed, the worker adopted a more contentious stance as 'just another contributor', throwing in ideas which were not credited with 'any automatic halo of expertise'.

The GAG worker, while engaging directly in debates about tactics, offered a primarily advisory role; for example, on how the group should present evidence to the public inquiry, and which council committees to contact. He did, however, advocate that the group should have direct access to decision makers and made it clear that he was not prepared to act as a broker between members of target bodies and the group. The WCAC worker maintained her activist role throughout, and was involved in directly representing the group's interests. As a matter of contingency, because members were not able to give up time at work, the worker attended meetings in Carlisle on their behalf.

The interaction between workers and groups in enacting strategies and tactics is particularly important because it is at this point in the problem solving process that aspirations for some desirable social change have to be translated into concrete goals and action to achieve them. In each of the groups, members possessed varying degrees of organisational expertise. The SCAG members had experience of self-help activities but were less conversant with conducting influence strategies. WCAC and GAG members similarly lacked technical information and knowledge about central and local government responsibilities and the political skills and knowhow to set about obtaining redress of grievances. It has also been noted that service and influence strategies tend to require different types of resource. The GAG and SCAG action systems which engaged in service strategies employed more material resources and needed an effective internal organisation. The CDP was able to supplement the former through, for example, small grants and the provision of premises; the latter the groups managed to sustain themselves. For influence strategies, practical aid such as the production of leaflets and campaign sheets was also provided by the CDP, but access to influentials (regarded as a key resource) had to be acquired through careful negotiation, bargaining and lobbying; and that meant that some GAG and SCAG members had to acquire certain political skills.

The WCAC worker on the other hand quite frequently performed this role on behalf of the group, apparently caught in the dilemma highlighted by Dearlove that:

> There is invariably a tension between getting things done and involving the poor. The middle-class activist may seek to assume a non-directive approach but he rapidly moves to assume a more positive and dominant role.[13]

In the WCAC case, tension particularly existed between both the group's and worker's respective diagnoses and plans of action and their preferred means of implementing strategies within the limited time and resources available.

Evaluating impact and monitoring process

It is clear that each of the workers recorded the development of the groups and used their records to consider both the overall direction of the group and their interaction with it. The meetings and debates on selection of strategies in respect of goals and organisational resources illustrated the workers' concern to help the groups constantly to evaluate their programme of activities. In addition, the GAG worker was supported by a research worker who sat in and observed group meetings; and, through the use of CDP resources, a small evaluative study was carried out on the work of SCAG and fed back to its members. The WCAC worker did not have the advantage of supplementary research and monitoring resources.

Summary
In summary, the following points can be made about the workers' role performance in relation to the groups and their target systems:

1 Each of the workers at one time or another assumed the roles of enabler, broker, advocate and activist. Enabler and broker roles tended to be more concerned with the internal organisational development of the groups, whilst advocate and activist roles were more related to the achievement of concrete tasks. The more the worker adopted an activist role, the less differentiation and distance there was between the worker's, and group members', operational involvement.

2 The workers focussed on both process/social relationship goals and task/social environment goals at all stages of the groups' development.

3 Both the SCAG and GAG workers adopted an advocate/activist role to help to stimulate group formation. The SCAG worker subsequently assumed an enabler role related to both process and task goals of group action. The GAG worker tended to act as both enabler and broker in the group development process but only as an advocate in ensuring that the group had a direct dialogue with decision makers.

4 The WCAC worker was initially required to act as an enabler but, in response to internal organisational conflict and the technical and political complexities of the bus pass issue, quickly assumed the roles of advocate and activist. It should be noted that this worker was not involved in the formative stages of the group, and it is probable that the members actually cast her in the role of 'expert' following their request for organisational help; her long-term role became one of group convenor and advocate to outside bodies.

5 This leads us to suggest that community workers who become involved with a group through its own expression of the need for aid may be more likely to adopt an activist role than those who are instrumental in a group's formation.

6 The community workers' resources and expertise seemed to be complementary to those possessed by group members. Each of the workers was more active in supporting, and making available resources to, action systems adopting influence strategies than those involved in service strategies; groups generally included members who had some previous experience of self-help organisations.

7 All three workers helped the groups to overcome internal conflict, through common definition of goals, relieving inter-personal tensions, and structuring internal organisations; only in the case of the WCAC worker was this achieved by adopting an official role within the group.

Agency goals and resources

The significance of the organisational context in which a worker operates has frequently been noted as a key source of influence on his actions.[14] Thomas and Warburton, for example, assert that

> The practice of community work is shaped by the nature of the organisation in which they (community workers) are employed – its goals, constitution, operating procedures, structure and its relationship with its consumers and other services . . . it is the task of the community worker to face up to the organisational constraints and to change them in order to promote more effective community work practice and/or improve the delivery of agency services to the community.[15]

Whether or not the three community workers in this study were bent on manipulating the structure of CDP to suit their practice is not a subject for debate here (though as all three workers were involved in staff management and policy discussions within CDP, no doubt at times they played a part in affecting this organisational environment). We are concerned to identify and ascertain the impact of the CDP on the workers' relationships with the groups and their adoption of enabler, broker, advocate and activist roles. The particular characteristics of CDP which we explore are: management structure; finance and resources; the duration of the projects; the locality base of CDP teams; and their policy and ideology.

Management structure

CDPs were set up by the Home Office in small localities as part of the Urban Programme to identify the causes of deprivation and to establish programmes supported by citizen involvement to meet the needs of local populations. The partnership between local and central government in the setting up and joint financing of the twelve local projects is significant in the management structures adopted. Both the Oldham and Cumbria CDP action teams were located in their respective local authority management structures. As an aid to communication between CDP and the local authority departments, it was decided that

> The Project Director's grading will preferably be such as will facilitate contact with the local authority's senior officials and that its (the project's) activities should be the responsibility of a special project management committee of the council, drawn from the chairmen or senior members of the council's main functional committees.[16]

In contrast to other local authority departments, the projects were set up on a decentralised basis, and there was intended to be easy access within and between other departments. The accountability of the teams was broadened because the research teams (of which the SCAG worker was a member) were, in our cases, both appointed by York University. The University, in theory, could have sent a representative to the projects' management committee meetings; in practice this was rarely taken up, but the local research workers did use the committees for the submission of reports. In both projects the action and research workers shared the same offices, and, notably in Cumbria, shared both action and research roles.

In practice the teams had a great deal of autonomy. Over the first two years of its operation, Cumbria CDP's management committee meetings were little more than rubber stamping operations for team reports and requests for finance. The pattern was similar in Oldham. In addition, the distance of both projects from York University and the infrequency of meetings with University staff meant that most of the action research programmes were planned and prepared, as well as executed, by the project staff.

Action and research teams enjoyed a considerable degree of

autonomy in determining the application of their brief; the case studies' account of Cumbria's and Oldham's initiatives with residents' groups suggest few, if any, directives from the projects' management committees and sponsors. The projects were not constrained from adopting either enabling or activist roles.[17] Project strategy and policy therefore originated from intra-team discussion. Team members' ideas, views and values were the most important constraint on the community workers.

Finance and resources

In community work terms, CDPs were characterised by the possession of generous financial and other resources. Cumbria CDP, for example, had a social action budget of approximately £40,000 per year, which was used to pay the salaries of special appointments (for example, to the Community Information and Action Centre where the WCAC worker was officially based) and to fund projects like adventure playgrounds and a housing association. In addition, the CDP possessed secretarial services, reprographic facilities, and research skills, all of which were taken up by the groups in our case studies. Indeed, for SCAG, the specific relevance of the small pump-priming grants to their activities led them to apply successfully for grants on a number of occasions. As a result of the availability of such resources and the group's direct association with a CDP worker, there was a tendency to call repeatedly on the services of this 'alternative bureaucracy' rather than press for resources from other agencies (though this also reflected the very real problems associated with raising cash and seeking grants from other sources).[18] Workers were clearly acting as brokers between their groups and their agencies' own resource allocation systems.

The duration of the CDPs

CDPs were set up for a period of five years in the first instance; and in practice no project continued in the same organisational form for longer. This time-span appears to have influenced the workers in their desire to become rapidly associated with community issues and local groups. The involvement with the CPO issue in Oldham and with the bus fares protest marches in Cleator Moor can be seen to have stemmed at least in part from the desire to give the projects an obvious presence. Both CDPs quickly produced publicity leaflets on arriving in their areas indicating the range of resources and services they felt able to offer. In particular, the Oldham CDP's publicity brochure emphasised the concern of staff to achieve changes rapidly: 'Time is not on our side – your problems are the problems of today' rang out the message. When a community worker's time is limited there is the 'temptation of wanting to achieve fairly tangible results in a short time; . . . the amount of time, care and attention given to organisational skill development (within community groups) . . . may be neglected'.[19] But, as all three of our study groups were formed during the early, rather than the later, years of the projects, time as an employment-related constraint does not appear to have promoted an activist and task-related approach as distinct from the process orientation implicit within the enabler role. Nevertheless, the initial launching of both CDPs in itself appears to have been a recipe for rapid involvement with grass-roots groups.

Locality

To say that workers became involved with groups in the locality in which the projects were based seems to be stating the obvious. But the West Cumberland Action Committee is an unusual example because the two protest groups which originated in Cleator Moor and Frizington became but part of a geographically federated organisation that stretched beyond the project area. However, the case study does indicate that the worker gave a higher degree of support to the locally based groups than to the others, for primarily geographical reasons. Face-to-face contact was reciprocated more frequently between the worker and these groups, whereas she contacted the others by telephone. The local groups also had greater accessibility to the project's resources, so that, for instance, it was easier for them to get to the West Cumberland Action Committee monthly meetings held in the CDP offices than it was for the Workington group who were dependent upon their own or pre-arranged transport.[20]

Many community workers find it essential to establish a base from which to work in the neighbourhoods or estates where they are active, so that residents can have easy access to them. The siting of the CDP offices, and the consequently greater personal contact that this promoted with the Cleator Moor protest group, is probably a significant factor in the prominence of that particular group during the first months of the West Cumberland Action Committee's life.

Ideology and policy orientation

How the projects, from a base of relative independence and in command of certain key resources, addressed themselves to the problems of their area, resulted almost entirely from staff members' internal clarification of policies and strategy formulation. Policies can be defined as sets of ideas (values and commitments) and rationales that agency uses to inform the way in which it offers services, resources and worker skills to its clients and consumers.

Values and commitment to citizen involvement: Both Oldham and Cumbria CDPs had a clear commitment to working with local grass-roots groups as part of their project strategies. In the Forward Plan, Oldham CDP stated: 'citizen involvement was seen as a central tool; . . . work with local resident and tenant groups has led to the establishment of eight groups with whom we work closely'.[21] Similarly, Cumbria CDP emphasised project members' concern 'to support local people in an increased involvement with community affairs and the local political process . . . to support local grass-roots groups in articulating needs, views and aspirations and in making demands on the general systems of resource allocation'.[22] These statements embodied the teams' interpretations of the Home Office's brief to CDPs to develop citizen involvement in community affairs.

Addressing problems: The rationale on which the projects formulated their strategies is significant in terms of the ways in which they became involved with, and actively supported, local groups. When the national CDP programme was set up, the problems of the local project areas were largely assumed to arise from local causes. Many of the difficulties experienced within these areas were attributed to the characteristics of the inhabitants themselves. Indeed, the indices for determining which local authorities might participate included areas' crime rates, numbers of children taken into care, unemployment rates and the percentage of dependants within the population. Less emphasis was placed on the level of services and facilities, including employment opportunities, actually available. It was felt that through encouragement of self-help within the community, together with improved co-ordination of existing local and central government services, many of the problems could be overcome. Within this perspective field-based community workers of the action teams might have been expected to adopt the neutral, apolitical roles of enabler and broker in their association with community groups.

By the time that the Oldham and Cumbria CDPs were established, these ideas had become seriously challenged by the findings of the projects which had been set up earlier. The causes of deprivation were coming to be seen as having much more to do with the economic, social and political structures of society than with intrinsically local factors. Structural conditions, it was argued, were more significant than pathological characteristics in causing area deprivation. Tackling social problems through a

strategy based on consensus, reasoned debate and a general
airing of opinions about local needs was not seen as productive
if fundamental changes were desired:

> At the local level this is likely to imply working more
> directly within local political processes rather than (CDP)
> simply being part of the bureaucratic apparatus. . . .
> Within this kind of analysis, action may take the
> following forms:
> (a) trying to service interest groups of the 'worst off'
> sections of the working class . . . with information,
> analysis and hard skills in order to develop greater
> consciousness of the nature and sources of inequality and
> to encourage collective struggle against oppression;
> (b) trying to develop connections and alliances between
> the Project, 'worst off' groups and the organised sections
> of the Labour movement . . . on issues of inequality and
> their eradication;
> (c) trying to use whatever opportunities the CDP
> framework provides to lodge propositions about the
> needs of people living in disadvantaged areas and to
> contribute to wider movements of political debate and
> action demanding:
> (1)   major increases and redistribution in public and
>   private investment, and
> (2)   increased levels of and new forms of control over
>   such investment.[23]

In working with community groups, the adoption of the roles of
advocacy and activism became seen as increasingly relevant
within such wide-ranging conflict strategies.

Getting started: Both the Oldham and Cumbria CDP teams
were aware of the shift in perspective that had been brought
about through the work of some of the other CDPs. Their initial
task, as we have seen, was to interpret the broad brief from the
Home Office; and for both projects this meant the need to begin
to identify the problems of their respective areas. Both Oldham
and Cumbria workers began by carrying out a community
profile.

In Oldham, the two field-based community workers split the
project area into two and began gathering information and making contacts. The area was found to contain problems which
were similar to those of Oldham as a whole, but noticeably more
acute. Furthermore, in each profile area there were neighbourhoods in which problems clustered. Glodwick was distinctive
both because of the prevalence of old and deteriorating houses,

reflecting one of the worst physical environments in Oldham, and because of the racial heterogeneity of the population, reflecting the presence of a significant Asian community. In the other fieldworker's patch Abbeyhills stood out as probably the most stigmatised council estate in Oldham. Of specific interest is the fact that having made some initial contacts and collected background information in these two areas, both workers subsequently became extensively involved in them. Glodwick was identified as a priority area for community-orientated intervention on the basis of the worker's initial profile and the impending CPO inquiry. These provided both a justification for the presence of CDP and opportunities for the project team to demonstrate the kinds of contribution it could make.

In Cumbria an initial profile of the two parishes had been published by the Project Director and his assistant before the two workers concerned with our case study groups were appointed. As in Oldham, the project area was assessed as having 'the same essential problems . . . shared with the whole coastal belt'[24] but in many ways more extreme.[25] The report described the problems and issues pertaining to the two parishes, and outlined a strategy of intervention.[26] A series of action-research programmes were proposed, concerned with housing, employment, the needs of young people and the elderly, and the lack of readily available information services and practical resources. This can clearly be seen to have had an impact on the way in which the community workers became involved; for example, the work with SCAG was seen as part of the project's work with the elderly.

Principles and practice in community work: So far we have examined the CDPs' policy orientations in terms of general assumptions about causes of deprivation and methods of identifying the needs and resources of areas. We now turn to the project teams' specific concerns in working with community groups.

In Oldham, the CDP director's interpretation of the Home Office brief placed particular emphasis on breakdown in communication between service providers and local communities. He was keen to facilitate the development of community based forums, groups and committees so that gradually 'a representative network or umbrella body can be built up. This would have pre-decision consultative status, would have the support of elected representatives and would be serviced by local authority officials or backed by the local authority'.[27]

An Area Councillors' Committee was established by CDP in Glodwick as part of the implementation of this policy. This was of interest because it revealed a difference in the perspectives of the director and community worker on the role which the worker should perform. The director wanted the community worker to adopt the broker role, acting as a thermometer of local views and feeding these to council representatives. The community worker, by contrast, believed that groups like GAG should have direct participative involvement in the committees and themselves speak on behalf of local people. The latter position presupposed the existence and some operational capacity of such groups; and it is worth noting that the development of GAG preoccupied the worker for the first eighteen months of his involvement with the project.

For the most part, Cumbria CDP's association with community groups was geared towards an issue rather than a neighbourhood focus. The workers intervened with local groups during the course of current action-research programmes and as a consequence of the operations of the two affiliated agencies, the Community Information and Action Centre and the Community Resource Centre.[28] Partly because the workers were all at some time involved with the action-research programmes, their initiatives were not unrelated. The project team set out to maintain an inter-relationship between 'top down' strategies (for example, analysing data, conducting surveys and policy analysis) and 'bottom up' strategies which, through work with local groups, promoted the articulation of residents' needs and aspirations. The worker associated with SCAG provides a good example of the integration of a 'bottom up' approach (facilitating group development) with a 'top down' survey into the social and economic life situations of pensioners.

The WCAC initiative also reflected the project's concern to relate diagnoses of the structural context of deprivation with the political mobilisation of residents. Because the school bus issue and related transport problems were as much a concern to people in the whole of West Cumbria and not just particular to Cleator Moor and Frizington, it made sense to support the West Cumbrian-based pressure campaign. Transport difficulties were validly seen in such a geographical context and, as a result of the lack of local authority and government finances to subsidise school bus routes, serious financial and access problems occurred for people living in rural areas. By being associated with the campaign the project was seeking solutions in a practical way to a local problem whose solution was ultimately dependent on structural rearrangements in the way that resources were allocated, in this instance to benefit users of public transport services. The project team's acceptance of the WCAC community

worker's activist role in part reflected an openness to a variety
of intervention approaches. But the role was also consistent with
the team's general structuralist perspectives and commitment to
the use of conflict tactics when these were considered
appropriate.

Summary
From our discussion of the CDPs' management structure, finance
and resources, duration, locality base and policy and ideology
the following points can be drawn out to summarise the agencies'
influence on the community worker's role and orientations:

1 The decentralised and remote sponsorship and
   management structures, and the broad Home Office
   brief, allowed project team members considerable
   independence in determining interventions applicable
   to the local setting. They were not restricted by their
   managers from adopting either enabler, broker,
   advocate or activist roles.

2 Because CDPs possessed a range of resources,
   community groups were, through their association
   with community workers, encouraged to make
   substantial use of them.

3 The limited duration of the projects stimulated
   workers to become involved in communities as soon
   as possible after their establishment. There is no
   evidence from our case studies that this encouraged
   workers to be more concerned with effecting changes
   in the social environment than in developing the
   organisational capacity of the groups.

4 The degree of worker support given to local groups
   related to their location within the project area; the
   more proximate and accessible groups received
   greater worker support.

5 Both projects' interpretation of the Home Office's
   brief led to a strong commitment to and an early
   association with the activities of community groups.

6 In Oldham the maintenance of the worker's presence
   in Glodwick stemmed from the urgency of the CPO
   issue as well as from a desire to build on the contacts
   which had already been established while carrying out
   the project area profile.

7 In Cumbria the workers' association with particular
   community groups stemmed from the way that the
   project was internally organised. Work with SCAG,

for example, was an integral aspect of the project's strategy in identifying and helping to meet the needs of the elderly. It also reflected Cumbria CDP team members' tendency to take on a mixture of roles associated with both the provision and development of services and direct work with community groups; in Oldham, by contrast, the team predominantly emphasised community work tasks.

8 In Oldham CDP there was a specific concern to facilitate the creation and maintenance of community problem solving structures (especially community groups) as a means of overcoming some of the difficulties in communicating the needs and wishes of residents. In Cumbria CDP there was an additional preparedness to identify with the interests of disadvantaged groups and adopt advocate and activist roles.

9 Both of the CDPs' workers were required to perform multiple roles, the Cumbria workers in terms of their other project commitments (for example, research and CIAC duties) and the Oldham workers in terms of different levels of activity within and between community structures.

10 The evidence of these two projects provides reinforcement for Rothman's conclusion

that a decentralised 'team' structure encouraged a broader role orientation . . . (and) that decentralised staffs brought into closer contact with community forces were to a greater degree confronting a non-uniform task environment; hence they were led to employ a greater range of roles in a more flexible way.[29]

Personal attributes of the workers

In order to understand the context of CDP work with community groups we have had to go beyond the case study material and examine the projects' features which guided the workers' interventions. This will also be necessary in this section. The workers' association with community groups was as much part of the attempt to fulfil the aims of the CDP as it was to achieve the objectives of the groups. The notion of citizen involvement put forward by the Home Office was picked up by the project teams in determining that work with community groups should form an important part of their overall strategies. Just as the projects were interpreters and executors of the Home Office brief, so too were individual team members of the projects' strategies. And yet,

> The community worker does not appear in a community out of a vacuum . . . he arrives there with both pre-conceptions and, as a rule, past experience of similar work. Though he will try to approach the problems of a new community in a neutral spirit . . . he cannot help but have a set of conceptual expectations, theoretical and practical, which affect his work.[30]

These expectations also affect the way that community workers develop and sustain their relationships with community groups. Rothman has suggested that three basic outlooks help to define those relationships. In his formulation,

> A professional orientation implies a high concern with professional values and standards, a bureaucratic orientation refers to a preoccupation with the policies and norms of the employing agency, and a client orientation connotes a primary attention to the needs of those served by the agency. Another way of stating this is in terms of expectancies; the focal reference groups conveying expectations regarding the character of job performance (hence 'accountability') may be professional peers, agency super-ordinates, or client populations.[31]

While not wishing to stereotype and force our three community workers into the straitjacket of these categories, they do provide a simple means of typifying worker relationships (and their jus-tification) with community groups. Clearly, all of our workers were highly committed to the specific groups with which they became associated. The WCAC worker 'identified completely with the aims and objectives' of the committee, the SCAG worker 'tried to remain fairly "non-directive" in approach while identifying with the group's general aims', and the GAG worker evidenced his commitment by the fortitude and staying power which his presence gave to the group. Their other responsibilities within the projects make it clear that this client orientation was coupled with a professional orientation in the case of the SCAG worker (through his research interests and inclination) and with a bureaucratic orientation on the part of the GAG worker, in that community group work was seen as the principal element of Oldham CDP's strategy. The WCAC worker, through her activist role, remained primarily client-orientated in her relationship with the group.

We now examine why each individual worker became involved with these groups. The workers' motivations, values, personal goals and ideologies, their previous working experience (and training) and their staffing position will be considered in relation to their orientation and selection of roles.

West Cumberland Action Committee

The worker's association with this group stemmed from her job brief and a commitment to the idea of CDP acting as a resource to the community. 'The Cleator Moor Bus Fares Protest Group, and subsequently the WCAC, were seen as the sort of groups that the resource centre should service.' At that time the project had not initiated any action-research programmes in the transport field and felt able to offer only organisational support in campaign planning and arranging meetings; initially the worker provided an 'extra pair of hands' to these ends. Later, however, one of the main functions which the worker performed was 'servicing the group with technical information', and she came to assume a more central position in the group than originally conceived by the project team. She gradually became the main co-ordinator of the group, passing information, letting the federated groups know what the others were doing, and arranging transport to meetings.

The worker's initial involvement with the group appears to have been based more on intuitive than rational criteria. She was one of the few local people employed as a member of the team and her job was particularly concerned with enquiries relating to personal problems. Brager has noted that 'the likeness of the indigenous worker to clients may facilitate rapport with them and encourage them to use the agency's programme whether it provides individual services or community action'; that such workers are 'less interested in or sensitive to the maintenance requirements of the agency that employs them', and that they tend to offer more active direction and assistance than 'professional workers', to share a 'we' identification with their clients, and draw on their own experience of dealing with similar problems.[32]

These remarks help to explain the worker's advocative and activist roles with WCAC. One implication is that the activist role need not be linked to politically held goals so much as to the close personal identification which indigenous workers are likely to share with their clients. Further, the implications of supporting the group in the execution of tactics may not have been clearly thought out, particularly in relation to possible repercussions on the agency. That such involvement was endorsed by her colleagues reflected their view that this was relevant to the particular issue. Different ideological positions may, therefore, be held within a team; and the justification for a particular strategy may be on both pragmatic (WCAC worker) and more rational (the team) grounds. In addition, the intense level of operation of this worker in her casework function was replicated in her work with the WCAC; for example, by giving socio-emotional support to the less confident members within the group. In effect, a limited role set was applied in each of the contrasting working situations.

Senior Citizens Action Group

The CDP worker who directly facilitated the formation of SCAG was a member of the research team. A background in social work teaching and research prior to joining the project meant that he brought certain analytical qualities to bear and approached community work with a mental framework which clearly linked goals with a variety of strategies. Indeed, one of his reasons for working with SCAG was that CDP's and his own research interests included the examination of factors influencing pensioners' 'predisposition to engage in collective action'.

The case study clearly spells out the worker's own ideological perspectives and reasons for devoting his energy to SCAG. Briefly, the worker identified the elderly as one population group experiencing cumulative disadvantage through their restricted ability to influence resource allocation in their favour. His involvement with SCAG was also justified because other groups of pensioners already enjoyed support from the CDP; because SCAG was ready to 'get on and do something'; and because it was newly formed and had no previous experience of community action which would determine the approach taken.

Face-to-face work with SCAG was therefore justified for the worker by the combination of a desire to seek redress of disadvantage for pensioners and a commitment to an experimental participative research programme to monitor constraints on their activities. The latter interest in part explains the worker's preference for an enabler role; this would not 'unduly influence the direction that the group took'. The worker was certainly concerned that the group should establish itself as an organisation; but he was less prepared than the WCAC worker to be actively involved in helping the group to tackle issues, make decisions and execute strategies. This relatively non-directive stance enabled the project team to develop an understanding of the group's tactical preferences and the reasons behind them.

Glodwick Action Group

Through his informal contacts and profile work in the Glodwick area the GAG worker identified three major issues confronting the neighbourhood: housing and redevelopment, general environmental problems, and lack of information and advice. He also became aware of some degree of racial disharmony and the existence of mutual suspicion between ethnic groups. Yet it was because a public inquiry on a compulsory purchase order in the area was due to be held within four months of his starting work in Glodwick (and because this affected and was likely to unite members of different ethnic groups) that the CPO issue was selected as the basis for resident organisation. Other aspects of the project's work were initially given a low priority because of the need to generate a rapid response to the imminent compulsory purchase order. Having had previous experience as a neighbourhood worker (and attended a full-time higher education course on community work), he was well aware of the likely disruption to people's lives if a wholesale clearance programme went ahead. While one aspect of his motivation was to get CDP known locally, he particularly felt that, through organising collective action in the area, the residents' interests would be articulated at the public inquiry. They would also acquire information about the technicalities and implications (for example, for compensation) of the compulsory purchase order, gain some experience of organising, and learn how to make use of bureaucratic procedures for the redress of grievances. The starting point for the GAG worker was to link his diagnosis of local problems with strategies by which to seek their solution. This led him to advocate strongly to local residents the potential of collective action as a way forward. That his diagnosis was correct is borne out by the large numbers of people who attended the public meetings.

The worker's emphasis was on an organisation building. After initially taking a directive approach to get residents involved in community action he advocated that GAG should gain access to established decision making circles and the Area Councillors' Committees. Within the group itself, while offering a considerable degree of technical advice (for example, on how to carry out a survey and prepare a report for the inquiry), he preferred to adopt an enabling role congruent with his belief that the group's decision making should be self-determined. There was an interplay between roles, the one complementing the other; once community involvement had been created and community participation in decision making established, the problems for the worker became concerned with process and social relation- ships. But to say that the worker at this stage was concerned solely with process or primarily with the individual growth of members within the group and their ability to achieve consensus (through his intra-group mediating role) would be an overstate- ment. Clearly, by helping to define issues and possible solutions the worker was drawing on his own ideological perspectives that groups without the power to express their wishes and demands are likely to suffer in the face of local policies which threaten fundamental upheavals in their lives. The GAG community worker saw his job as supplementing the resources of the area's residents so that their demands could be expressed and their interests advanced.[33]

Summary
Despite what has been said about the values, ideology and staff- ing position of the workers, their strong commitment to the groups should be re-emphasised. This is important because it is often said that community workers experience tension between what they actually do and what they would like to achieve.[34] For pragmatic, intuitive or rational reasons the community workers in our case studies subsumed their own private ambitions to the realistic gains which could be made by the three groups; and this in itself substantially influenced the roles which they adopted.

In summary, we can make the following points:

1   The degree of rationality or intuition that influences a worker's choice of roles depends significantly on his previous experience and training and the skills which he possesses. Untrained indigenous workers are likely to act more intuitively, while those with training and experience are more likely to adopt a rational orientation involving diagnosis of issues and selection of strategies related to explicitly determined goals.

2   The range of roles used in working with community groups appears to be closely related to the degree of specialism that workers have in an agency. The more specific their agency functions (in our examples, research and casework), the more limited will be the roles they perform. In contrast, the worker who maintains a loosely defined or generalist role within the agency is more likely to be able to adapt and vary his role in accordance with his values and ideological position.

3 Varying degrees of assertiveness are apparent between
   our three workers. Such variability seems to be
   associated with the extent of their personal
   identification with the life situations of clients and the
   degree of their ideological commitment to the goals of
   the group. Workers seem more likely to be assertive
   in their role when they have a strong personal or
   ideological commitment to the group's goals. Varying
   degrees of directiveness also seem to be related to the
   stage of a group's development and the nature of its
   structure; workers appear more likely to be directive
   when stimulating the formative stages of collective
   action or where internal conflict severely hampers
   members' identification with a group's goals and
   strategies.

4 When a community worker is not directly accountable
   to his superiors or colleagues, the strategies adopted
   both by him and by the group with which he is
   working may be accepted by his colleagues through
   being re-interpreted in accordance with their own
   values and ideologies rather than those actually held
   by the worker. The pragmatic but activist approach of
   the WCAC worker, for example, was accepted by
   other members of the Cumbria CDP team because of
   their perception of the relevance of campaign tactics
   to the seeking of structural solutions to local
   problems. However, when a community worker is
   more closely involved in the agency management
   structure, and yet holds different perspectives from his
   professional peers, his actions are less likely to be
   tolerated and disputes are more likely to ensue.

5 It would appear that community workers do not hold
   to a solely client, professional or bureaucratic
   orientation. They seem more likely to combine a
   general client orientation with either a bureaucratic or
   a professional perspective depending on their staffing
   position and the ways in which they utilise their skills
   in working with groups.

6 Terms such as enabler, broker, advocate and activist
   are usefully seen as associated skills and techniques
   rather than statements indicating the values of the
   worker or his orientation towards a group. It is
   possible to adopt an activist role through personal
   commitment and identification as well as ideological
   conviction; and an enabler can both facilitate decision

making and generate an awareness about structures that affect people's lives.

Conclusion

We have suggested that there are a variety of factors influencing workers' relationships with community groups, and have indicated some of the ways in which they operate. It would be naive to think that community workers are in any circumstances autonomous in defining their roles in relation to groups. In any case this would negate the strongly held value that workers should be accountable to group members. The CDPs' commitment to citizen involvement led workers to associate with residents' groups both to justify the projects' presence and to realise objectives concerned with promoting changes in social relationships and social environments. The workers' role performance varied considerably and was influenced by such factors as degree of involvement in agency management structures, training and previous experience, the extent of personal identification with group members, the duration of the project, and the skills, strategies, goals and resources of the groups. Each of the workers utilised a variety of roles along the enabler-activist continuum. The main dilemma for a worker is how and when to adopt particular roles in order to ensure that they are appropriate to changing circumstances.

Although in this chapter we have only been considering three of the five case study groups, we have been able to offer an extensive comparative analysis because the workers contrasted markedly in their orientations and actual role performance. In summary, the workers in each of the groups operated in the following ways:

West Cumberland Action Committee

As an information and advice worker she helped group members with problems and difficulties that arose as a consequence of their involvement in the group. As a local person she identified very strongly with group members and her pragmatic yet activist role was reinterpreted and accepted by other CDP colleagues who justified the role in terms of the need to adopt pressure group tactics in the face of structural problems. In general, more support was given to those groups in the immediate locality of Cleator Moor where the project was based.

When initially contacted for help, the worker responded in an enabling capacity, offering the local bus fares action group organisational aid in establishing the WCAC. As a result of the different perspectives on the problems held in the localities that WCAC represented, the worker came to act as a broker in defining commonly agreed goals. To mediate the incipient conflict between the various sub-groups the worker also acted as the organisation's secretary and took an activist role in arranging meetings and transport and in representing the group's interests directly to decision makers.

Senior Citizens Action Group
The worker's involvement with pensioners derived from both his research role and general position within CDP. This meant that involvement with SCAG ranked among a number of his duties. We can attribute his non-participative stance to his background in social work and research, which encouraged an objective and neutral outlook. Nevertheless, as the concern over odd jobs was insufficient in itself to galvanise collective action among pensioners, the worker facilitated this by adopting an advocate role. After the group's formation the worker assumed an enabling role both in ensuring organisational soundness and in the formation of subsequent goals and strategies; he resisted direct involvement in the execution of the group's tactics.

Glodwick Action Group
The worker became involved with GAG through his community profile brief from CDP, and subsequently maintained his presence in Glodwick to further continuity in contact building. However, because of his previous experience in community work, he held a different perspective from the director of the CDP in that the creation of problem solving structures was not for him an end in itself. Because he was embedded in the structure of CDP and in its formulation of policy some conflicts arose between himself and the director.

Initially, an activist role typified his approach to stimulating group formation because of the lack of prior organisational response to the CPO declaration. Later he adopted an enabling role to help the group acquire organisational expertise. He provided technical information and resolved internal strife by helping the group to draw specifically on some of the members' ability to run focussed meetings. Subsequently he acted as an advocate by pressing for GAG to have direct access to consultative meetings; he was not prepared to act on their behalf.

In all three cases, we noted that the CDP brief served as a spur for rapid involvement in supporting collective action. Workers were able to adopt a range of roles because of their relative independence from management accountability (caused by its remoteness, rather than, for example, its paternal benevolence).

We have explored aspects of the dynamic inter-relationships between group characteristics, workers' positions in their agency and their own personal attributes. Issues which seem to us particularly worthy of further exploration include: how the self-image of a worker (and that of his agency) affects his interaction with a group and their targets; the extent to which workers are aware of the roles they perform, and the factors which influence their choice of them; how workers are able to resist the dangers of being frozen in one role at the expense of others; and the effects of role strain on workers, and how they cope with it. We hope such issues will form the basis of research in the not too distant future.

Part four
Conclusion

Chapter 12
Summary findings and propositions

The activities of the five community groups presented in this book are not untypical of similar attempts elsewhere in this and other countries to resolve problems and issues in the community by collective effort. Whether as a reaction against prevailing public policies or from a desire to supplement them in order to meet needs, collective action necessitates a re-ordering of people's lives. It is with those factors accounting for and directing this populist involvement in the voluntary sector that we have been concerned. By focussing both descriptively and analytically on community groups, we have documented and explored the nature and purpose of, as well as constraints on, efforts to promote change in various communities.

Our methodological approach has been eclectic. We have obtained a variety of first-hand evidence on the development of five groups and subjected the data to comparative analysis. This necessitated the refinement of concepts to aid our understanding of the processes described in the case studies. The concepts provided the analytical tools with which a series of propositions were inductively drawn from the data. These propositions should be capable of testing through further studies of community groups.

This chapter is devoted to summarising and interpreting the findings from the study, underlining some of the problems and difficulties associated with our methods of research, and finally suggesting some possible areas of future research and development.

Findings and propositions relating to community groups

Both similarities and differences between the five case studies were analysed in the thematic section. We were conscious that, in the way the book was planned, there was likely to be some

247

overlap between these chapters. As it turned out, this overlap has been positive in that some of the general conclusions reached in one chapter are reinforced in another; yet they took different approaches or started from different perspectives. Following some general observations, the propositions are presented in the same order as they appeared in the commentary chapters. Overlaps have been merged so that the points relate explicitly to the goals, organisation, and strategy and resources of, and the role of the worker in, community groups. One value of the separation into these discrete headings is that it aids an understanding of evaluative criteria used in assessing the effectiveness of community groups. We list them, not as a set of universal propositions, but as a guide to further analysis and inductive testing.

1. *Community groups and their environment*

1.1 Community groups can be conceived as engaged in a series of group-environment exchanges which concern the attainment and deployment of resources.

1.2 Community groups may choose either to use their own resources to tackle and resolve problems directly or to seek to modify the performance of wider systems of resource allocation.

1.3 Community groups are neither wholly internally nor wholly externally orientated. In reality, groups have multiple concerns.

1.4 Community groups may be described as conglomerations of various interacting action systems (sub-systems within an overall group), each concerned with a particular issue or activity. Membership of action systems is likely to be overlapping and fluctuating. Their relationships may be formally or informally structured within the overall group.

1.5 Each action system is likely to engage in a triadic relationship between itself, beneficiaries and resource providers. At times an action system may be the same as the service provider or beneficiary.

1.6 The nature of an action system's deployment of resources in the wider environment may include:

(1) Using its own resources to tackle problems directly by
   (a) making services available for its own members (insiders);
   (b) making services available for a wider public (outsiders).

(2) Seeking to modify the allocation of resources by other bodies by

      (a) attempting to influence resource providers on their own behalf (self-directed);

      (b) attempting to influence resource providers on behalf of others (other-directed).

1.7   The approach adopted is likely to relate more to the specific goals of each action system of a group rather than those of the group as a whole. Nonetheless, the attributes of the groups of which they are a part are likely to predispose an action system to choose some goals rather than others, adopt particular organisational forms, and make use of certain resources in the execution of strategies.

2. *Goals*

2.1   As community groups are frequently coalitions of different interests they are likely to have multiple goals reflecting the activities pursued by different action systems.

2.2   System maintenance or process goals relate to community groups' need to maintain an adequate organisational structure from which to act; goals related to the achievement of a desired end product may be described as task goals.

2.3   At various times, community groups are likely to give greater or less emphasis to particular goals in relation to others. The goals of current concern may be described as focal goals.

2.4   A community group's official goals may be found within a constitution or charter; these are distinct from its operative goals, which comprise what the separate action systems are actually striving to achieve.

2.5   Change in goals seems a frequent occurrence in community groups.

2.6   Goal displacement occurs when system maintenance goals assume more importance than task goals.

2.7   Goal succession occurs when one focal operative goal is replaced by another (or others).

2.8   In the early stages of their development, community groups are often externally orientated in that they attempt to raise issues rather than provide services. At this stage the goals of a community group might receive the sanction of outside interests. Subsequently such support is liable to dissipate following the operationalising of goals or through the threat created by the strategies used by a group to achieve its goals.

2.9   As community groups are coalitions of different interests, the formulation of goals involves a process of resolution of internal conflict. Harmonisation of interests may be achieved by

(1) emphasising the significance of official or all-embracing goals, particularly when the group has a federated structure;

(2) emphasising goals of sufficient common concern to all parties to override other internal conflicts;

(3) accommodating simultaneously a number of focal goals by organising the different interests formally or informally into separate action systems.

2.10   The achievement of operative goals appears to be dependent on:

(1) the organisational experience, skills, time and commitment of the members of the community group;

(2) the ability of members both to locate and obtain multiple resources in order to provide services and to secure access to influentials to have an impact on other organisations' deployment of resources;

(3) the sensitivity maintained towards the actual or potential beneficiaries of a community group's services, or the ability to develop and demonstrate a power base to provide groups with political support;

(4) the ability both to overcome factors which inhibit the development of collective action in a community and to prevent sectional interests becoming polarised within a group;

(5) the expediency and fortitude which a community group's members can muster in managing their external relationships with other organisations, not least those which prove to be hostile.

2.11   The factors accounting for changes in a community group's operative goals may include: expected or unexpected consequences arising from the initial raising of an issue or problem; the raising of members' confidence following success in achieving goals; the highlighting of other needs, and generation of the motivation to tackle them, during the pursuit of a previous goal; incorporation of services provided by a group into the functions of another agency.

2.12   The changing of goals serves to sustain organisational survival and development and feature of community groups.

3   *Organisation*

3.1   A community group's organisation can be seen to encompass both the process of translating individual's intentions into collective action and the structures within which this occurs.

3.2 The initial stimulus that is likely to promote the formation of a community group is the existence of a provocative issue or shortcoming in people's lives which demands a concerted response. The provocative issue might include:
(1) a specific concrete decision made by a local political authority or public body;
(2) a persistent disposition of negligence by policy makers in relation to particular needs;
(3) a fundamental change in the way that policies are formulated and/or executed.

3.3 Promotional efforts by an outside agency might themselves lead to the formation of a community group; or a group might evolve following the facilitative efforts of an external resource such as a community worker.

3.4 The process of translating a provocative issue into collective action, in some cases supplemented by promotional or facilitative inputs, seems to involve: an appreciation by potential community group members that collective action is both possible and likely to be productive; individuals' motives being translated into a collective will to act; the identifying and mobilising of group members; and the development of knowledge about the extent of the problem to enhance the members' commitment and capacity to act.

3.5 Community groups seem particularly likely to form in response to a provocative issue when this is a specific concrete decision; promotional inputs seem more necessary when an issue is generalised; when an issue is weak or not pervasive, or there exist some other inhibiting factors in the community or local political arena, facilitative efforts seem likely to be needed to generate collective action.

3.6 Community groups often form in response to insensitive policies deriving from hierarchically organised bureaucracies; but community groups also have a tendency to develop a leadership pattern which is oligarchic.

3.7 A core leadership sub-system can help to maintain continuity in decision making and, in the early stages of group formation, a 'cadre' may prove indispensable to rapid organisation. Such a core leadership pattern may be maintained following acknowledgment by others of the initial impetus given by the core leaders to the setting up of a group through leaders' input of a disproportionate amount of time to the work of the group compared with other members, and through the reinforcement of leadership structures provided by close association and affiliation between group leaders.

3.8   A more participative structure of decision making in a group can serve to broaden the organisational experience of members, making for greater accessibility between members and leaders, and reduce the isolation of leaders from the rank and file. The desire to adopt a more participative style in decision making may arise from:

(1) the recognition of the value of power sharing and the will to distribute power by the leaders;

(2) the need for formally decentralised structures through which to manage a variety of organisation-environment exchanges;

(3) the need to prevent the fragmentation of a group into conflicting interests of equal power.

3.9   To facilitate the development of greater flexibility in leadership roles, community groups might find it helpful to discuss and decide the structure of their organisation at a time when members are sufficiently confident to make an equal contribution with others.

3.10   The more a group maximises its number of leadership roles, makes arrangements to rotate them, continuously recruits new members, and diversifies its functions through discrete action systems, the more likely is it that collective responsibility will be a manifestation of the whole group and not just of an oligarchic leadership.

4   Strategy and resources

4.1   Strategies are the ways in which community groups deploy their resources in order to achieve operative goals.

4.2   Just as community groups are comprised of several action systems with discrete goals, so they may employ a variety of strategies reflecting these multiple concerns.

4.3   Resources are an important factor for community groups to consider in their selection of strategies. These include (1) material and financial resources, (2) effective internal organisation for the formulation and execution of decisions, (3) a relevant power base comprising members and beneficiaries, (4) supportive public opinion, (5) access to influentials, (6) information, knowledge and expertise available to or within the group, (7) ideological sustenance to maintain group members' motivation and commitment.

4.4 Community groups' resources may change over time. The process of collective action can serve, for example, to increase the acquisition of skills in managing external relations, enhance members' commitment and create access to influentials.

4.5 In managing their external organisation-environment exchanges community groups may adopt either a service strategy or an influence strategy.

4.6 Service strategies are concerned to exploit community groups' own resources in tackling problems or issues directly through self-help or voluntary service schemes. These may be conceptually distinguished as:
(1) complementary strategies, which augment existing service provisions;
(2) alternative strategies, which demonstrate a new way of meeting a need and compete with existing services;
(3) substitute strategies, which attempt to replace existing forms of service provision and challenge the legitimacy of existing methods of meeting needs.

4.7 Action systems which engage in service strategies tend to make use of a wide variety of resources, though most notably material resources, which may be obtained from external sources, and an effective internal organisation.

4.8 In terms of tactics, effective planning, the assessment of needs, and matching resources to needs appear to be crucial to the success of a service strategy.

4.9 Influence strategies are concerned to modify the performance of wider systems of resource allocation. These may be conceptually distinguished as:
(1) collaborative strategies, where both the community group and the target for change agree on the existence of need but the group argues for further action and resources;
(2) campaign strategies, where the community group seeks to demonstrate the need for additional resources when an authority is not committed to the legitimacy of the needs to be met;
(3) coercive strategies, where a group seeks to replace or destroy the existing target system or, at the very least, to confront and force it to make concessions.

4.10 The essential resource of influence strategies appears to be access to influentials; the acquisition of a power base and ready sources of information, knowledge and expertise also seem important. In comparison with service strategies an effective internal organisation and possession of material resources are less significant. Material resources used tend to be more significant in the formative stages of the community group and may be acquired from external sources.

4.11   The range of tactics used in the execution of influence strategies is fluid and varies along a continuum from persuasion (e.g., lobbying, petitioning) to force (e.g., boycotts, sit-ins) in line with the degree of threat suggested in the three types of strategy.

4.12   In general the more resources available to a community group in executing both service and influence strategies, the greater appear its chances of success.

5   *Community worker role*

5.1   A worker may be seen as an additional external resource to a community group, principally supplying information, knowledge and expertise, as well as access to the material resources available within his employing organisation. His role is to facilitate and maximise the use of resources by the group; to help to generate an effective internal organisation, a relevant power base, and access to influentials; and to maintain members' commitment in the course of the group's definition of goals and execution of strategies.

5.2   The resources available through a community worker can offset deficiencies in the group's own possession of, or access to, resources. In terms of resources, the worker's contributions often complement those of group members.

5.3   Community workers are not autonomous in defining their role with community groups. The interplay between a community group, the employing agency and a worker's own attributes determines the range and nature of the roles he performs.

5.4   In working with community groups, community workers employ the roles of enabler, broker, advocate and activist. Workers seem likely to adopt a variety of these roles in the course of their association with a community group.

5.5   In the initial stages of group formation a worker may play a significant facilitative role and advocate collective action as a means of resolving community problems.

5.6   When there has been little experience of collective action, or when a community group's strategy involves overt conflict with resource providers community workers seem likely to undertake activist roles.

5.7 The level of a community worker's involvement in a group is likely to be greater when he has been involved in establishing it, and when group members have easy access to his office or the immediate area of his activity.

5.8 A prime concern for a community worker is to sustain a group's cohesion as a basis for collective action. In extreme cases where internal conflicts of interest militate against a minimal level of agreement, the community worker may adopt official positions within the group as a means of neutralising conflict.

5.9 Where sponsorship or management structures are remote or decentralised, the community worker's selection of roles for working with community groups (enabler, broker, advocate, activist) is likely to be minimally restricted.

5.10 A limited time frame for community work activity may be a recipe for rapid involvement, but in itself it is insufficient to prejudge the use of an activist as distinct from enabler role; nor does it necessarily lead to an emphasis on achievement of task goals at the expense of process goals.

5.11 The more decentralised the execution of an agency's functions, the broader is likely to be the role orientation of its community workers.

5.12 The more specialised a worker's function within an agency, the more limited is his role set likely to be in working with community groups.

5.13 When agency decision making structures are more hierarchical, differences in perspectives over the legitimacy of workers' roles are unlikely to be tolerated and intra-agency conflict is likely to occur.

5.14 When the motivations or ideological commitment of a worker differ from those of an agency whose structure is decentralised, the acceptance of the adoption of that worker's roles in relation to community groups may be rationalised to accord with agency policies.

5.15 Community workers select the roles which they perform in relation to community groups on the basis either of rational criteria derived from previous training or experience, or from their own intuition; the latter seems particularly the case amongst indigenous workers.

5.16 The stronger a personal commitment or identification with group members, or an ideological motivation relating to collective action, the more likely are community workers to be predisposed to adopt advocative or activist roles;

those with preference for a more neutral relationship tend to adopt enabler roles.

5.17 While community workers may perceive that their accountability is primarily to the community group with which they associate, they are likely to couple this client orientation with either a professional or an agency orientation in their overall frame of reference towards their activities.

Research

At a relatively early stage of this project we decided that the focus of enquiry should be community groups' own effectiveness in relation to the formulation of aims, organisation, selection and implementation of strategies, and use of both internal and external resources. Our main concern has been to explore the dynamics of the groups and their component parts rather than to analyse them either in the context of community worker roles or in relation to broader social and political phenomena. These aspects have not, however, been ignored; their importance is recognised both in Chapter 10 and in frequent references to groups' relationships with political target systems.

At the beginning of the study, we were unable to discover in the literature any real attempts at comparative analysis of community groups drawing on original data, and deliberately decided to try out a variety of research methods. This proved to be both stimulating and frustrating. For example, our earlier case studies (SCAG and WCAC) were written largely on the basis of our first draft of the checklist. As additional explanatory material was drawn out in the further studies, so the checklist was modified. Similarly, it became clear that the nature of the information which could be obtained by a participant and a non-participant research worker varied. The closer the research worker was involved, the more aware he was of the social norms which influenced a group's decision making. But a non-participative role seemed more conducive to conducting interviews with a range of participants and, through that, to reach more evaluative interpretations. While we think that the variety of methods used has sharpened the overall analysis without detracting from the substantive comparability of the case study material, it is nevertheless true that differences in emphasis in the accounts might in part reflect the stage reached in the development of the checklist when each was written, and the different relationships between the research workers and the groups.

We hope that the checklist will be used and developed in further studies, providing the basis for observation recording forms and interview questionnaires. Its application should be flexible and appropriate to the circumstances and purposes of individual research projects. Three major areas which might valuably be added are:

1   The perceptions of group members, beneficiaries, the community worker (if relevant) and members of the group's target bodies.
2   The historical background of collective action relevant to the initiative.
3   The social and political context within which the group determines and develops its management of group-environment relationships, and in particular the detailed characteristics of the target bodies on which groups might be trying to exert influence.

Conclusion

The refinement and development of new conceptual tools and the testing and development of the propositions arising from this study present challenges to this field of research. Conceptual models and evaluative frameworks are only slowly being developed and it is important that research tools used are clarified so that others might test and develop both the concepts and conclusions. In the plethora of jargon that surrounds an embryonic area of study, the validity of the terminology rests in its ability to communicate clearly and accurately, both within and between recognised disciplines in the social and political sciences. A logical step to follow up the study would be a wider survey of the activities of community groups than has been possible in our intensive case study approach. A comparison could be made of a range of community groups operating in more varied localities, or selected according to predetermined categorisations of membership, goals, strategies, organisations, structure or other characteristics.

If evaluation is to address the very real questions concerning community groups' effectiveness in relation to their goals, organisation, strategies and resources, time must be built in to enable the groups to benefit from such assessment. How often do community groups consider the degree of convergence between their official and operative goals? How much are the strategies and tactics espoused by a group the reflection of its own oligarchic leadership pattern? To what extent are the resources of a group not being supplemented by external resources to mount an effective campaign?

Evaluation is not indulgent or mere navel-gazing. It is an analytical tool for assessing effectiveness. To be of any worth it must be applied by community groups themselves.

Appendix
The resources used by different action systems

Group	Campaign or issue	Resources used (see list on p. 202)
SCAG	Social activities	1 Material resources: pump-priming grant (CDP), transport (CDP and Social Services) 2 Effective internal organisation – to run events
SCAG	HELP cards	1 Material resources to prepare cards (CDP) 2 Effective internal organisation to run scheme
GAG	Information and advice service	1 Material resources: salary of worker, premises, secretarial help (all CDP) 6 Information and expertise (Citizens' Advice Bureaux service and CDP worker)
SCAG	Welfare rights course	1 Material resources (CDP) 2 Effective internal organisation – to run course 6 Information and expertise, of a technical nature
Joint Working Party	Setting up shelter	1 Material resources for rehabilitating and running shelter 2 Effective internal organisation 3 Support from volunteers, sponsoring organisations and affiliates 5 Access to influentials – for planning permission, etc. 6 Information, knowledge, expertise – for survey 7 Ideology
SCAG	Food and household goods club	1 Material resources: pump-priming grant (CDP) 2 Effective internal organisation – to run scheme 6 Information and expertise, about commercial methods and practices

Group	Campaign or issue	Resources used (see list on p. 202)
SCAG	Small jobs scheme	1 Material resources for organisation (CDP) 2 Effective internal organisation – to administer scheme 5 Access to influentials
GAG	Issues arising from public inquiry	1 Material resources (CDP) 3 Power base – evidence from survey 5 Access to influentials – local authority 6 Information, knowledge, expertise – from survey and from community worker (CDP) 7 Ideology: strong feeling that residents should have a say in developments in the area
SCAG	Improving chiropody service in area	5 Access to influentials
SCAG	Time restrictions on free bus passes	5 Access to influentials
SCAG	Pedestrian safety	5 Access to influentials
Joint Working Party	Threat to close shelter	1 Material resources: building itself 2 Effective internal organisation 3 Power base: support from constituents/beneficiaries 4 Supportive public opinion 5 Access to influentials: local authority and press 6 Information, knowledge, expertise: feeling that this was a resource which should not be lost 7 Ideology: commitment to maintaining shelter
Failsworth Community Association	Provision of community hall	3 Power base: from constituent organisations and presumably tacit support of people in Failsworth 5 Access to influentials: councillors and officers 6 Information, knowledge and expertise: ex-councillors on deputation
FCA	Territorial Army's request to use quarry for training	3 Power base – again tacit support from member organisations and local people 5 Access to influentials: Planning Department
GAG	Survey and evidence to public inquiry	1 Material resources: community worker, secretarial help, etc. (CDP)

Group	Campaign or issue	Resources used (see list on p. 202)
		3 Power base: claimed support from potential beneficiaries by survey 5 Access to influentials: public inquiry inspector 6 Information, knowledge, expertise: from survey, and from community worker (CDP) about Compulsory Purchase Order procedure and group organisation
GAG	Re-letting of council-owned empty houses in good condition, managed by Family Housing Association	5 Access to influentials: officers, councillors 6 Information, knowledge and expertise: Family Housing Association and community worker (CDP)
West Cumberland Action Committee	Children's bus passes – local issues	1 Material resources from Resource Centre (CDP) 3 Power base: many people involved locally 5 Access to influentials: MPs, councillors 6 Information and expertise from community worker (CDP), especially about decision making channels 7 Ideology
WCAC	Public transport – national issues	1 Material resources as above 5 Access to influentials 6 Information, knowledge and expertise from community worker (CDP)

Notes

Preface

1 P. Jenkins, 'Commentary', *Guardian*, 5 May 1978.
2 Calouste Gulbenkian Foundation, *Current Issues in Community Work*, Routledge & Kegan Paul, London, 1973, pp. 71–7.
3 Calouste Gulbenkian Foundation, *Community Work and Social Change*, Longman, London, 1968, p. 3.
4 Calouste Gulbenkian Foundation, *Current Issues in Community Work*, p. 110.
5 Central Council for Education and Training in Social Work, *The Teaching of Community Work (the Pinker Report)*, Social Work Curriculum Study Paper 8, London, 1975, p. 30.

Chapter 1 The background to the study

1 K. Newton, *Second City Politics: Democratic Processes and Decision Making in Birmingham*, Clarendon Press, Oxford, 1971, pp. 34–6. Formidable difficulties confront those who set out to enumerate the number and types of voluntary organisations in a given community. Newton was by no means confident that his own listing was exhaustive, and as his study progressed he became convinced that there were probably at least a further 1,000 voluntary organisations in the city that met his criteria, 'and there may well be another 4,000'.
2 A. Barker, 'Local Amenity Societies – a survey and outline report', in *The Local Amenity Movement*, Civic Trust, London, 1976, pp. 21ff. There were 1,250 societies 'registered in early 1976 with the Civic Trust . . . and possibly several hundred more which are, in practical terms, very similar in their work and interests'. Eighty five per cent of the societies which Barker surveyed 'have begun since 1957'.
3 K. Newton, 'Voluntary Organisations in Community Politics: the Hidden 90% of the Iceberg'; *Social Science Research Council Newsletter*, no.24, London, July 1974, p. 5.
4 One commentator has labelled the 1970s the 'self-help decade', and another has identified self-help groups as the 'emerging church of

the 21st century'. See D. Robinson and S. Henry, *Self-Help and Health*, Martin Robertson, London, 1977; and A. H. Katz and E. I. Bender, *The Strength in Us*, New Viewpoints, New York, 1976. Although this trend seems to have proceeded further in the USA than elsewhere, the growth in what we later on call voluntary service groups has proceeded apace in Britain too.

5 We are referring, for example, to the establishment of the Home Office Community Development Projects, the growing trend towards citizen participation in the welfare state, and advocacy by the Wolfenden Committee and others of substantial central government funding to local intermediary bodies. See K. Jones, J. Brown and J. Bradshaw, *Issues in Social Policy*, Routledge & Kegan Paul, London, 1978, particularly pp. 98–113, a chapter on citizen participation; *The Future of Voluntary Organisations*, Report of the Wolfenden Committee, Croom Helm, London, 1977; Home Office, *CDP: A General Outline*, London, 1969; C. Cockburn, *The Local State*, Pluto Press, London, 1977.

6 A working party set up by the Calouste Gulbenkian Foundation drew attention to the growth of local groups employing community action approaches to problem solving, and some commentators have seen the new forms of local protest and organising as the emergence of a new style of political action. See Calouste Gulbenkian Foundation, *Current Issues in Community Work*, op. cit., ch. 4; and R. Hain, 'The Future of Community Politics', in P. Hain (ed.), *Community Politics*, John Calder, London, 1976, pp. 9–32.

7 See, for example: M. N. Zald, 'Organizations as Polities: an Analysis of Community Organization Agencies', in F. M. Cox, J. L. Erlich, J. Rothman and J. E. Tropman (eds), *Strategies of Community Organization*, 2nd edn., F. E. Peacock, Itasca, Illinois, 1974, pp. 95–104; V. M. Sieder, 'Community Organization in the Direct Service Agency', and W. J. Reid, 'Inter-Organizational Co-ordination in Social Welfare: a Theoretical Approach to Analysis and Intervention', both in R. M. Kramer and H. Specht (eds), *Readings in Community Organization Practice*, Prentice-Hall, Englewood Cliffs, New Jersey, 1969, pp. 154–61 and 176–87.

8 Home Office, op. cit., p. 1. Local CDPs comprised part of a national action-research programme designed to secure

better understanding and more comprehensive tackling of social needs, especially in local communities within the older urban areas, through closer co-ordination of central and local official and unofficial effort informed and stimulated by citizen initiative and involvement.

Each local project team consisted of a group of community workers and a complementary team of research workers. The research teams were required to provide a research service to action teams as well as to evaluate the effectiveness of project interventions. Each action team embarked upon a wide-ranging programme of work encompassing intervention in the fields of housing and planning, employment and transport, welfare rights, play and educational provision.

All the teams invested substantial time and other resources in working with local voluntary groups and organisations. Concerning the national programme, see R. Lees and G. Smith, *Action Research in Community Development*, Routledge & Kegan Paul, London, 1975; and National Community Development Project, *Forward Plan 1975–76*, CDP Information and Intelligence Unit, London, 1975. Concerning the Cumbria and Oldham projects see H. Butcher, J. Pearce, I. Cole with A. Glen, *Community Participation and Poverty: the Final Report of the Cumbria CDP*, Paper in Community Studies, no.22, Department of Social Administration and Social Work, University of York, York, 1979; and L. Corina, P. Collis and C. Crosby, *The Final Report: Oldham CDP*, Paper in Community Studies, no.23, Department of Social Administration and Social Work, University of York, 1979.

9   The community development projects at Oldham, Cumbria and Batley.

10 K. Newton, *Second City Politics*, op. cit., p. 35.

11 The term 'target body' parallels Pincus and Minahan's notion of a 'target system', meaning the person, people or institution 'that will have to be changed if . . . goals are to be reached'. See A. Pincus and A. Minahan, *Social Work Practice: Model and Method*, F. E. Peacock, Itasca, Illinois, 1973, p. 59.

12 G. W. Goetschius, *Working with Community Groups: Using Community Development as a Method of Social Work*, Routledge and Kegan Paul, London, 1969, p. 129.

13 G. Brager and H. Specht, *Community Organizing*, Columbia University Press, New York, 1973. M. Taylor, A. Kestenbaum and B. Symons, *Principles and Practice of Community Work in a British Town*, Young Volunteer Force Foundation, London, 1976, p. 19.

14 C. G. Pickvance, 'Voluntary Association', in E. Gittus (ed.), *Key Variables in Social Research*. Vol. 2, Heinemann, forthcoming. Privately circulated script, p. 1.

15 P. Baldock, *Community Work and Social Work*, Routledge & Kegan Paul, London, 1974, p. 60.

16 N. Derricourt, 'Linking Learning to Experience in Community Work Training', in C. Briscoe and D. Thomas (eds), *Community Work: Learning and Supervision*, Allen & Unwin, London, 1977, p. 142.

17 N. McCaughan, 'Group Behaviour: Some Theories for Practice', in C. Briscoe and D. Thomas (eds), op. cit., pp. 82–103.

18 Calouste Gulbenkian Foundation, *Current Issues in Community Work*, op. cit., p. 66; P. Baldock, op. cit., p. 61.

19 F. Milson, *An Introduction to Community Work*, Routledge & Kegan Paul, London, 1974, p. 146.

20 See, for example, D. N. Thomas, 'Chaucer House Tenants' Association: a Case Study' and J. Benington, 'Gosford Green Residents' Association: a Case Study', in P. Leonard (ed.), *The Sociology of Community Action*, Sociological Review Monograph 21, University

of Keele, 1975, pp. 185–203, 205–45; S. Jacobs, *The Right to a Decent House*, Routledge & Kegan Paul, London, 1976; I. M. Hall, *Community Action Versus Pollution: A Study of a Residents' Group in a Welsh Urban Area*, University of Wales Board of Celtic Studies, Social Science Monograph 2, University of Wales Press, Cardiff, 1976; J. O'Malley, *The Politics of Community Action*, Spokesman Books, Nottingham, 1977.

21 Calouste Gulbenkian Foundation, *Current Issues in Community Work*, op. cit., p. 68.

22 Ibid. p. 69.

23 B. G. Glaser and A. L. Strauss, *The Discovery of Grounded Theory: Strategies for Qualitative Research*, Aldine Atherton, Chicago, 1971, p. 6.

24 N. P. Mouzelis, *Organization and Bureaucracy: An Analysis of Modern Theories*, Routledge & Kegan Paul, London, 1967, pp. 68–70.

25 See H. Butcher *et al.*, op. cit., and R. Barber, *Iron Ore and After; Boom Time, Depression and Survival in a West Cumbrian Town; Cleator Moor 1840–1960*, Cleator Moor Local Studies Group, Cleator Moor, Cumbria, 1976.

26 Department of the Environment, *Making Towns Better: The Oldham Study – Environmental Planning and Management*, HMSO, London, 1973, pp. 3–4.

27 A. Barr, *Housing Improvement and the Multi-racial Community*, Paper in Community Studies, no. 16, Department of Social Administration and Social Work, University of York, 1978.

28 At the request of group members the name and location of the group that forms the basis for our fifth case study is not divulged.

29 P. Marris, 'Experimenting in Social Reform', in D. Jones and M. Mayo (eds), *Community Work One*, Routledge & Kegan Paul, London, 1974, pp. 256–8.

30 Calouste Gulbenkian Foundation, *Current Issues in Community Work*, op. cit., p. 68.

31 P. Marris, op. cit., p. 258.

32 It is 'the author's role in the events described and interpreted' which items in the first section of the checklist are intended to clarify. It will have been noted that, for the purposes of this book, the information on these items for the five groups studied has been presented in composite form in the penultimate section of this first chapter.

Chapter 2 The Senior Citizens Action Group

1 Community Industry operates in a number of areas in the country where there is high unemployment among young people. The West Cumbria scheme employed 50 young people who worked, under supervision, in teams of eight or so on projects 'of benefit to the community'. It is sponsored by local and central government. Central government pays the wage bill for the youngsters; people and

organisations who benefit from the scheme generally only have to meet the cost of materials.

2 The CDP-sponsored community resource centre existed to service community groups. Besides the minibus, it also loaned out slide projectors, video television and exhibition stands. It also helped, for instance, to make posters and duplicate agendas for meetings.

3 J. Pearce and A. Tweedie, *Initial Study of the Two Parishes of Cleator Moor and Arlecdon/Frizington*, Cumberland CDP, Cleator Moor, 1973.

4 Core members were those who regularly attended group meetings along with those who undertook the bulk of between-meeting work.

5 Two members were recruited from the local OAPA; they became interested when SCAG negotiated for the use of the OAPA hut.

6 R. Miliband, 'Politics and Poverty', in D. Wedderburn (ed.); *Poverty, Inequality and Class Structure*, Cambridge University Press, London, 1974, p. 187.

7 H. Butcher and D. Crosbie, *Pensioned Off: A Study of the Needs of Elderly People in Cleator Moor*, Paper in Community Studies, no. 15, Department of Social Administration and Social Work, University of York, 1978.

8 Before Community Industry can undertake a new project a 'responsible authority' has to agree to sponsor the scheme. Sponsorship involves making guarantees about fidelity insurance and providing assurances that the project is of 'benefit to the community'.

9 Internal review of SCAG's progress, Cumbria CDP, unpublished paper, 1975.

10 It is ironic that one defensive ploy of councillors was to suggest that many action groups are mere fronts for the community worker (or the CDP); their legitimacy questioned, the councillor could choose to ignore them.

Chapter 3 West Cumberland Action Committee

1 Such a report was requested from all county councils by the Department of the Environment, to be submitted by November 1974.

2 J. Pearce and A. Tweedie, op. cit.

3 Ibid., p. 48.

4 R. Sugden, *Unskilled and Unemployed in West Cumbria: a Study of Unemployment in Relation to Economic Planning and Public Transportation Policies*, Paper in Community Studies, no. 3, Department of Social Administration and Social Work, University of York, 1975.

5 The advertisement for the public meeting in Whitehaven stated: 'We would welcome the support of all mothers in the area'.

6 The marches occurred during the last two weeks of the summer term and did not begin again in the autumn.

7 At a full Cumberland County Council meeting in July 1973, while agreeing with any immediate and appropriate action to reduce school bus fares, two councillors made a proviso that this should not mean

'free travel to school'. They commented that it could cost £40–£80,000 a year, which was 'equal to all the money available for new education development'. (*Cumberland Times and Star*, 17 July 1973).

8 Department of Education and Science, *School Transport*, Green Paper, London, December 1973.

9 In October 1975, the Minister of Transport announced a proposal to abolish the mileage limits and replace them with a 7p flat-rate fare, with means-testing on cases of financial hardship. In the *Guardian* (6 May 1976) the Education Under-Secretary was reported as saying that the Government was looking into free bus travel for children within three miles of school. And so it goes on. . . .

Chapter 4 Glodwick Action Group

1 A. Barr (in consultation with the Glodwick Action Group), *Evidence for a CPO*, Oldham Community Development Project, Oldham, 1973.

2 Two Area Councillors' Committees were set up by CDP in the Project area, one of which covered the whole of Glodwick. These committees provided a forum for discussion between councillors, council officers, and local groups. Agendas were drawn up by CDP in co-operation with local groups.

3 M. Clifton, *Not in Permanent Accommodation*, Oldham Community Development Project, Oldham, 1975.

4 A. Barr, *Housing Improvement and the Racial Conundrum*, Oldham Community Development Project, Oldham, 1975.

5 N. Shenton and P. Collis (eds), *Neighbourhood Information and Advice Centres: Oldham CDP*, Oldham Community Development Project, Oldham, 1977. The first four paragraphs of this section on the context of Glodwick Action Group are based on the community worker's description of the area for this project paper.

6 A. Barr, *Housing Improvement and the Multi-racial Community*, op. cit.

7 Oldham Metropolitan Borough Council, *The South Hill Street Area – the Case for a Housing Action Area*, Oldham, 1976.

8 S. Baillie, N. Shenton, A. Barr and S. Swidenbank, *Oldham CDP: a First Report*, Oldham Community Development Project, Oldham, 1973.

9 C. Crosby, *Intra-Urban Migration: A Study of Housing Mobility in the Clarksfield and Glodwick Districts of Oldham*, Paper in Community Studies, no. 17, Department of Social Administration and Social Work, University of York, 1978.

10 The questions put by the group to the local authority as a result of its first meeting, and the Borough Solicitor's replies, were:
(a) When will demolition begin?
When blocks of property are completely empty. In any event, not for at least another 12 to 18 months.

(b) Will all public services be maintained?

Yes. Every effort will be made to avoid inconvenience.

(c) Will all houses be bricked up and made secure?
Once the properties have been vested in the council, empty houses will be boarded up and made secure if considered necessary by the Borough Engineer and Surveyor.

(d) What plans do the council have for the area?
Residential, shopping and public open space. Detailed plans will not be prepared until after it is known whether the Order has been confirmed.

(e) What rights do residents have when offers of rehousing are made?
A choice is usually offered by the Housing Manager, but this depends on the houses then available.

(f) Is there a disturbance allowance?
Tenants receive a contribution towards removal expenses. A home loss payment of three times the rateable value will be payable to owner-occupiers or tenants with at least 5 years' continuous occupation.

(g) Are there any plans for a social centre, youth club, further playing space?
See answer to question (d).

(h) What shops and services will be maintained?
This will be better dealt with at the Public Inquiry. Shopping and other facilities will be provided if there is a need.

(i) At what price will shops be rented?
This information cannot be given at present.

(j) Why is 101, Waterloo Street, not included in the Compulsory Purchase Order?
This will be dealt with at the Public Inquiry.

(k) Why did the council allow lodging houses to develop in the area, and what is going to happen to them?
This will be dealt with at the Public Inquiry.

(l) Will rehousing be offered locally?
This cannot be answered at the moment.

11 S. Baillie et al., op. cit.
12 A committee of local authority officers, usually second or third tier, set up to discuss CDP issues.
13 The officer said that there had been one attempt to get local rehousing for people in a clearance area in the borough before but this had been unsuccessful because there had been a large movement of residents from the area, causing it to run down quickly, and there had been no community group there to try to mitigate the effects. Almost certainly a similar acceleration of the run-down process would have occurred in Glodwick in 1974 had the group not been vigilant and active in seeking the rectification of difficulties as soon as they came to light.

14 M. Clifton, op. cit.

Chapter 5 Failsworth Community Association

1 The population of Failsworth in 1951 was 18,705 and in 1971 was
23,279. Oldham's population declined from 123,218 in 1951 to 105,913
in 1971. If each population is said to have been 100 per cent in 1951,
Failsworth's 1971 population was 124.4 per cent and Oldham's 85.9
per cent.

2 The respective housing tenure patterns shown by the 1971 census
were:

	Failsworth	Oldham
Owner-occupied	67%	47%
Rented from the council	16%	36%
Rented unfurnished from private landlord	16%	16%
Rented furnished	1%	1%

3 81 per cent of the households in Failsworth had exclusive use of hot
water, fixed bath and inside lavatory, compared with 69 per cent of
those in Oldham (1971 census).

4 It may be worth noting that a member of the executive committee
who was asked to check the case study for accuracy was concerned
that the several references to ex-councillors being members of the
association could give an erroneous impression. He thought that

> The emphasis on ex-councillors in various parts of the report
> could be interpreted in two ways, both misleading and incorrect:
>
> (a) that the ex-councillors were important to the successful run-
>   ning and operation of a voluntary group;
> (b) that the association was run by men that had lost their seats
>   on the council and were only there to exercise outside control
>   of the local authority.

Both views were wrong, because most groups in Failsworth, with
some exceptions (where the authority had financial interests, for
example, through grant aid) were set up and operated over many
years without ex-councillors, and the Failsworth Community Association had over twenty active members, and out of these there were
only three or four ex-councillors.

5 Profiles of those who held offices in the Failsworth Community
Association in December 1975 are as follows:

Executive committee

Chairman	– electrical engineer with television company, JP.
Vice-chairman	– self-employed chiropodist, member of community health council; former councillor and chairman of one committee of the former Failsworth Urban District Council.
Secretary	– research technician at the University of

Manchester Institute of Science and Technology,
former councillor and chairman of a former
Failsworth UDC committee.

Planning sub-committee

Chairman   – systems planning engineer with GPO, ex-
chairman of housing committee of Failsworth
UDC.

Secretary   – sales/service department of car suppliers.

Personal social services and welfare sub-committee

Chairman   – local organiser of WRVS, member of community
health council, vice-chairman of Townswomen's
Guild.

Secretary   – police officer, churchwarden, secretary of
Failsworth Council of Churches.

Finance sub-committee

Chairman   – Manchester Corporation Housing Department
official, JP, ex-chairman of a number of
Failsworth UDC committees, holder of
numerous committee posts on other bodies.

Secretary   – secretary in computer section of Ferranti.

6 In June 1974 the Oldham council deferred for two years any decision
on whether neighbourhood councils should be set up throughout the
borough. In the interim a working party on neighbourhood councils
was set up, and a special meeting of the policy and resources committee in April 1976 to consider the working party's report decided
to recommend that the council should not take the initiative in setting
up such councils but that consideration should be given to the local
authority's supporting voluntary and community groups which had
functions similar to neighbourhood councils.

7 A chronological summary of events is not included because, as outlined in Chapter 1, this case study was conducted in large part to test
the checklist as an interviewing tool for use with relatively unfamiliar
groups. The intention was to produce a contemporary portrayal of
the group; detailed records of recent historical events were not therefore drawn on.

Chapter 6 The Joint Working Party on Vagrants

1 As mentioned in Chapter 1, neither the town nor the voluntary
organisation are identified in this case study. This is honouring the
research worker's agreement with the members that any material
published on the group would preserve confidentiality and anonymity.

2 S. Trench, *Bury Me in My Boots*, Hodder & Stoughton, London,
1973, p. 49. A Wallich-Clifford, *No Fixed Abode*, Macmillan,
London, 1974.

3 Department of Health and Social Security, *Homeless Single Persons in Need of Care and Support, Circular 37/72,* London, September 1972, pp. 1–2.

4 This is a quotation from the minutes of one of the working parties. Further unnumbered quotations are taken from project records, press reports and research notes.

5 F. M. Cox, J. L. Erlich, J. Rothman and J. E. Tropman (eds), op. cit., p. 7.

6 P. Marris and M. Rein, *Dilemmas of Social Reform: Poverty and Community Action in the United States,* Penguin, Harmondsworth, 1974, p. 329.

7 J. R. Seeley *et. al.,* 'Laymen and Professionals', in W. A. Glaser and D. L. Sills (eds), *The Government of Associations: Selections from the Behavioural Sciences,* Bedminster Press, New Jersey, 1966, p. 213.

8 Those who join a community group are by their nature self-selecting; control, and if necessary rejection, at the point of entry, is not an option generally available to organisational leaders.

Chapter 7 Groups and their environment

1 R. K. Merton, *Social Theory and Social Structure,* Free Press, New York, 1968, p. 143.

2 See, for example, J. Rothman, 'Three Models of Community Organization Practice', in F. M. Cox *et al.* (eds), op. cit., pp. 22–39; I. A. Spergel, *Community Problem Solving – The Delinquency Example,* University of Chicago Press, 1969; R. Perlman and A. Gurin, *Community Organization and Social Planning,* John Wiley and The Council for Social Work Education, New York, 1972. For overviews of practice models and goals in the British context see, for example, the two Calouste Gulbenkian Foundation Reports: *Community Work and Social Change,* op. cit., and *Current Issues in Community Work,* op. cit.; see also D. Jones, 'Community Work in the United Kingdom', and C. Briscoe, 'Community Work and Social Work in the United Kingdom', both in H. Specht and A. Vickery (eds), *Integrating Social Work Methods,* Allen & Unwin, London, 1977, pp. 164–81 and 182–94.

3 R. Perlman and A. Gurin, op. cit., p. 53.

4 J. Rothman, op. cit., p. 28.

5 Ibid., p. 27.

6 J. Rothman, op. cit., p. 30.

7 See, for example, R. L. Warren, 'Types of Purposive Change at the Community Level', in R.M. Kramer and H. Specht (eds), op. cit., pp. 205–22; R. E. Walton, 'Two Strategies of Social Change and their Dilemmas', in F.M. Cox *et al.* (eds), op. cit., pp. 365–71; P. Kotler, 'The Elements of Social Action', in G. Zaltman, P. Kotler and I. Kaufman (eds), *Creating Social Change,* Holt, Rinehart & Winston, New York, 1972, pp. 172–86; R. Bryant, 'Community

Action', in R. Kimber and J. J. Richardson, *Pressure Groups in Britain: A Reader*, Dent, London, 1974, pp. 242–54.

8 The National Community Development Project: *Inter-Project Report*, CDP Information and Intelligence Unit, London, 1974, p. 24.

9 See R. M. Kanter, *Commitment and Community: Communes and Utopias in Sociological Perspective*, Harvard University Press, Cambridge, Massachusetts, 1972; P. Abrams, *Communes, Sociology and Society*, Cambridge University Press, London, 1976; and A. Rigby, *Alternative Realities: A Study of Communes and their Members*, Routledge & Kegan Paul, London, 1974, for interesting insights and analysis on this theme.

10 D. Thorns, *The Quest for Community*, Allen & Unwin, London, 1976, p. 145.

Chapter 8 Goals and goal achievement

1 See C. Perrow, 'The Analysis of Goals in Complex Organizations', *American Sociological Review*, vol. 26, no. 6, 1961, pp. 854–66, and C. Perrow, *Organizational Analysis: A Sociological View*, Tavistock Publications, London, 1970, in particular ch. 5 on organisational goals, pp. 133–74.

2 J. Rothman, *Planning and Organizing for Social Change: Action Principles from Social Science Research*, Columbia University Press, New York, 1974, p. 132.

3 R. Michels, *Political Parties: a Sociological Study of the Oligarchical Tendencies in Modern Democracy*, Free Press, Chicago, 1958.

4 R. Perlman and A. Gurin, op. cit., p. 218.

5 J. B. Turner (ed.), *Neighbourhood Organization for Community Action*, National Association of Social Workers, New York, 1968, p. 14.

6 Ibid.

7 See for example, A. Etzioni, *Modern Organizations*, Prentice-Hall, Englewood Cliffs, New Jersey, 1964, pp. 16–19.

8 R. H. Hall, *Organizations, Structure and Process*, Prentice-Hall, Englewood Cliffs, New Jersey, 1972, pp. 85–94.

Chapter 9 Organisation: process and structure

1 D. Silverman, *The Theory of Organisations*, Heinemann, London, 1970, p. 126.

2 D. Dickinson (ed.), *Voluntary Action*, British Broadcasting Corporation, London, 1973, p. 22.

3 R. Bryant, op. cit., p. 247.

4 A. A. Milne, *The House at Pooh Corner*, Methuen, London, eleventh paperback reprint, 1976, p. 37.

5 R. H. Hall, op. cit., p. 9.

6 P. Clark is an industrial organisational theorist who has rejected 'the structure-process dichotomy' and is undertaking a project which 'argues that structure varies in cyclical fashion through time. . . . This approach can be referred to as the theory of structural activation because it seeks to establish when and how structures are activated'. See P. Clark, 'Time, Control and Structures: The Theory of Structural Activation', in *Annual Report of the Organisational Analysis Research Unit*, Management Centre, University of Bradford, 1976/7, p. 13.

7 M. J. Hill and R. Issacharoff, *Community Action and Race Relations: A Study of Community Relations Committees in Britain*, Oxford University Press, London, 1971, p. 74.

8 This confidence is generated by our practical awareness that community organisation is most readily built on and round issues; and from familiarity with, for example, the bi-monthly journal, *Community Action*, whose reports predominantly concern groups which come together in reaction to specific issues.

9 W. A. Glaser and D. L. Sills (eds), op. cit., p. 3.

10 H. Eckstein, *Pressure Group Politics: The Case of the British Medical Association*, Allen & Unwin, London, 1960, pp. 26–7.

11 P. Sills, *Community Groups and Political Decision Making*, unpublished research paper retained for reference in the Department of Social Administration and Social Work, University of York, July 1974, p. 13.

12 It will be clear that we share Cox *et al.*'s view that community organisation can be 'performed by professionals from a number of disciplines . . . as well as by citizen volunteers in civic associations and political action groups'. See F. M. Cox, J. L. Erlich, J. Rothman and J. E. Tropman (eds), op. cit., p. 3.

13 S. Kahn, *How People Get Power: Organizing Oppressed Communities for Action*, McGraw-Hill, New York, 1970, p. 45.

14 R. Michels, op. cit., pp. vii, 418.

15 J. Freeman, *The Tyranny of Structurelessness*, Agitprop, London, 1972, p. 4.

16 O. Grusky, 'The Effects of Succession: A Comparative Study of Military and Business Organization', in O. Grusky and G. A. Miller, *The Sociology of Organizations: Basic Studies*, The Free Press, New York, 1970, p. 454.

17 P. Bachrach and M. S. Baratz, *Power and Poverty: Theory and Practice*, Oxford University Press, New York, 1970, p. 8. In the chapter 'Two Faces of Power', Bachrach and Baratz argue that 'non-decision making' is one of the faces, in that 'to the extent that a person or group – consciously or unconsciously – creates or reinforces barriers to the public airing of policy conflicts, that person or group has power'.

18 G. Brager and H. Specht, op. cit., p. 142.

Chapter 10 Strategy, tactics and resources

1 It is worth noting that Richard Bryant suggests a division into only two categories: bargaining and confrontation:
> 'Bargaining strategies are conventionally employed in situations where negotiation is possible between the various interests involved and the framework for action is defined by the institutionalised processes of formal and pressure group politics.'

Tactics here include lobbying, petitions, and information and publicity campaigns.

> 'In contrast, confrontation strategies are employed in situations where a polarisation of interests exists and the conventional processes of political representation are viewed, by community groups, as being unproductive or dysfunctional for the pursuit of their ends. The accommodated conflict of the bargaining situation is replaced by an open conflict or warfare situation and recourse is likely to be made to tactics of an extra-parliamentary and extra-legal nature; for example, street demonstrations, sit-ins, muck-raking campaigns, rent strikes, the takeover of private property and, on occasions, the threat and use of physical violence. (R. Bryant, op. cit., pp. 245–6).

2 T. N. Clark (ed.), *Community Structure and Decision-Making: Comparative Analyses*, Chandler, Scranton, Pennsylvania, 1968, p. 61; J. Dearlove, *The Politics of Policy in Local Government*, Cambridge University Press, 1973, p. 56; H. Eckstein, op. cit., pp. 34–5; P. H. Rossi, 'Theory, Research, and Practice in Community Organization', in R. Kramer and H. Specht (eds), op. cit., pp. 51–2. P. Sills, 'Power and Community Groups' in *Community Development Journal*, vol. 10, no. 1, January 1975, pp. 24–8.

3 C. J. Ham, *Protest Group Politics: the case of the A2 Group*, Unpublished MPhil thesis, University of Kent, Canterbury, 1976.

4 For a discussion about how resources provided by CDP were used in the Cleator Moor area see A. Glen, J. Pearce and A. Booth, *Resources for Social Change*, Paper in Community Studies, no. 14, Department of Social Administration and Social Work, University of York, 1977.

5 J. Dearlove, op. cit., p. 58.

6 C. J. Ham, op. cit.

7 L. Corina, *Local Government Decision Making*, Paper in Community Studies, no. 2, Department of Social Administration and Social Work, University of York, 1975; L. Corina, 'Community Work and Local Authority Decision Making: Potential and Problems', *Community Development Journal*, vol. 11, no. 3, October 1976, pp. 174–84; L. Corina, *Oldham CDP: An Assessment of its Impact and Influence on the Local Authority*, Paper in Community Studies, no. 9, Department of Social Administration and Social Work, University of York, 1977; H. Butcher, J. Pearce, I. Cole with A. Glen, op. cit; L. Corina, P. Collis and C. Crosby, op. cit.

Chapter 11 The role of the community worker

1 Association of Community Workers, *Knowledge and Skills for Community Work*, ACW, London, 1975, p. 5.
2 Association of Community Workers, *Some Guidelines for the Appointment of a Community Worker*, ACW, London, 1973, p. 1.
3 R. Perlman and A. Gurin, op. cit., pp. 37–8.
4 See, for example, I. T. Sanders, 'Professional Roles in Planned Change', in R. M. Kramer and H. Specht (eds), op. cit., pp. 269–77; R. Morris and R. Binstock, *Feasible Planning for Social Change*, Columbia University Press, New York, 1966; A. Barr, *The Practice of Neighbourhood Community Work*, Paper in Community Studies, no. 12, Department of Social Administration and Social Work, University of York, 1977.
5 J. Rothman, 'Three Models of Community Organization Practice', op. cit.
6 A. Barr, *The Practice of Neighbourhood Community Work*, op. cit.
7 C. Grosser, 'Neighbourhood Community Development Programmes Serving the Urban Poor', in G. Brager and F. P. Purcell (eds), *Community Action against Poverty; Readings from the Mobilization Experience*, College and University Press, New Haven, 1967, pp. 243–52.
8 See J. Rothman, 'Analysis of Goals and Roles in Community Organisation Practice', in *Social Work*, vol. 9, no. 2 (April 1964), pp. 24–31, where he elaborates the democratic issues involved in a community worker adopting both directive and non-directive methods.
9 Some writers have linked the 'enabler' role with a process-orientated, apolitical stance which aims to help individuals and groups cope with change in their social environment. Others have suggested that this enabling process should be directed towards the raising of consciousness and the helping of groups to take political action. Examples of this latter, comparatively recent, emphasis include: C. Smith and B. Anderson, 'Political Participation through Community Action', in G. Parry (ed.), *Participation in Politics*, Manchester University Press, 1972, pp. 303–18; T. Woolley, 'The Politics of Intervention', in J. Cowley, A. Kaye, M. Mayo and Thompson (eds), *Community or Class Struggle?* Stage One, London, 1977, pp. 210–21; C. McConnell, *The Community Worker as Politicizer of the Deprived*, Centre for Environmental Studies, Edinburgh, 1977; P. Freire, *Pedagogy of the Oppressed*, Penguin, Harmondsworth, 1972; J. B. Taylor and J. Randolph, *Community Worker*, Jason Aronson, New York, 1975.
10 See, for example, R. Perlman and A. Gurin, op. cit., pp. 58–75; and F. M. Cox *et al.* op. cit., Appendix: A Suggestive Framework for Community Problem Solving, pp. 425–44.
11 Other lists of tasks may be found in: Association of Community Workers, *Knowledge and Skills for Community Work*, op. cit.; M. Naish and E. Filkin, *What does a Community Worker Need to*

Know?, Occasional Papers in Community and Youth Work, no. 2, Goldsmiths College, London, 1974; Calouste Gulbenkian Foundation, *Community Work and Social Change*, op. cit: G. Goetschius, op. cit.

12 W. C. Haggstromm, 'Can the Poor Transform the World?' in I. Deutscher and E. J. Thompson (eds), *Among the People: Encounters with the Poor*, Basic Books, New York, 1968, pp. 67–110.

13 J. Dearlove, 'The Control of Change and the Regulation of Community Action', in D. Jes and M. Mayo (eds), op. cit., p. 28.

14 See, for example, J. Rothman, *Planning and Organising for Social Change: Action Principles from Social Science Research*, op. cit., pp. 115–94; M. N. Zald, op. cit.; and R. Perlman and A. Gurin, 'The Importance of the Organisational Context', in R. M. Kramer and H. Specht, *Readings in Community Organisation Practice, 2nd edn*. Prentice-Hall, Englewood Cliffs, New Jersey, 1975, pp. 75–80.

15 D. N. Thomas and R. W. Warburton, *Community Workers in a Social Service Department: A Case Study*, Personal Social Services Council and National Institute for Social Work, Allen & Unwin, 1977, p. 67.

16 Home Office, *CDP: A General Outline*, p. 2.

17 As it turned out, the closure of the Cumbria CDP in 1976 can be seen as a result of local political élites who were certainly hostile to the employment of activist roles. During the period covered by the SCAG and WCAC case studies, however, such opposition to advocacy and activist styles of operation was muted. For a fuller account of the closure of Cumbria CDP see H. Butcher, J. Pearce, I. Cole with A. Glen, op. cit.

18 For a detailed discussion of the impact and take up of Cumbria CDP resources, see: A. Glen, J. Pearce and A. Booth, op. cit.

19 D. Thomas, *Organising for Social Change: A study in the theory and practice of community work*, National Institute Social Services Library, no. 30, Allen & Unwin, London, 1976, pp. 108, 109.

20 At this time in the life of Cumbria CDP the geographical location of workers' activities was not constrained by the management committee. Later in its life, the staff were restricted to providing services to organisations solely based in the CDP area. For further discussion see A. Glen, J. Pearce and A. Booth, op. cit.

21 National Community Development Project, *Forward Plan*, op. cit., p. 54.

22 Ibid. p. 30.

23 J. Benington, 'Strategies for Change at the Local Level: some Reflections' in D. Jones and M. Mayo (eds), op. cit., pp. 276–7.

24 National Community Development Project, *Forward Plan*, op. cit., p. 31.

25 R. Sugden, op. cit. In this the project area is described as a deprived part of a deprived area (West Cumbria) of a deprived region (The North).

26 J. Pearce and A. Tweedie, op. cit.

27 CDP Information and Intelligence Unit, *CDPs – Perspectives and Strategies*, CDP IIU, London, September 1974, p. 22.
28 See A. Glen, J. Pearce and A. Booth, op. cit; and Cumbria CDP, *Community Information and Action Centre*, Paper in Community Studies, no.1, Department of Social Administration and Social Work, University of York, 1975.
29 J. Rothman, *Planning and Organising for Social Change*, op. cit., p. 63.
30 M. Taylor, B. Kestenbaum and B. Symons, op. cit., p. 13.
31 J. Rothman, *Planning and Organising for Social Change*, op. cit., p. 83.
32 G. Brager, 'The Low Income Non-Professional' in G. Brager and F. P. Purcell (eds), op. cit., pp. 163–74.
33 Many of these points are discussed (though using a different conceptual framework) with reference to the neighbourhood strategies of Oldham CDP in A. Barr, *The Practice of Neighbourhood Community Work*, op. cit.
34 See J. Cheetham and M. Hill, 'Community Work – Social Realities and Ethical Dilemmas', *British Journal of Social Work*, vol. 3, no. 2, Autumn 1973; and A. Barr, *The Practice of Neighbourhood Community Work*, op. cit.

Bibliography

This bibliography provides a list of sources referred to in the text. Its sections are: books; papers and articles; and reports.

Books

Abrams, P., *Communes, Sociology and Society*, Cambridge University Press, 1976.
Bachrach, P. and Baratz, M. S., *Power and Poverty: Theory and Practice*, Oxford University Press, New York, 1970.
Baldock, P., *Community Work and Social Work*, Routledge and Kegan Paul, London, 1974.
Brager, G. and Specht, H., *Community Organizing*, Columbia University Press, New York, 1973.
Clark, T. N. (ed.), *Community Structure and Decision Making: Comparative Analysis*, Chandler, Scranton, Pennsylvania, 1968.
Cockburn, C., *The Local State*, Pluto Press, London, 1977.
Cox, F. M., Erlich, J. L., Rothman, J., and Tropman, J. E. (eds), *Strategies of Community Organization*, 2nd edn, F. E. Peacock, Itasca, Illinois, 1974.
Dearlove, J., *The Politics of Policy in Local Government*, Cambridge University Press, 1973.
Dickinson, D. (ed.), *Voluntary Action*, British Broadcasting Corporation, London, 1973.
Eckstein, H., *Pressure Group Politics: The Case of the British Medical Association*, Allen & Unwin, London, 1960.
Etzioni, A., *Modern Organizations*, Prentice-Hall, Englewood Cliffs, New Jersey, 1964.
Freire, P., *Pedagogy of the Oppressed*, Penguin, Harmondsworth, 1972.
Glaser, B. G. and Strauss, A. L., *The Discovery of Grounded Theory: Strategies for Qualitative Research*, Aldine Atherton, Chicago, 1971.
Glaser, W. A. and Sills, D. L. (eds), *The Government of Associations: Selections from the Behavioural Sciences*, Bedminster Press, Tutowa, New Jersey, 1966.
Goetschius, G. W., *Working with Community Groups: Using Com-*

munity Development as a Method of Social Work, Routledge & Kegan Paul, London, 1969.

Hall, I. M., *Community Action Versus Pollution: A Study of a Residents' Group in a Welsh Urban Area*, University of Wales Board of Celtic Studies, Social Science Monograph, No. 2, University of Wales Press, Cardiff, 1976.

Hall, R. H., *Organizations, Structure and Process*, Prentice-Hall, Englewood Cliffs, New Jersey, 1972.

Hill, M. J., and Issacharoff, R., *Community Action and Race Relations: A Study of Community Relations Committees in Britain*, Oxford University Press, London, 1971.

Jacobs, S., *The Right to a Decent House*, Routledge & Kegan Paul, London, 1976.

Jones, K., Brown, J. and Bradshaw, J., *Issues in Social Policy*, Routledge & Kegan Paul, London, 1978.

Kahn, S., *How People Get Power: Organizing Oppressed Communities for Action*, McGraw-Hill, New York, 1970.

Kanter, R. M., *Commitment and Community: Communes and Utopias in Sociological Perspective*, Harvard University Press, Cambridge, Massachusetts, 1972.

Katz, A. H. and Bender, E. I., *The Strength in Us*, New Viewpoints, New York, 1976.

Lees, R. and Smith, G., *Action Research in Community Development*, Routledge & Kegan Paul, London, 1975.

Marris, P. and Rein, M., *Dilemmas of Social Reform: Poverty and Community Action in the United States*, Penguin, Harmondsworth, 1974.

McConnell, C., *The Community Worker as Politicizer of the Deprived*, Centre for Environmental Studies, Edinburgh, 1977.

Merton, R. K., *Social Theory and Social Structure*, Free Press, New York, 1968.

Michels, R., *Political Parties: a Sociological Study of the Oligarchical Tendencies in Modern Democracy*, Free Press, Chicago, 1958.

Milson, F., *An Introduction to Community Work*, Routledge & Kegan Paul, London, 1974.

Morris, R. and Binstock, R., *Feasible Planning for Social Change*, Columbia University Press, New York, 1966.

Mouzelis, N. P., *Organization and Bureaucracy: An Analysis of Modern Theories*, Routledge & Kegan Paul, London, 1967.

Newton, K., *Second City Politics: Democratic Processes and Decision Making in Birmingham*, Clarendon Press, Oxford, 1971.

O'Malley, J., *The Politics of Community Action*, Spokesman Books, Nottingham, 1977.

Perlman, R. and Gurin, A., *Community Organization and Social Planning*, John Wiley and The Council for Social Work Education, New York, 1972.

Perrow, C., *Organizational Analysis: A Sociological View*, Tavistock Publications, London, 1970.

Pincus, A. and Minahan, A., *Social Work Practice: Model and Method*, F. E. Peacock, Itasca, Illinois, 1973.

Rigby, A., *Alternative Realities: A Study of Communes and their Members*, Routledge & Kegan Paul, London, 1974.

Robinson, D. and Henry, S., *Self-Help and Health*, Martin Robertson, London, 1977.

Rothman, J., *Planning and Organizing for Social Change: Action Principles from Social Science Research*, Columbia University Press, New York, 1974.

Silverman, D., *The Theory of Organisations*, Heinemann, London, 1970.

Spergel, I. A., *Community Problem Solving – The Deliquency Example*, University of Chicago Press, 1969.

Taylor, J. B. and Randolph, J., *Community Worker*, Jason Aronson, New York, 1975.

Taylor, M., Kestenbaum, A. and Symons, B., *Principles and Practice of Community Work in a British Town*, Young Volunteer Force Foundation, London, 1976.

Thomas, D., *Organising for Social Change: A study in the theory and practice of community work*, National Institute Social Services Library, no. 30, Allen & Unwin, London, 1976.

Thomas, D. and Warburton, R. W., *Community Workers in a Social Service Department: A Case Study*, Personal Social Services Council and National Institute for Social Work, Allen & Unwin, London, 1977.

Thorns, D., *The Quest for Community*, Allen & Unwin, London, 1976.

Trench, S., *Bury Me in My Boots*, Hodder & Stoughton, London, 1973.

Turner, J. B. (ed.), *Neighbourhood Organization for Community Action*, National Association of Social Workers, New York, 1968.

Wallich-Clifford, A., *No Fixed Abode*, Macmillan, London, 1974.

Papers and articles

Barber, R., *Iron Ore and After: Boom Time, Depression and Survival in a West Cumbrian Town; Cleator Moor 1840–1960*, Cleator Moor Local Studies Group, Cleator Moor, Cumbria, 1976.

Barker, A., 'Local Amenity Societies – a survey and outline report', in *The Local Amenity Movement*, Civic Trust, London, 1976.

Barr, A., *The Practice of Neighbourhood Community Work*, Paper in Community Studies, no. 12, Department of Social Administration and Social Work, University of York, 1977.

Barr, A., *Housing Improvement and the Multi-racial Community*, Paper in Community Studies, no. 16, Department of Social Administration and Social Work, University of York, 1978.

Benington, J., 'Strategies for Change at the Local Level: some Reflections', in D. Jones and M. Mayo (eds), *Community Work One*, Routledge & Kegan Paul, London, 1974.

Benington, J., 'Gosford Green Residents' Association: a Case Study', in P. Leonard (ed.), *The Sociology of Community Action*, Sociological Review Monograph 21, University of Keele, 1975.

Brager, G., 'The Low Income Non-Professional', in G. Brager and F. P. Purcell (eds), *Community Action against Poverty: Readings from the Mobilization Experience*, College and University Press, New Haven, 1967.

Briscoe, C., 'Community Work and Social Work in the United Kingdom', in H. Specht and A. Vickery (eds), *Integrating Social Work Methods*, Allen & Unwin, London, 1977.

Bryant, R., 'Community Action', in R. Kimber and J. J. Richardson, *Pressure Groups in Britain: A Reader*, Dent, London, 1974.

Butcher, H. and Crosbie, D., *Pensioned Off: A Study of the Needs of Elderly People in Cleator Moor*, Paper in Community Studies, no. 15, Department of Social Administration and Social Work, University of York, 1978.

Butcher, H., Pearce, J., Cole, I. with Glen, A., *Community Participation and Poverty: the Final Report of the Cumbria CDP*, Paper in Community Studies, no. 22, Department of Social Administration and Social Work, University of York, 1979.

Cheetham, J. and Hill, M., 'Community Work – Social Realities and Ethical Dilemmas', *British Journal of Social Work*, vol. 3, no. 2, Autumn 1973.

Clark, P., 'Time, Control and Structures: The Theory of Structural Activation', in *Annual Report of the Organisational Analysis Research Unit*, Management Centre, University of Bradford, 1976/7.

Corina, L., *Local Government Decision Making*, Paper in Community Studies, no. 2, Department of Social Administration and Social Work, University of York, 1975.

Corina, L., 'Community Work and Local Authority Decision Making: Potential and Problems', *Community Development Journal*, vol. 11, no. 3, October 1976.

Corina, L., *Oldham CDP: An Assessment of Its Impact and Influence on the Local Authority*, Paper in Community Studies, no. 9, Department of Social Administration and Social Work, University of York, 1977.

Corina, L., Collis, P. and Crosby, C., *The Final Report: Oldham CDP*, Paper in Community Studies, no. 23, Department of Social Administration and Social Work, University of York, 1979.

Crosby, C., *Intra-Urban Migration: A Study of Housing Mobility in the Clarksfield and Glodwick Districts of Oldham*, Paper in Community Studies, no. 17, Department of Social Administration and Social Work, University of York, 1978.

Cumbria CDP, *Community Information and Action Centre*, Paper in Community Studies, no. 1, Department of Social Administration and Social Work, University of York, 1975.

Dearlove, J., 'The Control of Change and the Regulation of Community Action', in D. Jones and M. Mayo (eds), *Community Work One*, Routledge & Kegan Paul, London, 1974.

Derricourt, N., 'Linking Learning to Experience in Community Work

Training', in C. Briscoe and D. N. Thomas (eds), *Community Work: Learning and Supervision*, Allen & Unwin, London, 1977.

Freeman, J., *The Tyranny of Structurelessness*, Agitprop, London, 1972.

Glen, A., Pearce J. and Booth, A., *Resources for Social Change*, Paper in Community Studies, no. 14, Department of Social Administration and Social Work, University of York, 1977.

Grosser, C., 'Neighbourhood Community Development Programmes Serving the Urban Poor', in G. Brager and F. P. Purcell (eds), *Community Action against Poverty: Readings from the Mobilization Experience*, College and University Press, New Haven, 1967.

Grusky, O., 'The Effects of Succession: A Comparative Study of Military and Business Organisation', in O. Grusky and G. A. Miller, *The Sociology of Organisations: Basic Studies*, Free Press, New York, 1970.

Haggstromm, W. C., 'Can the Poor Transform the World?' in I. Deutscher and E. J. Thompson (eds), *Among the People: Encounters with the Poor*, Basic Books, New York, 1968.

Hain, P., 'The Future of Community Politics', in P. Hain (ed.), *Community Politics*, John Calder, London, 1976.

Ham, C. J., *Protest Group Politics: the case of the A2 Group*, unpublished MPhil thesis, University of Kent, Canterbury, 1976.

Jenkins, P. 'Commentary' *Guardian*, 5 May 1978.

Jones, D. 'Community Work in the United Kingdom' in H. Specht and A. Vickery (eds), *Integrating Social Work Methods*, Allen & Unwin, London, 1977.

Kotler, P., 'The Elements of Social Action', in G. Zaltman, P. Kotler and I. Kaufman (eds), *Creating Social Change*, Holt, Rinehart & Winston, New York, 1972.

Marris, P., 'Experimenting in Social Reform', in D. Jones and M. Mayo (eds), *Community Work One*, Routledge & Kegan Paul, London, 1974.

McCaughan, N., 'Group Behaviour: Some Theories for Practice', in C. Briscoe and D. N. Thomas (eds), *Community Work: Learning and Supervision*, Allen & Unwin, London, 1977.

Miliband, R., 'Politics and Poverty', in D. Wedderburn (ed.), *Poverty, Inequality and Class Structure*, Cambridge University Press, London, 1974.

Naish, M. and Filkin, E., *What does a Community Worker Need to Know?* Occasional Papers in Community and Youth Work, no. 2, Goldsmiths College, London, 1974.

Newton K., 'Voluntary Organisations in Community Politics: the Hidden 90% of the Iceberg', *Social Science Research Council Newsletter*, no. 24, London, July 1974.

Perlman, R. and Gurin, A., 'The Importance of the Organizational Context', in R. M. Kramer and H. Specht (eds), *Readings in Community Organization Practice*; 2nd edn., Prentice-Hall, Englewood Cliffs, New Jersey, 1975.

Perrow, C., 'The Analysis of Goals in Complex Organizations', *American Sociological Review*, vol. 26, no. 6, 1961.

Pickvance, C. G., 'Voluntary Associations' in E. Gittus (ed.), *Key Variables in Social Research*, vol. 2, Heinemann, forthcoming.

Reid, W. J., 'Inter-Organizational Co-ordination in Social Welfare: a Theoretical Approach to Analysis and Intervention', in R. M. Kramer and H. Specht (eds), *Readings in Community Organization Practice*, Prentice-Hall, Englewood Cliffs, New Jersey, 1969.

Rossi, P. H., 'Theory, Research and Practice in Community Organization', in R. M. Kramer and H. Specht (eds), *Readings in Community Organization Practice*, Prentice-Hall, Englewood Cliffs, New Jersey, 1969.

Rothman, J., 'Analysis of Goals and Roles in Community Organization Practice', in *Social Work*, vol. 9, no. 2 (April 1964).

Rothman, J., 'Three Models of Community Organization Practice' in F. M. Cox, J. L. Erlich, J. Rothman and J. E. Tropman (eds), *Strategies of Community Organization*, 2nd edn, Peacock, Itasca, Illinois, 1974.

Sanders, I. T., 'Professional Roles in Planned Change', in R. M. Kramer and H. Specht (eds), *Readings in Community Organization Practice*, Prentice-Hall, Englewood Cliffs, New Jersey, 1969.

Seeley, J. H., *et al.*, 'Laymen and Professionals', in W. A. Glaser and D. L. Sills (eds), *The Government of Associations: Selections from the Behavioural Sciences*, Bedminster Press, New Jersey, 1966.

Sieder, V. M., 'Community Organization in the Direct Service Agency', in R. M. Kramer and H. Specht (eds), *Readings in Community Organization Practice*, Prentice-Hall, Englewood Cliffs, New Jersey, 1969.

Sills, P., *Community Groups and Political Decision Making*, unpublished research paper retained for reference in the Department of Social Administration and Social Work, University of York, July 1974.

Sills, P., 'Power and Community Groups' in *Community Development Journal*, vol. 10, no. 1, January 1975.

Smith C. and Anderson B., 'Political Participation through Community Action', in G. Parry (ed.), *Participation in Politics*, Manchester University Press, 1972.

Sugden, R., *Unskilled and Unemployed in West Cumbria: a Study of Unemployment in Relation to Economic Planning and Public Transportation Policies*, Paper in Community Studies, no. 3, Department of Social Administration and Social Work, University of York, 1975.

Thomas, D., 'Chaucer House Tenants' Association: a Case Study', in P. Leonard (ed.), *The Sociology of Community Action*, Sociological Review Monograph 21, University of Keele, 1975.

Walton, R. E., 'Two Strategies of Social Change and their Dilemmas', in F. M. Cox, J. R. Erlich, J. Rothman and J. E. Tropman (eds), *Strategies of Community Organization*, 2nd edn, F. E. Peacock, Itasca, Illinois, 1974.

Warren, R. L., 'Types of Purposive Change at the Community Level', in R. M. Kramer and H. Specht (eds), *Readings in Community*

Organization Practice, Prentice-Hall, Englewood Cliffs, New Jersey, 1969.
Woolley, T., 'The Politics of Intervention', in J. Cowley, A. Kaye, M. Mayo and M. Thompson (eds), *Community or Class Struggle?* Stage One, London, 1977.
Zald, M. N. 'Organizations as Polities: an Analysis of Community Organization Agencies', in F. M. Cox, J. R. Erlich, J. Rothman and J. E. Tropman (eds), *Strategies of Community Organizations*, 2nd edn., F. E. Peacock, Itasca, Illinois, 1974.

Reports

Association of Community Workers, *Some Guidelines for the Appointment of a Community Worker*, ACW, London, 1973.
Association of Community Workers, *Knowledge and Skills for Community Work*, ACW, London, 1975.
Baillie, S., Shenton, N., Barr, A. and Swidenbank, S., *Oldham CDP: a First Report*, Oldham Community Development Project, Oldham, 1973.
Barr, A., (in consultation with the Glodwick Action Group), *Evidence for a CPO*, Oldham Community Development Project, Oldham, 1973.
Barr, A., *Housing Improvement and the Racial Conundrum*, Oldham Community Development Project, Oldham, 1975.
Calouste Gulbenkian Foundation, *Community Work and Social Change*, Longman, London, 1968.
Calouste Gulbenkian Foundation, *Current Issues in Community Work*, Routledge & Kegan Paul, London, 1973.
Central Council for Education and Training in Social Work, *The Teaching of Community Work* (the Pinker Report), Social Work Curriculum Study Paper 8, London, 1975.
CDP Information and Intelligence Unit, *CDPs – Perspectives and Strategies*, CDP IIU, London, September 1974.
Clifton, M., *Not in Permanent Accommodation*, Oldham Community Development Project, Oldham, 1975.
Department of Education and Science, *School Transport*, Green Paper, London, December 1973. Department of the Environment, *Making Towns Better: The Oldham Study – Environmental Planning and Management*, HMSO, London, 1973.
Department of Health and Social Security, *Homeless Single Persons in Need of Care and Support*, Circular 37/72, London, September 1972.
Home Office, *CDP: A General Outline*, London, 1969.
National Community Development Project: *Inter-Project Report*, CDP Information and Intelligence Unit, London, 1974.
National Community Development Project, *Forward Plan 1975–76*, CDP Information and Intelligence Unit, London, 1975.
Oldham Metropolitan Borough Council, *The South Hill Street Area – the Case for a Housing Action Area*, Oldham, 1976.

Pearce, J. and Tweedie, A., *Initial Study of the Two Parishes of Cleator Moor and Arlecdon/Frizington*, Cumberland CDP, Cleator Moor, 1973.

Shenton, N. and Collis, P., (eds), *Neighbourhood Information and Advice Centres: Oldham CDP*, Oldham Community Development Project, Oldham, 1977.

Wolfenden Committee, *The Future of Voluntary Organisations*, Croom Helm, London, 1977.

Index